FUN TO MAKE

Wooden Toys & Games

Jeff & Jennie Loader

Guild of Master Craftsman Publications Ltd

For Luke and Sam

Acknowledgements

Our grateful thanks go to the following companies who have generously supported this venture: Humbrol Ltd, Hobbies (Dereham) Ltd, and Yandle and Sons Ltd.

First published 1997 by
Guild of Master Craftsman Publications Ltd,
166 High Street · Lewes · East Sussex · BN7 1XU

Reprinted 1999

ISBN 1 86108 049 2

Photography by Jennie Loader, except as follows
Photography on pages 34, 35, 44, 45, 50, 56, 64, 65, 74, 75, 86, 96, 106, 107, 118, 119, 144 by Dennis Bunn
Line drawings by Jeff Loader

Designed by Lovelock & Co
Typeface: Caslon
Colour separation by Global Colour (Malaysia)
Printed in Singapore under the supervision of MRM Graphics, Winslow, Buckinghamshire, UK

B 4

FUN TO MAKE

Wooden Toys & Games

Contents

Notes

Constructional complexity grading

The projects in this book are graded in terms of constructional complexity. Those with one star (★) are the simpler projects, while those with three are the most difficult.

The time required to complete a project is broadly proportional to its constructional complexity: one star indicates a day or weekend project, while three signify a project that may take several evenings plus weekends to complete.

The one exception to this is the Play Roadway (Chapter 7), where the time taken depends on the amount of roadway constructed.

Measurements

Although care has been taken to ensure that imperial measurements are true and accurate, they are only conversions from metric. Throughout the book instances may be found where a metric measurement has slightly varying imperial equivalents, because in each particular case the closest imperial equivalent has been given. Care should be taken to use either imperial or metric measurements consistently (*see also* the Metric Conversion Table, page 167).

For clarity, only metric measurements (all in millimetres) have been given on the line drawings, though metric measurements and their imperial equivalents are given throughout the text.

Please note

Within the instructions given in this book, the personal pronoun 'he' has been used. This is purely for convenience and consistency; it is not our intention to exclude or offend lady readers.

Introduction

This book will enable you to construct wooden toys and games, based on a variety of subjects and themes. We have tried to give each project a 'traditional' feel, yet not allow it to look out of place alongside modern, shop-bought toys.

All our projects have been designed to excite and stimulate children's imaginations. It is our intention that some of the projects will also appeal to adults – for example, the Fortune-telling Money Box or Chinese Acrobat would be suitable to make as an unusual present for an adult.

We strongly recommend that you thoroughly read through the entire instructions for a project before beginning work on it.

In the construction details for each project certain obvious instructions are taken as said, in order to avoid tedious repetition. These are general points such as planing smooth a freshly sawn straight edge, smoothing away any unevenness from a fretted shape, or filling a pin hole after driving the pin below the surface of the workpiece, and so forth.

We hope you will have as much fun making these toys and games as children (and you?) will have in playing with them.

CHAPTER 1

Materials

Birch plywood

Birch plywood is a sheet material with an odd number of plys. The grain direction of each ply is bonded perpendicularly to its neighbour. This helps to give it equal strength and stiffness in both length and width. The face surfaces are fine, straight grained and visually appealing.

Due to its versatility and strength birch plywood allows small and fine components to be produced. This makes it ideal for toymaking. Toys made entirely from regular solid hardwood have a 'chunkier' appearance, as intricate shapes and features tend to break off during play. For these reasons the majority of our toys are produced from birch plywood (*see* Fig 1.1). Various thicknesses are available, the following being used in this book:

1.5mm (1⁄16in)
3mm (1⁄8in)
6mm (1⁄4in)
9mm (3⁄8in)
12mm (1⁄2in)

The last three thicknesses are usually sold in 2440 x 1220mm (8 x 4ft) sheets. The smaller thicknesses are also available in large sheets, but more manageable sizes; for example, 600 x 300mm (24 x 12in) can be obtained from hobbyist suppliers.

Most timber merchants will cut a large sheet down into more manageable sizes for you, but they may add a small additional charge for this service. Some may even sell half or quarter sheets.

When purchasing birch plywood for the first time you may think it a little expensive (especially the thicker and larger sheet sizes). However, bear in mind that, as most toys are relatively small, a little goes a long way.

Shop around for the best prices before buying your sheets. We are always surprised at the disparity of price between merchants!

If you need to have your plywood delivered, find out if there is a delivery charge. Timber merchants will often deliver free in their local area.

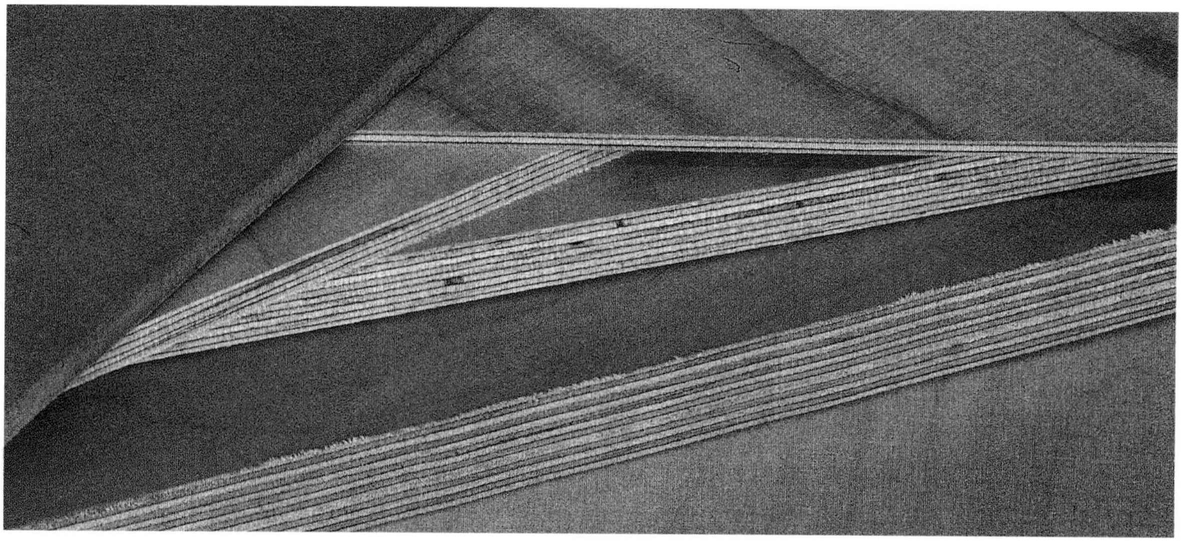

Fig 1.1 A selection of materials. From top: 6mm (¼in) MDF; 3mm (⅛in), 6mm (¼in) and 12mm (½in) birch plywood; 18mm (¾in) birch plywood constructed by joining 6mm (¼in) and 12mm (½in) sheets together.

One note of caution. Do not be tempted to purchase a less expensive and inferior plywood. This will invariably prove more difficult to work, will not be as strong, and will be awkward to finish.

Medium-density fibreboard (MDF)

Wood fibres are bonded together with a synthetic resin adhesive to produce this board, which has two smooth surfaces.

It is a relatively new material and is available in a variety of thicknesses and sheet sizes. Because of its economical price and versatility it has become popular and widely used.

In some instances you can use it as a less expensive alternative to birch plywood. For instance, the Play Roadway (*see* pages 51 – 5) has been constructed entirely from 6mm (¼in) MDF.

However, you should be aware that MDF is generally not as structurally strong as birch plywood. Furthermore, the edges do not take pins or screws being driven into them as well as birch plywood.

Hardboard

A small amount of standard hardboard 3mm (⅛in) thick is required for Snargon's Wrath (*see* pages 107 –17). It is used as a less expensive alternative to birch plywood.

Hardwood

Some projects require certain components to be produced from a suitable hardwood. Beech is ideal for this purpose as it is strong and hard wearing.

Many good timber merchants have a selection of small strips and offcuts. As the components required are relatively small in size, there is no need to buy large quantities of hardwood.

Brass

A small amount of 1.5mm (1/16in) sheet brass is used in the Chinese Acrobat and Fortune-telling Money Box projects. It is not essential to use brass, however, as plywood could be substituted.

Sheet brass can be purchased from good model suppliers.

Wooden moulding/edging

A variety of styles of these items can be purchased from most timber merchants and DIY suppliers. They are frequently available in either softwoods or hardwoods.

Dowel rods

Round, sectioned lengths of softwood and hardwood dowel rods are available in a variety of diameters from timber merchants, DIY stores and hobbyist outlets.

It is advisable to use hardwood doweling for the smaller diameters you need, as this is stronger than softwood.

Abrasive paper

You will find it necessary to keep a stock of assorted grades, from very fine to coarse abrasive paper.

Aluminium oxide paper and silicon carbide paper (known as wet-and-dry paper) are the ideal types to use.

Sanding sticks

These are a useful aid when sanding intricate shapes or surfaces which are not easily accessible. They are simply constructed from thin strips of birch plywood, with abrasive paper glued to them.

You can amass a useful range of lengths, widths and abrasive grades (*see* Fig 1.2). The most useful thicknesses of plywood for this purpose are 3mm (1/8in) and 6mm (1/4in). If you use anything thinner than this, such as 1.5mm (1/16in), be extremely careful as these may bend or snap when in use.

Wire wool

Wire wool is a useful item to keep at hand, 0000 grade being particularly useful for lightly sanding (or de-nibbing) a varnished or painted finish before applying the final coat.

Pins

A variety of small moulding, panel and/or fret pins are required. You will find 12mm (1/2in), 18mm (3/4in) and 25mm (1in) to be useful sizes.

Fig 1.2 Sanding sticks and assorted abrasive paper.

Filler

After moulding pins have been driven below the surface of the wood using a pin punch, you will need to fill the resulting recess with filler.

There are many brands, types and shades of wood filler on the market. Choose one that suits your particular needs best. If in doubt, most retail outlets will advise you.

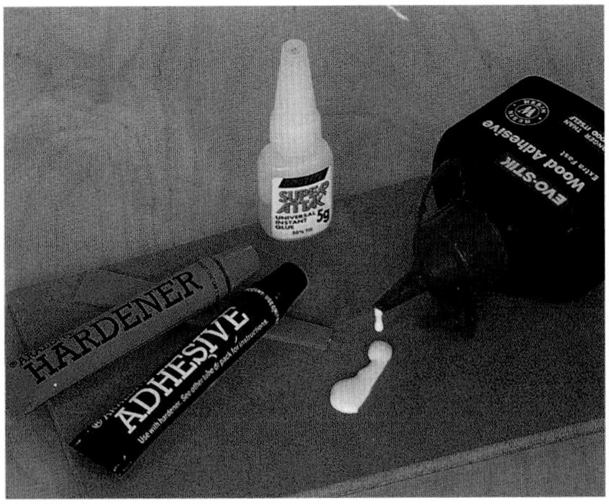

Fig 1.3 Types of adhesive. From left: epoxy resin, instant glue and PVA wood glue.

Glue

Woodworking PVA adhesive (or 'white glue') can be used in the construction of the toys and games. It is available in various quantities and styles of container. The most useful for the toymaking hobbyist comes in conveniently sized bottles with a nozzle top (*see* Fig 1.3).

You may find a universal instant glue (the type that bonds in seconds) useful, especially on small components, or where a fast setting time is required or where clamping is not possible.

A couple of the projects require metal to be stuck to wood. For these operations an epoxy resin adhesive is useful.

CHAPTER 2

Tools

Pencils

We have granted pencils premier position in this section, as they are one of the most important yet most neglected hand tools! Compared with the cost of other tools pencils are inexpensive, so try to use good-quality ones. We find 2H pencils to be an ideal compromise between a softer grade (which gives a nice bold line, but blunts much too easily), and a harder grade (which does not blunt so easily, but may indent the wood too readily and does not draw a bold line so well).

Accurate measuring and marking out is absolutely essential, so it is vital that you always keep a sharp, regular point on your pencil (*see* Fig 2.1). It is amazing how many people fail to do this.

> **TIP**
>
> To sharpen a pencil well, use a sharp knife, and first pare the wood away from around the lead at an acute angle until a reasonable length of lead is exposed (*see* Fig 2.1). Then sharpen the lead to a regular point either with a small file or fine abrasive paper. If using abrasive paper lay it on a flat surface and rub the lead across it.

Rules

You will need a 300mm (12in) and, if possible, a 600mm (24in) steel rule.

Retractable measuring tape

A retractable measuring tape, preferably one with a locking device, is useful when measuring large lengths and widths. A 3m (10ft) size is a useful length to have.

Fig 2.1 Blunt and sharpened pencils. It is easier to mark accurate lines with a sharp pencil.

Try squares

For marking and checking 90° angles.

A traditional woodworkers' try square has a steel blade with a hardwood stock incorporating a brass edge.

A combination square is more versatile, as it measures and tests mitres as well as levels and squareness. The blade is usually adjustable in length.

A small steel engineers' precision square, 50mm (2in) or 100mm (4in) in size, is more manageable when checking the squareness of small work (*see* Fig 2.2).

Knives

You will find a craft/modellers' knife and/or a scalpel invaluable for various cutting and trimming tasks (*see* Fig 2.3).

Planes

A smoothing plane is useful to have, but not essential. As the majority of planing operations involve relatively small pieces of plywood, we recommend that you use a block plane (*see* Fig 2.4).

A block plane has its blade set at a lower angle, thus allowing it to trim plywood edges (which includes end grain faces) cleanly and easily. If you do not already

Fig 2.2 Squares. Two try squares (top), a mitre square (bottom left), a 50mm (2in) engineer's square (bottom) and a combination square (right).

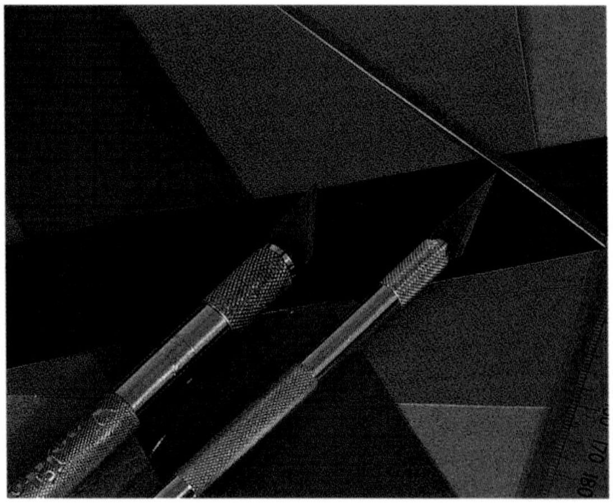

Fig 2.3 Craft knives.

Fig 2.4 A smoothing plane (top) and a block plane (bottom).

own one, we recommend that you buy one. Although they may seem expensive, it is well worth purchasing a top of the range model that has a depth adjustment screw and a throat adjustment lever. The cheaper and less sophisticated models are not as simple to adjust and may prove tiresome to use.

Chisels

You will find one or two bevel-edged chisels useful, but not essential, to produce the toys and games in this book. Chisels can be used for various trimming applications where a craft knife would be too delicate.

A 6mm (¼in) and a 12mm (½in) are good sizes to have. A 3mm (⅛in) is useful for smaller tasks.

Hand saws

Apart from a fretsaw (*see* Chapter 3) you will require a fine-toothed crosscut saw and a fine-toothed back saw (*see* Fig 2.5).

Crosscut saw

It is preferable to use a panel saw, which is a large hand saw that has fine teeth, usually 10–12 TPI (teeth per inch). This makes it an ideal tool for cutting out larger sheets of plywood.

Back saw

Of the range of back saws the tenon saw is probably the most versatile, with 13–15 TPI. However, if possible, a finer-toothed back saw, such as a dovetail saw (22 TPI+) is desirable, especially when cutting small toy components.

Gent's saw

For really small and delicate sawing operations a very fine-toothed gent's saw will prove invaluable.

Hacksaw

A junior hacksaw is needed for cutting steel axle rods and rivets.

Hammers

The majority of hammering tasks required involve the driving of moulding pins, so a

Fig 2.5 Hand saws. From top: tenon saw, dovetail saw, crosscut panel saw and gent's saw.

lightweight pin hammer should suffice (*see* Fig 2.6).

If you intend to construct any of the projects requiring riveting, you will need a light to middle-weight ball-peen hammer.

Files

A selection of small files, needle files and rasps are useful when making wooden toys.

Pin punch

A pin punch is used for driving pins slightly below the surface of the timber. Many sizes are available (*see* Fig 2.6). Ensure you choose the correct punch for the size of pins you use.

Centre punch

Used to make a small indentation in the surface of a metal workpiece (*see* Fig 2.6). This is usually to mark the exact centre point of a hole to be drilled. It also aids the drill bit to stay 'on line' when starting to drill the hole.

Pincers

Pincers will be required for removing any pins that bend during driving (*see* Fig 2.6).

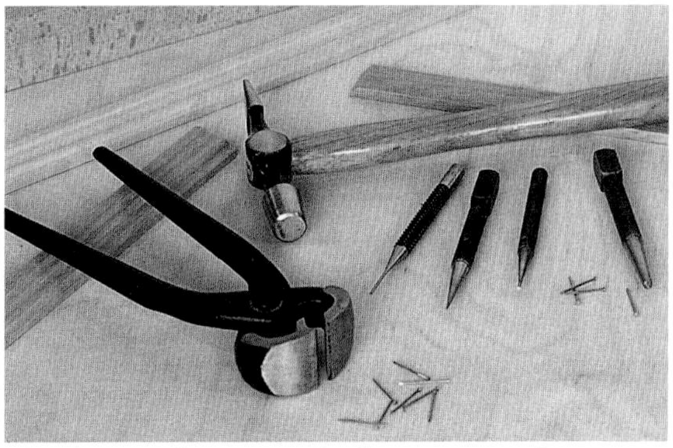

Fig 2.6 Pincers, pin hammer, pin punches and a centre punch.

Screwdrivers

In general, you will only require a couple of the smaller-sized, straight-tip variety to fit the range of small brass screws used in the projects (*see* Fig 2.7).

Awl

An awl is useful for marking the centre point of holes in timber prior to drilling, and for boring a starting hole for small screws (*see* Fig 2.7).

Fig 2.7 An awl and three screwdrivers of varying sizes.

Marking gauge

This is an invaluable tool when a line needs to be marked parallel to a square edge (*see* Fig 2.8).

Fig 2.8 Marking gauge (left) and a combined mortise and marking gauge (right).

Hand drill

For many the portable power drill has replaced the need for this tool. However, the hand drill has many advantages over a power drill. It is usually lighter in weight and therefore easier to handle. It is also easier to control when drilling small holes (such as pilot holes for small screws) on intricate items, as you can stop the bit cutting almost instantaneously. A hand-held portable power drill inevitably 'runs on' for a short while after the power has been shut off.

The hand drill is ideal for many toymaking operations and we thoroughly recommend that you have one (*see* Fig 2.9).

Drill bits

You will need a variety of these. It is a good idea to have a range of bits, the size of which are in between and around the diameters most frequently used in toymaking. These are: 1.5mm (1/16in); 3mm (1/8in); 6mm (1/4in); and 9mm (3/8in).

For example, when drilling a hole to receive a 3mm (1/8in) dowel you may find that the diameter of the actual dowel is considerably oversized. As reducing this diameter can prove problematical a simple solution is to drill the hole fractionally larger, say 3.3mm.

There are two main types of bit: conventional twist bits and dowel bits (*see* Fig 2.10).

Dowel bits, as the name suggests, are specially designed to drill a flat-bottomed hole to receive dowels. They are similar to a twist bit except that they have a central-led point and two cutting spurs. This enables the bits to cut through wood without being deflected by the grain.

Fig 2.9 A hand drill and a selection of drill bits.

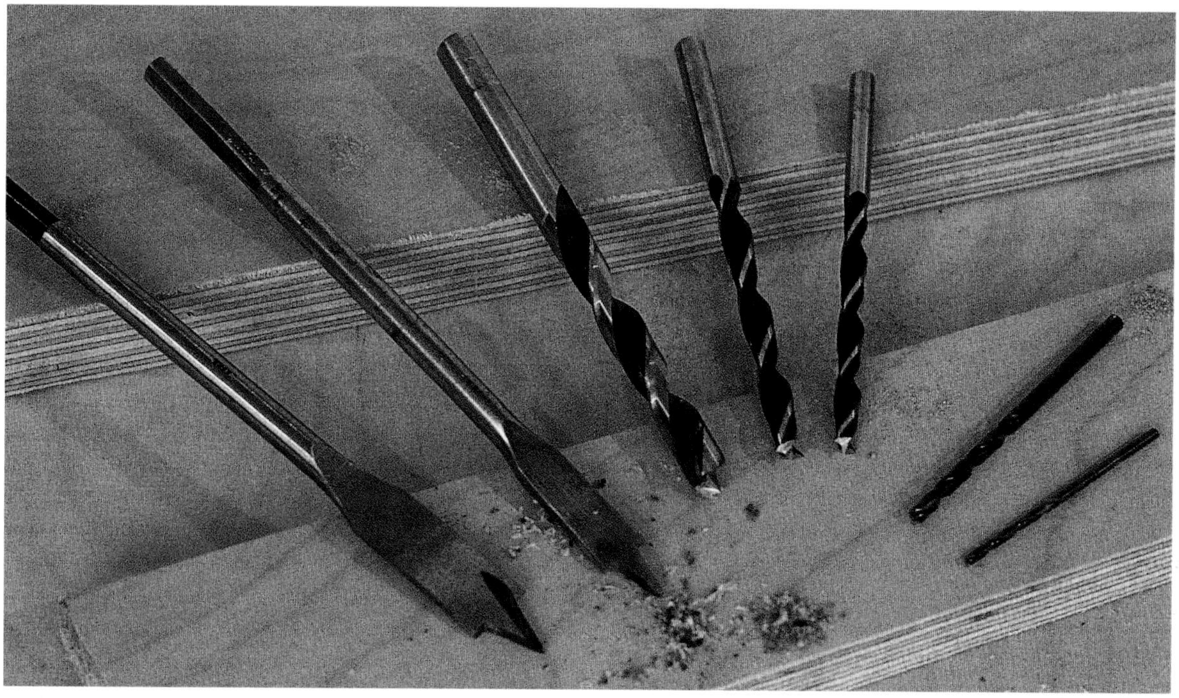

Fig 2.10 From left: two spade bits, three wood or dowel bits and two standard twist bits.

Spade bits

These are also known as zip bits or flat bits. They must be used in conjunction with a power drill (*see* Fig 2.10).

Each bit has a long central-led point that enables it to be fed positively through the workpiece. They are usually available in sizes ranging from 6mm (¼in) to 38mm (1½in).

Archimedes fret drill

This tool is used for boring small holes in thin material, in order to allow a fretsaw blade to be threaded through when undertaking any internal cutting tasks (*see* Fig 2.11).

It can hold fine twist bits or drill points. Many of these drills have hollowed handles for bit storage.

To operate, hold the end handle in one hand while moving the central handle backwards and forwards with the other. This will cause the bit to rotate.

The possession of this tool is not essential, especially if you own a hand drill. However, they cost surprisingly little and may prove a very useful addition to your toolkit.

Bench hook

This is a useful workbench aid used when sawing timber with a back saw.

They are usually made from scrap wood rather than being shop bought (*see* Fig 2.12).

Mitre box

Used for cutting mitres on the edging. There are numerous jigs and aids available to enable accurate mitres to be cut, and a

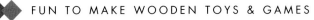

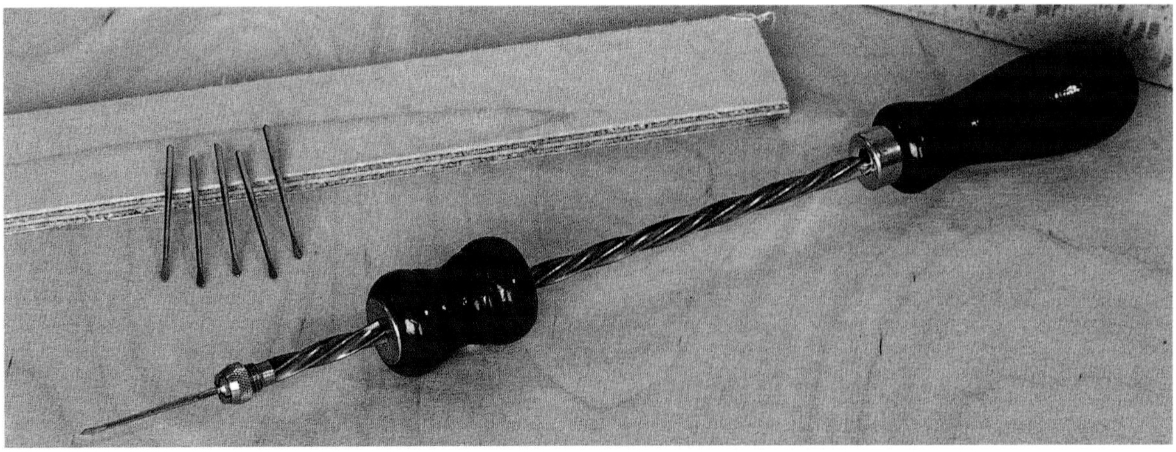

Fig 2.11 An Archimedes fret drill and drill points.

mitre box is one of the most inexpensive. They are usually made from hardwood such as beech (*see* Fig 2.13).

The photograph on page 94 (Fig 11.9) shows the use of a mitre jig to cut the mitres on the edging for the Snail Racing game board. If you intend to do much mitre cutting it may be worth investing in one of these jigs.

G-cramps

These are useful for holding workpieces together while waiting for glue to set, and for other general clamping tasks (*see* Fig 2.14).

Portable power tools and machinery

One of the joys of the pastime of making wooden toys is that you do not necessarily need large or expensive items of machinery.

If you intend to undertake a large amount of wooden toymaking then a powered fretsaw is a must. Advice on purchasing and using such a machine is given in the Construction Techniques chapter, pages 16 – 22.

A power drill and stand (or preferably a bench-mounted pillar drill) is very useful and as you do more toymaking you will probably wish to purchase a small bandsaw. You are unlikely to need many more machines, though a glance through

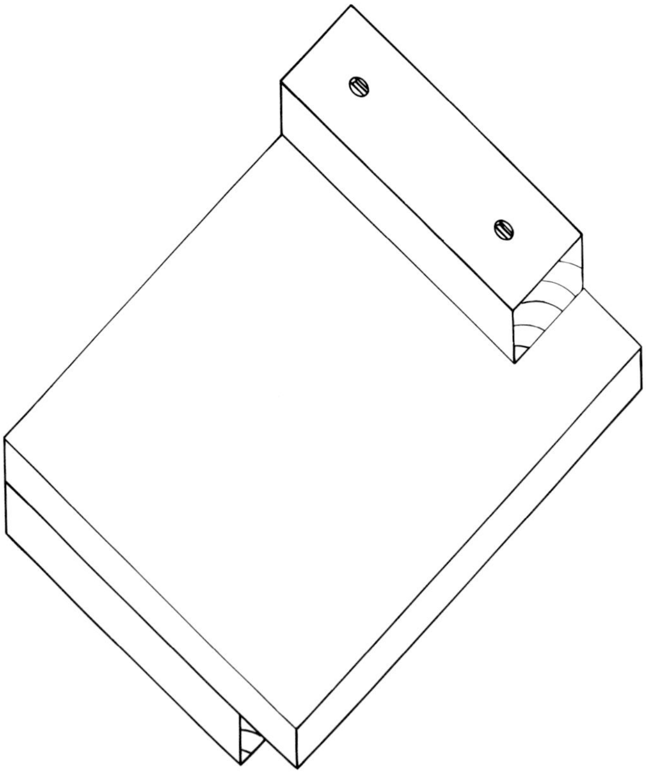

Fig 2.12 An easy-to-make bench hook.

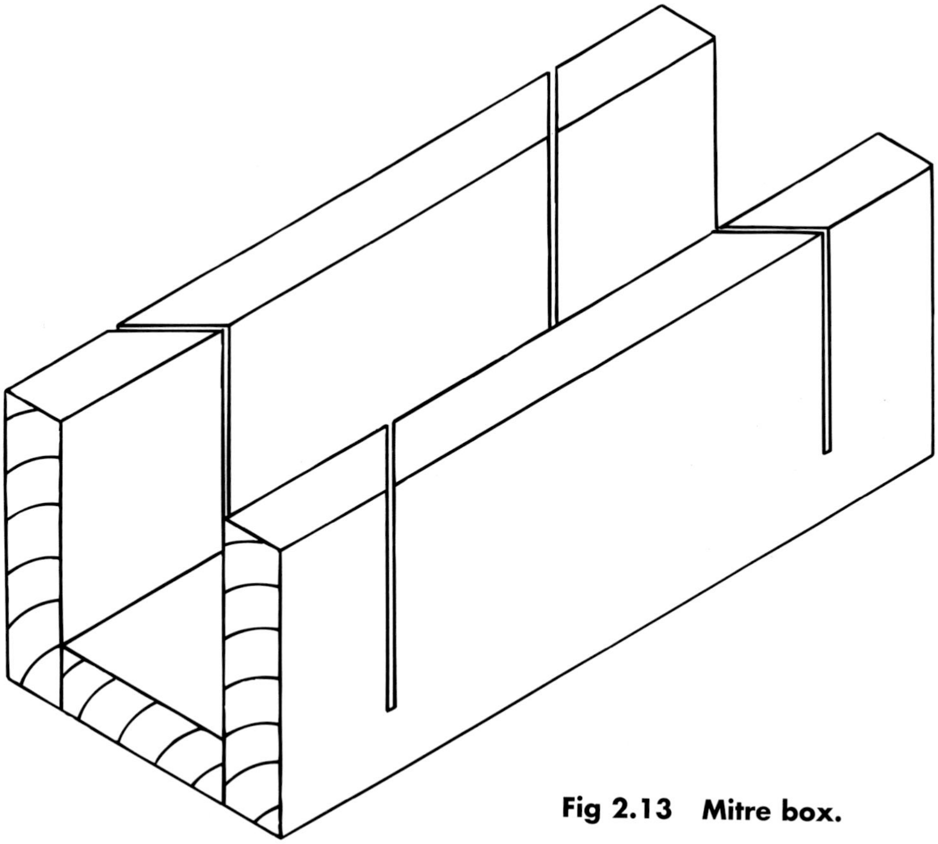

Fig 2.13 Mitre box.

machine or trade catalogues, or a visit to a woodworking show, can leave you prone to the 'if only I had that . . . and that . . . and . . .' syndrome.

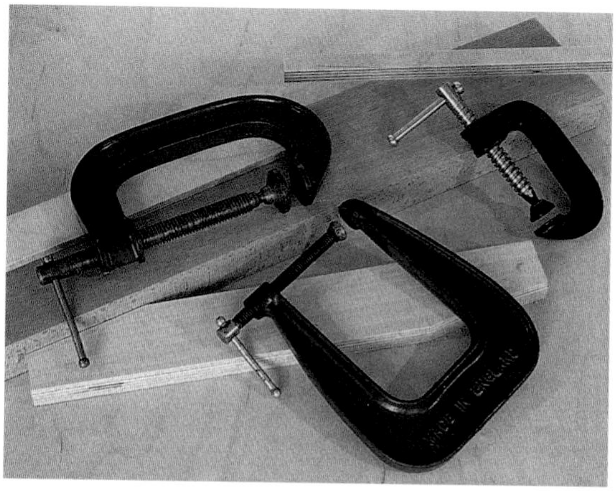

Fig 2.14 Cramps. From left: a 102mm (4in) capacity G-cramp; a 76mm (3in) C-cramp, and a 51mm (2in) G-cramp.

Workspace

Few of us are fortunate enough to have a purpose-built and fully equipped workshop for toymaking. Luckily, however, you will not need very large items of equipment, but you will need a workbench. This may be as basic as a table with a vice bolted to it, but it must be strong and stable. Not only is it difficult to work on a surface that wobbles, it is also dangerous as tools can easily slip and cause a nasty accident.

Good lighting is important, and so too is cleanliness and tidiness. An untidy workspace is dangerous, and cutting tools in particular should be kept in racks when not in use but within easy reach.

CHAPTER 3

Construction Techniques

INTRODUCTION

This section provides guidelines for the use of some of the tools and machines previously mentioned, and some of the techniques required for the construction of the toys and games. However, it does not, and cannot fairly be expected to, instruct the reader in every process and workshop practice.

If you are at all unsure how to use a tool or undertake a task correctly, please seek some expert advice. Many colleges run evening classes which can instruct you. There are also many excellent books available to inform you.

FRETSAWING

Fretsawing is used many times during the construction of the toys in this book. We have gone into some detail for those new to fretsawing and have included tips and techniques.

Fretsawing can be an enjoyable practice and often becomes a popular pastime in its own right.

Basically, fretsawing is the process of cutting small curves and shapes from wood with a thin and narrow blade. There are two main categories of fretsawing: hand powered and machine powered.

Hand fretsawing

A hand-held fretsaw has a deep-bowed metal frame. The spring of the frame tensions the blade. The blade is clamped to the frame by two thumbscrews. It is usually fitted with its teeth pointing towards the handle as it cuts on the downstroke.

It is best to sit at the workbench when cutting. The work should be supported by a jig which is clamped to the edge of the bench (*see* Fig 3.1). Ready-made jigs may

Fig 3.1 This home-made jig is simply clamped to the workbench.

be purchased, or jigs can easily be made from some scrap plywood (*see* Fig 3.2). Make the dimensions of the jig to your own requirements.

The more substantial jig shown in Fig 3.2 is held in the workbench vice while in use (*see* Fig 3.3). The longer back piece of the jig will enable height adjustment and give clearance between your hand and the vice top on each downstroke cut.

With a little practice, cutting with a hand-held fretsaw should not prove too difficult.

Fig 3.2 Two very simple fretsawing platforms that can be made from scrap plywood.

Fig 3.3 The height of this home-made jig can be adjusted.

Never force the blade through the work, and try to maintain a smooth, rhythmic cutting action.

When cutting internal shapes and holes, drill a hole through the waste part first. Then unclamp one end of the blade, pass it through the hole, reclamp the blade and begin cutting.

Machine fretsawing

If you intend to make wooden toys regularly and you were given the option of owning only one machine, then a powered fretsaw would prove a wise choice.

It is one of the most versatile machines in the workshop. Many models can cut intricate curves in various materials such as plywood, hard- and softwoods, plastics and some metals. On some machines you can tilt the cutting table through 45°. The blades can often be turned through 90°, enabling long cuts to be made. Some manufacturers supply machines with variable-speed control, which is a very useful facility.

Most fretsaws are powered by a small and, usually, relatively quiet electric motor, but there are one or two treadle machines on the market. These are relatively inexpensive machines with the added plus that they help you keep fit as you have to pedal them with your feet to drive the blade! Don't scoff if you have not come across one of these machines before – they require little maintenance, are economical, quiet and produce a fine finish of cut.

If you are intending to purchase a powered fretsaw for the first time you should take great care in choosing the right machine. Here are some of the basic questions you should ask yourself and/or a dealer.

What will it cost?

As with the rest of life, you get what you pay for. It will usually prove a false economy to purchase an inexpensive machine, or one with a capacity unsuited to your needs. Chat to a group of toymaking enthusiasts and invariably one or two will bemoan the purchase of an inferior machine that now gathers dust in the corner of their workshop. That said, there are nevertheless one or two less expensive models on the market that are reputedly quite good.

The best advice we can give is to shop around, and get as much advice and information as you can – woodworking shows and exhibitions are a great place to meet fellow enthusiasts.

Remember that, if you are intending to make wooden toys only, a fretsaw machine could be the most expensive purchase for your workshop.

What size and type of machine will I need?

This will depend upon the size of material and components you will need to cut.

Look at the size of the machine's table and the throat depth. Also check whether the table will tilt for angled cutting.

If you intend to cut large sheets, find out if the blade and its holder can be rotated.

Is it user friendly?

Find out how easy it is to change a blade. If you intend to do a lot of pierced work (internal cuts) a machine with awkward-to-use bladeholders will frustrate you.

Check that your prospective machine has an adjustable air blower. You will need one to clear dust from your work during cutting. As you should always wear a dust mask during cutting, you will be unable to blow the dust away yourself.

What cutting speeds does it have?

Some machines are single speed. Others have a selection of speeds, but the best machines (in our opinion) have a variable-speed facility.

How easy is it to stop the machine?

This may seem an odd question, but does merit some thought. During use you will probably not be able to reach the socket switch, so find out how accessible the machine's on and off switches are. Bear in mind that you will need to keep your eyes and one hand on the workpiece while your other hand searches for the switch.

We would strongly recommend that you purchase a machine that has a foot control switch fitted. We would not like to use a machine without one!

Does it run smoothly?

Not only is it irritating if a machine does not run smoothly, it is unlikely that you will achieve accurate cutting if excessive vibration is evident. This leads us to one of the most important questions.

Can I test it, or view a demonstration before buying?

A good dealer and/or manufacturer ought to be able to arrange this for you. You may have to travel to do this but it would probably prove worth your while.

Having purchased your machine here are some tips on how to get the most from your fretsaw.

Blade choice and installation

Blade sizes are graded from 00 (very fine) to 12 (coarse). The grade you choose will be dependent upon various factors – the smoothness of the finish required, the thickness of the workpiece material and the speed of the cut. Generally, the finer the cut and thinner the material then the finer the blade you will need. Blade manufacturers and suppliers provide details of which grade is best suited to which material. They also give information regarding which type of blade tooth arrangement is best for the job in hand. The most popular blades for fretsawing thin wood and plywood are skip-tooth or double-tooth blades.

Other blades worth noting are reverse-tooth blades. These have a few teeth, at the bottom of the blade, pointing back upwards. These are intended to create a smooth, splinter-free finish to the underside of the workpiece being cut.

When fitting a blade follow the manufacturer's instruction issued with your machine, always ensuring that the teeth of the blade point downwards.

The table overleaf will help you choose the correct blade to use.

Fretsaw blade sizes and usage

GRADE	MATERIAL THICKNESS
00	For veneers and wood up to 3mm (⅛in), 26 TPI
0	As above
1	For 3mm (⅛in) wood
2	For 4.5mm (3/16in) wood
3	For 6mm (¼in) wood
4	For 9mm (⅜in) wood
5	For 12mm (½in) wood
6	For 18mm (¾in) wood
7	As above
8	As above
9, 10	For cutting larger thickness from 18mm (¾in) to 50mm (2in) wood
11	As above, 10 TPI
12	As above

Blade tensioning

There is no substitute for the experience and practice which will teach you how to assess the correct tensioning for your blades. Too little tension will make it difficult for you to cut to a line, too much and your blade will soon break.

Think of blade tensioning as 'tuning up', because you 'ping' the back of the fitted blade with a finger nail while increasing the tension on the blade. Listen to the increasing pitch of the blade and stop when you hear the correct 'ping' note which you recognize as being right for the blade grade and the job in hand. While 'pinging' the blade, you can also feel the increasing tension. This method may not be very technical, but it works very well for us!

Table squareness

For general cutting operations the blade must be square (at a right angle) to the table surface.

To check this, move the upper arm of your machine to its uppermost position and place a small try square next to the blade (*see* Fig 3.4). Any discrepancy will be obvious, and can be rectified by loosening the knob which clamps the table-tilting mechanism (*see* Fig 3.5), gently tilting the table until it is square with the blade, and retightening the knob.

Angled cuts

Most machine tables can be tilted from 0° through to 45°, thus allowing you to make a series of angled cuts. The tilting mechanisms on some machines are graded in degrees and accurate adjustment is straightforward.

For machines which do not have graduated degrees marked, Fig 3.6 illustrates a simple homemade protractor jig which will assist you to set the blade quickly to the required angle. This jig simply consists of a piece of

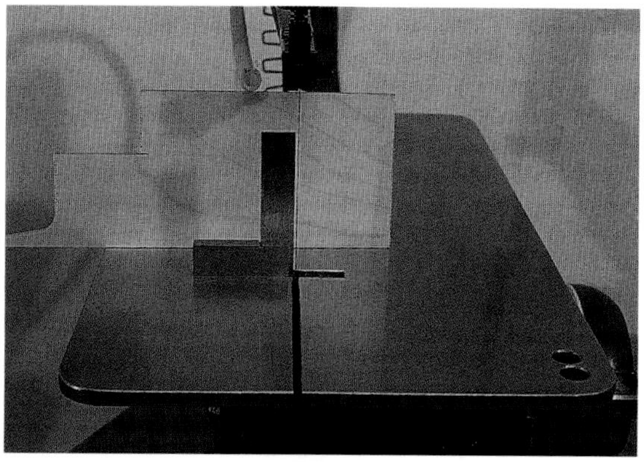

Fig 3.4 Checking that the table is square.

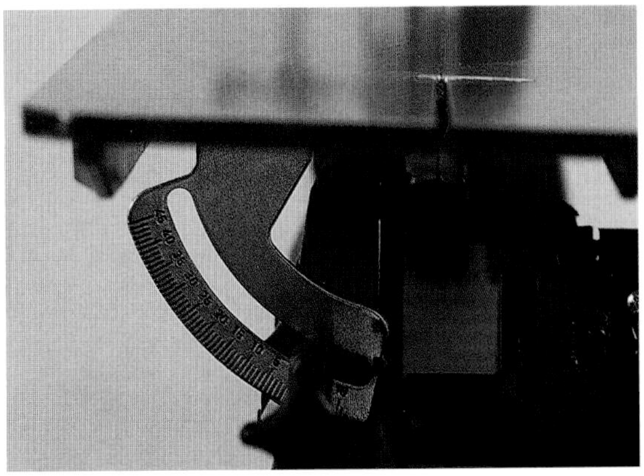

Fig 3.5 The table-tilting mechanism.

white card with lines drawn from one central, bottom point at the cutting angles most used. Place the card on the table and tilt the table until the blade is in line with the angled line of your choice.

Cutting speeds

Some machines operate at a fixed speed, but most have a selection of speeds or a variable-speed facility.

It is difficult to advise on speed selection as, once again, experience will instruct you what speed to use. Generally, choose a speed that you feel comfortable with for the job you are undertaking.

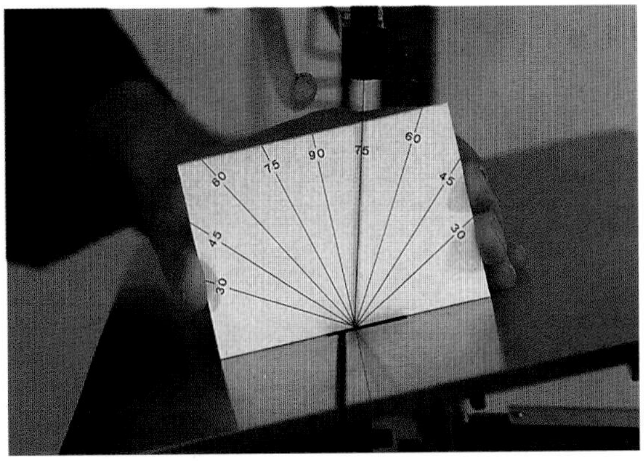

Fig 3.6 Using a home-made jig to set the blade for an angled cut.

Body position

Whether you are standing or sitting at your machine you must be comfortable. Not only can it be dangerous if you are not, but it may prove difficult to achieve accurate cutting. You should be positioned directly in front of your machine with your torso parallel to its table.

When cutting, the fingers and thumbs of each hand should be either side of the blade respectively (*see* Fig 3.7). Ideally, when feeding work into the blade, you should never place any part of either hand in front of it, though in reality this is not always practically possible. However, never have a finger or thumb in front of the blade as it breaks through the workpiece at the end of a cut. Remember, you can always replace a component or workpiece but never a finger or thumb!

Cutting curves

When cutting a curve the blade should just stroke the outline of your workpiece.

You should be relaxed (sometimes very difficult when cutting intricate patterns!) and not hold the workpiece too tightly – just hold it firmly enough so that it will not be picked up by the blade on the upstroke causing 'chatter'. Always let the blade cut freely, do not force the workpiece on to it.

If you do happen to let the blade wander off line it is better to let it come back gently. Trying to bring it back in a jerky movement can make it difficult for you to get the blade cutting smoothly again. This

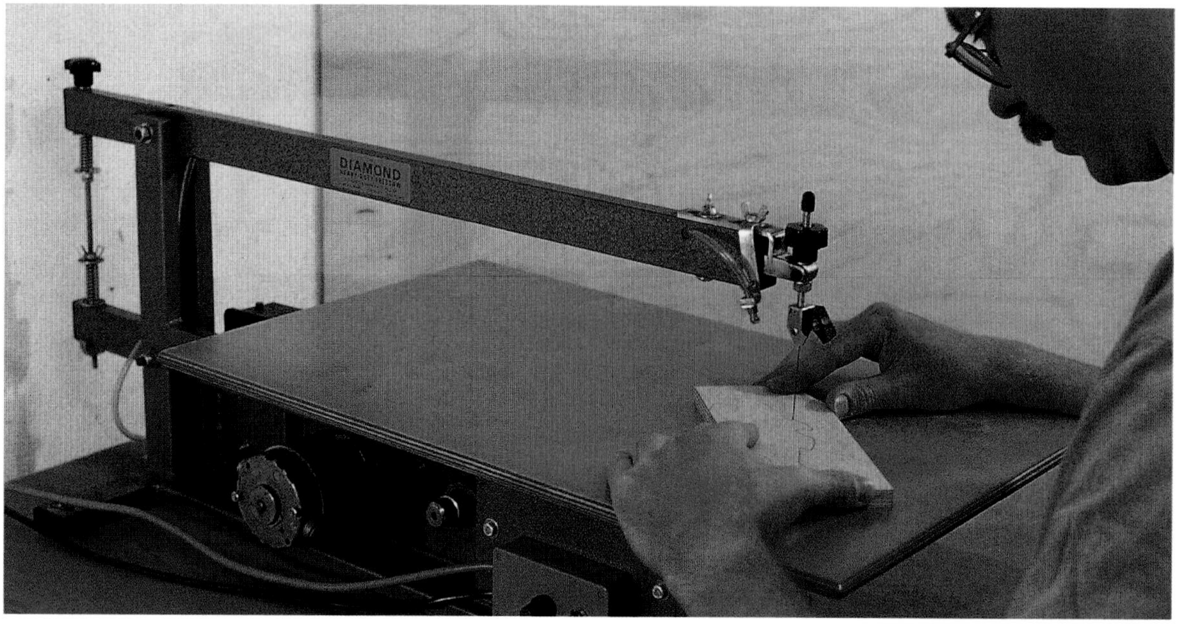

Fig 3.7 A good position for fretsawing – note the position of the hands.

will result in a jerky or wobbly section to the outline of your workpiece.

Straight cutting

Theoretically it is possible to clamp a square piece of batten to the fretsaw's table, parallel with the blade, and use this as a cutting fence.

We do not find this method satisfactory, however, and prefer to cut straight lines freehand. Invariably, with a fretwork project or task, a straight line is connected to a curved line anyway, thus rendering the use of a fence impractical.

With practice you will be able to cut straights as easily as curves.

Cutting tight curves

When cutting a tight turn or corner it is easy to imagine that the blade is running away from your control. Remember, on a good machine, if you stop feeding the workpiece into the blade it will not be cut. The blade will simply idle up and down. Therefore, to cut a tight corner, stop feeding the workpiece as the blade reaches the corner. Then, with the finger of one hand positioned on the workpiece behind the blade, acting as a pivot, spin the workpiece around steadily with your other hand. This will become easier with practice. Ensure that the blade you use is fine enough to turn the corner adequately.

Internal cutting

To cut an internal shape from your workpiece you will first need to drill a hole, large enough for the blade to fit through, into the last section of the shape. Some thought ought to be given to deciding where to drill the hole (*see* Fig 3.8).

Drilling the hole as in Fig 3.8A will make it more awkward to get the blade cutting in line than in Fig 3.8B.

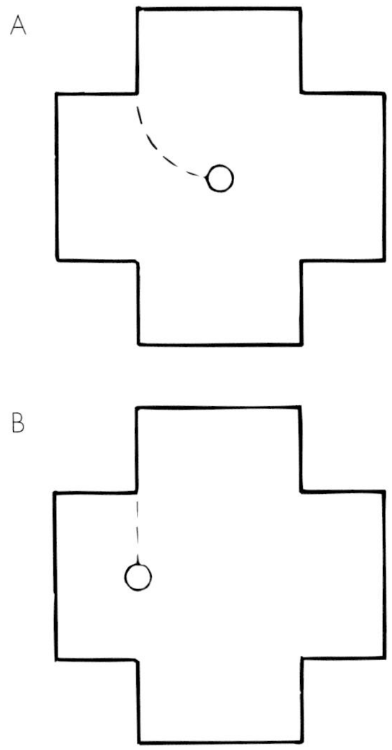

– – – indicates line of cut

Fig 3.8 Blade-hole positioning.

Thread the blade through the hole and clamp it into the blade holders of the machine. Ensure that the blade is sufficiently tensioned before cutting.

Cutting small components

You may find that the blade aperture on the table of your machine is too large to cut small items comfortably and safely. While cutting, this could result in the blade trying to pull a small component down into the aperture; there is then a risk that you could cut your fingers.

As a remedy, you can securely tape a temporary overlay on to the table top (*see* Fig 3.9). This consists of a piece of 3mm (⅛in) material (such as ply or hardboard) with a hole drilled through it for the blade.

Fig 3.9 Temporary table overlay.

The diameter of this hole needs to be marginally larger than the width of the blade. The size of the overlay required depends upon your preference and the size of your machine's table.

If you regularly work on small components it may prove useful to make an overlay with sides which fit entirely over the table of your machine. I would suggest that such an overlay be made from 12mm (½in) birch plywood, with sides constructed from suitable pieces of batten which would secure it to the top of the table.

Multiple cutting

Occasionally you may need to cut multiples of a shape in thin material. You can save time by stacking and securing several sheets together and cutting one thick shape from it. When the shape is unstacked you will have multiples of that shape. See, for example, the animals on Acorn Farm (page 79).

Blade changing

Obviously you will need to change blades when one breaks, though blade breakages become a rare occurrence the more experience you gain using your machine.

As a blade blunts you will be able to feel that it is not cutting so well. By listening carefully you may also be able to detect a change in the cutting sound. With the blade stopped you can visually gauge wear. With time you will be able to determine easily when the blade is no longer effective and requires replacing.

The length of cutting stroke of fretsaw machines is relatively short, so frequently only a small proportion of a blade tends to be worn. To further the usefulness of a blade you can make use of an unworn section. To do this fit an overlay table as described in the section on cutting small components (page 21). This should be more than 18mm (¾in) thickness.

Applying patterns to the timber

Here are four useful methods to assist you in transferring a design on to your workpiece:

Photocopies

Use artist's temporary spray adhesive to glue a full-size photocopy of your design on to the timber. The paper can easily be removed when cutting is finished.

Tracing paper

Good old tracing paper is a bit fiddly but works well.

Transfer paper

This is used like carbon paper but is less messy.

Templates

If you plan to cut the same shape repeatedly, make a template from hardboard or thin plywood. Draw around this on to your timber.

DRILLING

The process of drilling accurate holes is required for most of the toys in this book.

Provided you use the appropriate bits (*see* Chapter 2), drilling should be a relatively straightforward process.

Whether you own a large bench-mounted pillar drill or a vertical drill stand and power drill, or if you have a hand drill or brace, a few simple precautions should be taken.

Always ensure that the workpiece is firmly held, preferably in a vice or by a cramp, while drilling takes place.

Beware of loose clothing, jewellery, hair or flex coming near the drilling operation.

Always wear eye protection, and ear protection if necessary. In addition, wear a dust mask appropriate to the material being drilled.

Make sure that your drilling equipment is in good order and that your drill/boring bits are sharp.

When using any type of drill press, ensure that it is bolted securely to a stable, solid surface.

When you are drilling right through a piece of wood, place a scrap piece at the back or base of it. This will help prevent splintering when the bit breaks through the workpiece.

When a hole needs to be drilled partway through the workpiece to a precise depth, some means of gauging the depth is required. Large drill presses and vertical drill stands often have a depth gauge and a depth stop fitted. The latter, when set, will prevent the drill from going deeper when the correct depth has been obtained.

If your drill does not have this facility, or you are using a hand drill, you can indicate the desired depth by wrapping a piece of coloured sticky tape around the drill bit. The depth required will be the distance from the tip of the drill bit spurs (if using a wood bit) to the leading edge of the sticky tape. Stop drilling when the leading edge of the sticky tape reaches the surface of the workpiece (*see* Fig 3.10).

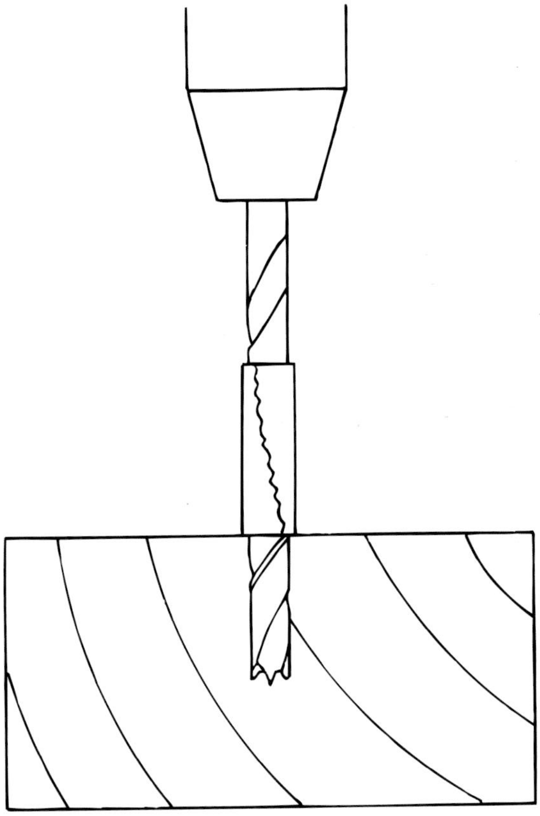

Fig 3.10 Drilling a peg hole using a piece of coloured sticky tape as a depth stop.

RIVETING

Some of the toys in this book, such as Chris Clown's Tricky Trike and the Chinese Acrobat, have jointed limbs. An unusual method of loose riveting has been used to allow the free movement of these limbs.

The rivets used are called snap rivets and are available in a variety of lengths and widths. It is advisable to obtain a few of varying sizes, as you will find that bigger rivets are more suited to bigger jointing tasks than smaller ones and vice versa.

Normally, snap rivets are fixed with a hand-operated riveter. For the construction of the toys in this book it will not be necessary to use one of these.

As an example of the technique required, the jointing of Chris Clown's arms is described below. Please note that this process of riveting may sound difficult and tedious to those who have not done it before. However, it really is a surprisingly quick and neat method of loose jointing.

Items required

An assortment of snap rivets
A small ball-peen hammer
A small hacksaw
A metal-working vice
A homemade rivet set (optional)

Take two 4 x 5.6mm ($\frac{5}{32}$ x $\frac{7}{32}$in) snap rivets. Using a hammer, tap out the central pin of each rivet. Hold the rivets in a vice when doing this. Now slide one of the rivet pins back into position, but make sure that it is reversed (*see* Fig 3.11).

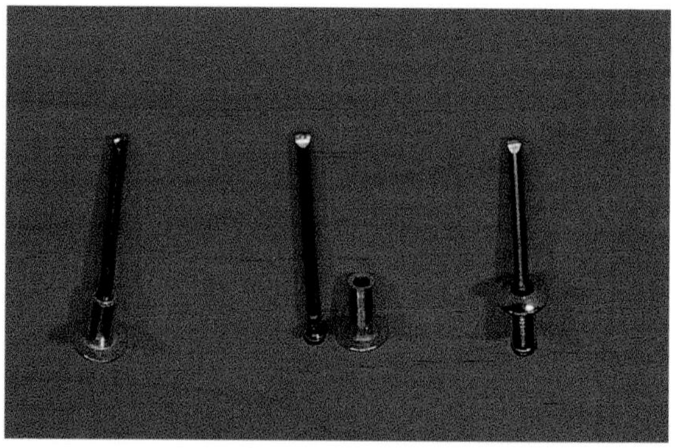

Fig 3.11 Stages in reversing the rivet assembly. From right: original rivet, central pin of rivet removed, reversed rivet.

Make sure that all the holes drilled into Chris's body parts are of a suitable size to enable free movement when riveted. Drill trial-size holes in scrap wood to determine the perfect drill diameter to suit your chosen rivets.

Pass the newly assembled rivet through the appropriate arm, fit a suitable washer and fit it into Chris's body.

Take the disassembled rivet head, pass it through the other arm, thread a washer onto it and thread this onto the other rivet's pin. This pin should be protruding out of the armhole in Chris's body. You should now have an arrangement as shown in Fig 3.12.

Mark the protruding pin a little way away from the domed rivet head. This is the point where you will cut the pin. The remaining short length of pin is to be

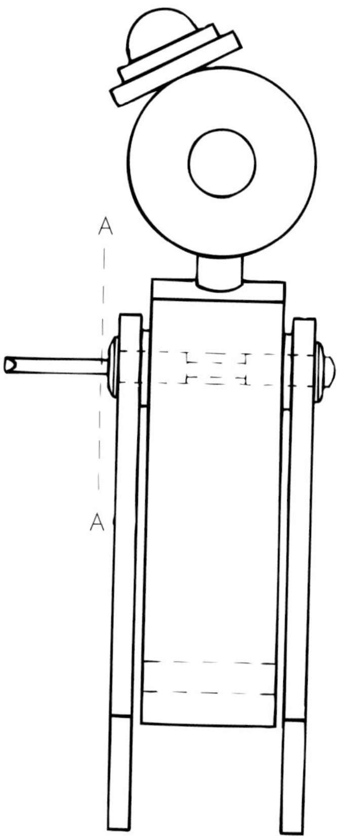

Mark the protruding pin at the dashed line (A–A) for cutting

Fig 3.12 Front view of Chris Clown's head, torso and arms, showing rivet assembly.

riveted over. Experience will tell you where to cut the pin. Practise riveting some scrap wood first if you are unsure.

With the pin marked, disassemble the arms and body, hold the pin in the vice and cut to length. Then reassemble the arms, body and rivet arrangement.

The small protruding length of pin must now be hammered over to hold the entire assembly together. To do this the pin's round head should be placed on a hard, metal surface. Alternatively, a homemade 'set' can be made by drilling a very shallow hole (to form a cup-like depression) into the top surface of the head of a large bolt (*see* Fig 3.13). The hole should just allow the round rivet pin head to fit snugly into it.

Securely hold the 'set' in a vice and place Chris appropriately on to it.

Using the ball end of the hammer, repeatedly tap the protruding pin gently. You must try to round the pin over on all sides and fill the slight countersunk hole that most rivet heads have. When complete, check that you haven't left any sharp edges on the pin.

Chris's arms should now move freely. If they are too stiff, or they will not move at all, this can easily be rectified by drilling the rivets out and re-riveting.

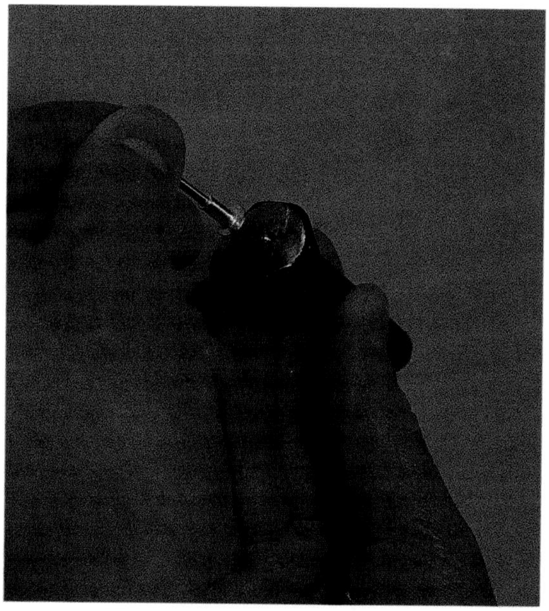

Fig 3.13 Placing a rivet into a home-made set.

To do this, centre punch the newly hammered end. Then use a suitably sized drill bit and drill this out, thus enabling the assembly to come apart.

On some riveting tasks you may find that the shanks of your rivets are too long and protrude too much from your workpiece. This would create much too loose a fit. Therefore, simply cut or file away any surplus before fitting.

WORKING WITH BIRCH PLYWOOD

The two face surfaces of birch plywood are already fairly smooth, so they require minimal preparatory sanding.

Use a block plane to smooth any freshly sawn edges; the low angle of blade will shave the end grain plys more easily than a larger smoothing or jack plane.

One drawback of working plywood is that it tends to blunt the cutting edges of your tools fairly quickly, so be prepared to sharpen them regularly.

Splintering

Occasionally, the corner edge of a piece of birch plywood will splinter away. This can sometimes be caused by a blunt or incorrect type of saw blade being used (though occasionally you might be unlucky and have a rogue sheet with a tendency to do this). Here are two methods to deal with this problem.

1 Use instant glue (carefully) to stick the splinter down, thus enabling you to use the plywood almost immediately.

2 Sometimes, with a rogue piece, just sanding the surface can result in many tiny splinters being raised from the edge. To save the sheet and make it usable, give both face surfaces a sealing coat of gloss varnish. The varnish will act as glue and prevent the corner edges from splintering, thus enabling you to produce a crisp, clean edge. However, you cannot use this method if you wish to apply a stain to the plywood later.

If you have a sheet of plywood which splinters badly whatever precautions you take, then there is probably a fault in its manufacture. In such rare cases you should take the matter up with the supplier.

Making a thicker sheet from two thinner sheets

Occasionally, you may need to glue two plywood sheets together. For instance, you may need a small piece of 18mm (¾in) thick birch plywood. Purchasing a whole sheet can be expensive, so you could glue a sheet of 12mm (½in) and a sheet of 6mm (¼in) together, thus producing an 18mm (¾in) piece.

To do this, spread PVA adhesive on one surface. Then join the two pieces and place them on a flat surface. Place a weight (any suitably heavy object) evenly on top. Then leave until the adhesive has fully set.

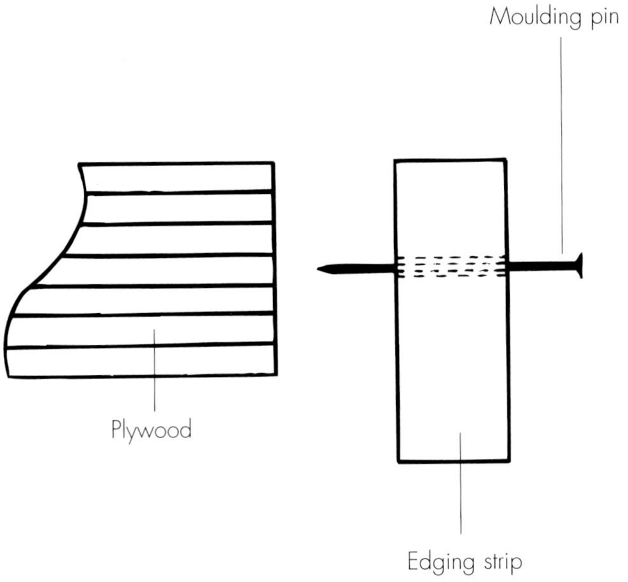

Fig 3.14 Pinning edging.

PRE-DRILLING PIN HOLES

When applying a length of moulding, or another piece of plywood or sheet material, to the edge of birch plywood, the moulding pins used may deflect away from one of the denser-face plys into an adjacent softer, end-grain ply. When this happens, the result is to raise or lower the moulding, or other material being pinned, making it impossible to achieve a flush finish. To help prevent this, drill a hole larger than the shaft of the moulding pin, but narrower than the diameter of the pin head, into the moulding or plywood before pinning (*see* Fig 3.14). This will provide you with some leeway when driving in the pin.

Use a pin punch to drive the pin below the surface to secure the two pieces until the glue sets.

DOWEL JOINTS

In some of the projects it is suggested that a glue joint be reinforced by using dowel pegs. You may be familiar with this jointing method from furniture-making, where it is primarily used for carcass joints, framing joints and edge-to-edge joints.

The pegs required for these joints depend upon the thickness of timber used. Usually needed are 6mm (¼in), 8mm (5/16in), 10mm (⅜in) or 12mm (½in) diameter pegs.

Due to either size or intricate shape, our projects will only require 3mm (⅛in) or 6mm (¼in) pegs. The latter may be bought ready made, usually in 25mm (1in) or 30mm (1 3/16in) lengths, fluted and with their ends chamfered. The former you will need to make yourself, scoring your own flutes with a sharp implement such as an awl or knife. These flutes alleviate the hole pressure when gluing and prevent the timber from splitting.

Accurate marking out of where the dowel holes are to be drilled is vital. When using the 6mm (¼in) dowel pegs the dowel centre points may be used as an aid (*see* Fig 3.15).

Simply insert them into previously drilled dowel holes in one workpiece. Then push this workpiece against the other in the desired position. When taken apart small indentations will be left on the other workpiece. These indicate the centres of the dowel holes to be drilled.

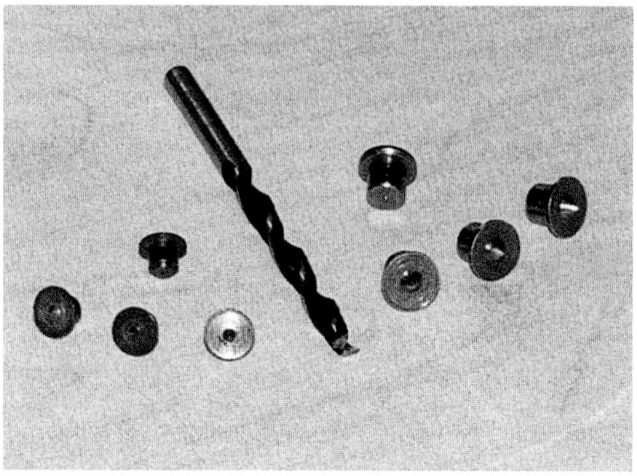

Fig 3.15 Wood twist bit and centre points.

SHARPNESS

The degree of sharpness of your tools with cutting edges is vital. Whether you are new to woodwork or not, you have probably heard the phrase, 'Blunt tools are dangerous'. This is absolutely true! Sharp, well-maintained tools save time, trouble and accidents.

A cutting tool with a blunt edge will require greater force in order to make it cut, and it will be more likely to deflect away from (or in the case of a plane, skim over the surface of) the workpiece.

Whole books have been written on the sharpening of tools, and it would be impossible for us to give full instructions on how to undertake all sharpening tasks in this brief section.

There are many places, such as saw-sharpening specialists, that will sharpen and, if necessary, regrind the cutting edges of your tools. Your local commercial telephone book should have a list. Failing that, your local independent tool or hardware store will often know of someone who can do this service for you if you do not wish to do it yourself.

CHAPTER 4

Painting & Finishing

Painting and finishing your own handmade wooden toys and games can be the most satisfying, and sometimes the most frustrating, process! More often than not we find that the finishing of a toy or game takes much more time than its construction.

Take time to plan your colour schemes for each toy. Of course, you could copy ours, but children really appreciate a toy that has been personalized for them. For instance, using transfer lettering, you could put a child's name and address on the side of the Breakdown Recovery Truck.

Good stationers, hobby shops and some toy shops stock a range of transfers and stickers which can be used to decorate the toys. In addition, most hardware and decorating shops sell sticky-backed plastic sheets in various colours, enabling you to make some designs of your own.

The design and style of some stickers or transfers may influence the whole colour scheme and theme of the toy.

Remember that transfers may need one or two coats of varnish to protect them.

Do not be afraid to experiment with colour. It is said that, under the right conditions, it is possible for someone with good eyesight to be able to detect up to 10 million different colours!

Understandably, most suppliers tend not to stock paint colours in a very wide range, so have a go at mixing and matching. An old white plate serves as an excellent palette and may be cleaned easily and reused.

Before applying paint make absolutely sure that the workpiece surface is as clean and sound as possible. It is nigh on impossible to achieve a good finish if you do not prepare thoroughly first.

Ensure that the environment you choose for painting in is well ventilated, warm, tidy and as clean and dust free as possible. A good light source is also essential – daylight is the best.

Take your time when applying a finish. As we have previously said, quite often generally finishing and painting a project takes longer than the actual construction. It may be a bit of an old chestnut, but the adage, 'Several light coats of paint are far better than one or two heavy ones' is on the whole true! After all the overall effect and appeal of a design is largely influenced by the colour scheme and quality of finish.

When painting a decorative symbol or shape, try to paint boldly and with confidence. You will find you make fewer mistakes this way than when you are nervous – a tense hand will make it difficult to paint flowing, even lines.

Keeping your paint at the right consistency will help. If a paint pot has been in use for a while, and has been opened and closed frequently, the paint will invariably be too thick. Simply thin the paint with the appropriate solvent to the required viscosity.

Before finishing a project, think about how you will store the workpieces while their freshly painted surfaces are drying. You may find that you will have to make a few jigs or holding devices. These need not be elaborate. A few nails or dowel rods partly set into a length of timber and clamped to a table will act as a hanger for a multitude of items. You will often be able to use a drying jig many times for various projects.

Whatever paint, varnish or colouring medium you choose to use, make absolutely sure it is safe for children's toys. Most are safe nowadays, but if you are unsure contact the manufacturers. They are usually pleased to advise you on their product.

Try to relax and enjoy finishing your toys – after all, you will have lavished time and care in their making. Quite often painting is forgiving. If you make a mistake you can usually paint over it later!

MATERIALS, TECHNIQUES AND TIPS

Paint

There is a vast array of paints available on the market, so we shall therefore concentrate on the types we find most useful for toymaking (*see* Fig 4.1).

Primer

It is advisable to prime the bare wood or plywood of a toy before painting. Ensure that you use child-safe primer.

Acrylic paint

The type that is convenient to use is Humbrol's Acrylic Colour. A wide range of colours are readily available in 12ml and 30ml sizes. It is water based, quick drying and easy to apply. All the colours are intermixable, and brushes may be cleaned

Fig 4.1 Paint, varnish and finished toys.

with water. Most colours are available in matt and gloss.

Acrylic varnish and some useful metallic colours are also available.

Modelling enamels

Humbrol produce an excellent range of this non-toxic, oil-based paint, available in both matt and gloss finishes. They come in convenient-sized tins such as 14ml and 50ml.

All the colours are intermixable and fairly robust; they resist steam, boiling water, salt water, fumes, oil and dirt (though we hope that your toys will not be subjected to such elements and substances).

Safety

Whatever type and make of paints you choose to use, do find out if they are child safe. Manufacturers are usually only too pleased to advise you.

Brushes

There is a wide range of brushes available (*see* Fig 4.2). The size, style and make you pick is a matter of personal preference.

You may find one type of brush used for a certain job suits one person, but not another. So buy brushes that you feel comfortable with.

A useful tip if you find some fine brush handles too thin is to wrap adhesive tape

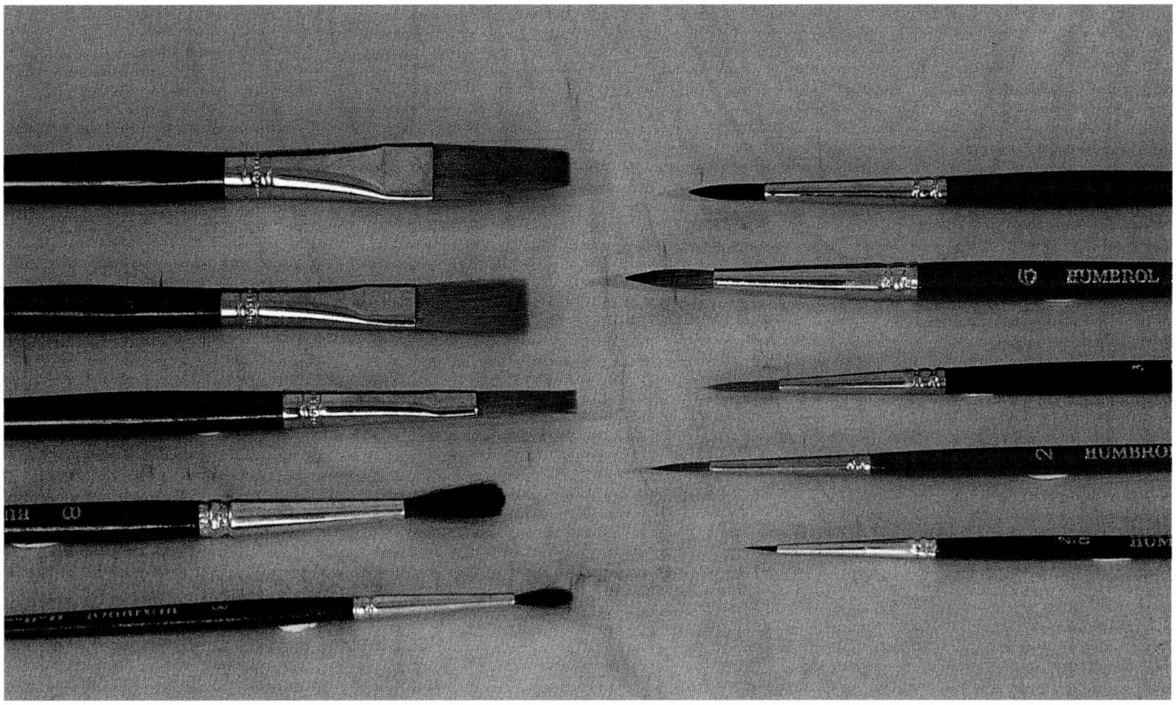

Fig 4.2 Assorted paintbrushes.

around the handle until you achieve a more comfortable thickness.

When using new brushes for the first time, you may find it advantageous to clean them first. This will not only ensure that they are clean for use, it will also take away the odd loose hair or two which may otherwise spoil the painted finish.

Whatever brushes you choose to use, always try to ensure they are of good quality. It is a false economy to buy cheap brushes – they will not last, and a satisfactory finish will be harder to achieve.

Varnish

The varnish that we need concern ourselves with is available in two forms: polyurethane and acrylic. The former is a synthetic resin that may be thinned with white spirit. The latter may be thinned with water.

Both types are available in matt, satin and gloss finishes. Gloss varnish offers greater protection than matt or satin. If you prefer these latter finishes use a gloss varnish for the first few coats, followed by matt or satin for the last one or two coats.

Both have advantages and disadvantages over each other. Personal preference will determine which to use.

Applying varnish

Whatever type of varnish you choose to use, apply it with a good-quality, clean, soft-bristled brush. Do not overload the brush and do not wipe it on the rim of the can – this will create small air bubbles that will transfer to the surface of the workpiece.

On large flat areas, spread the varnish evenly in different directions, finishing with light 'laying off' strokes in the direction of the wood grain. Do this in small sections at a time.

When varnishing near an edge, brush towards it to prevent any surplus running down the sides.

Between coats lightly sand away any dust particles or imperfections with a very fine-grade abrasive paper and/or 0000 grade wire wool.

Velour

Self-adhesive green velour with its nylon pile provides an excellent covering material for the bases of some of the toys. It is readily available in roll or sheet form from most hardware stores and hobby suppliers.

Dolls' house cladding paper

Available from hobby and dolls' house accessory suppliers in a variety of colours and effects, this paper can be a very useful finishing material (*see* Fig 4.3). Use wallpaper adhesive to attach it. In this book it has been used on the Corner House, Snargon's Wrath and Acorn Farm. Decorative sticky-back plastic is used on part of the Magic Box.

Fig 4.3 Dolls' house decorative paper and sticky-back plastic.

CHAPTER 5

Magic Box

Whether on television, in the theatre, or at a party, most children love watching magic tricks. With this Magic Box they will be able to perform a professional-looking illusion themselves.

On a table, in front of his audience, the magician has a box on a stand. The front of the box has a series of 'windows' fretted out of it. Through these the front of another box may be viewed. The magician removes the outer, open ended box and shows the audience that it is empty. He then replaces it over the inner box. The inner box is likewise removed, shown to be empty, and replaced. The magician then holds both boxes together and lifts them clear of the stand. Magically, a tiger cub has appeared and is sitting on the stand!

EQUIPMENT

Secret box

This is the secret to the illusion. It is this box which conceals the tiger cub. The box is four sided, open ended and painted matt black inside and out.

Inner box

This is also a four sided, open ended box. Inside it is painted matt black. Outside it is decorated with a striking and contrasting colour to that of the outer box.

Outer box

This is again four sided and open ended, and has a fretted 'window' pattern cut out of its front side. It is painted matt black on the inside. The outside should be finished using a bold colour – we chose bright red.

Stand

This is simply a piece of painted plywood supported by four feet.

The tiger cub

This is a shop-bought child's soft toy.

PERFORMANCE

Preparation

Place the tiger cub centrally on the stand. Carefully place the secret box over it. Then place the inner and outer boxes over the secret box. Ensure that the windows in the outer box will face the audience.

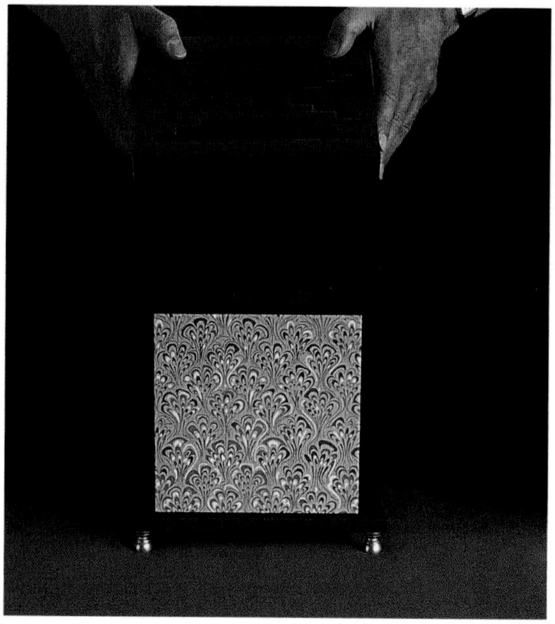

Fig 5.1 The outer box is shown to be empty.

The performance method

1 Introduce your audience to your equipment. Lift the outer box from the stand and show that it is empty (*see* Fig 5.1).

2 Replace the outer box, ensuring that the windows still face the audience, and carefully remove the inner box (*see* Fig 5.2). Show the audience that this is also empty.

This is the point where the secret of the illusion works. When the inner box is removed the audience will not notice the secret box through the fretted windows, because both it and the interior of the outer box are matt black. As matt black does not reflect light well, the outer box appears to be completely empty (*see* Fig 5.3).

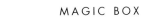

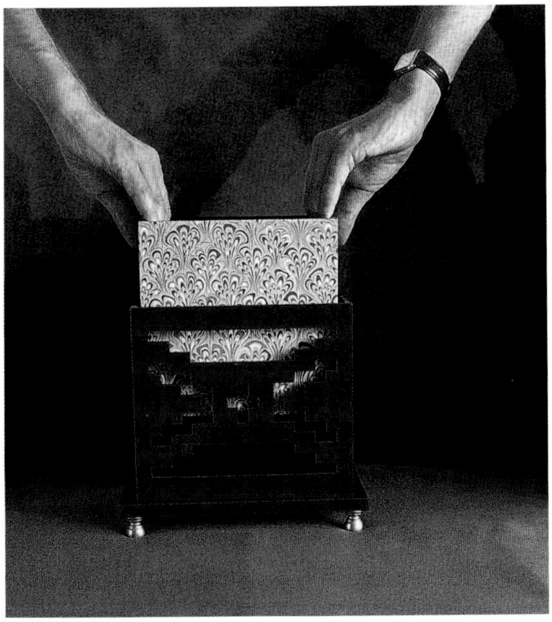

Fig 5.2 The inner box is removed to show . . .

Fig 5.3 . . . that there is absolutely nothing in the box.

3 Replace the inner box (over the secret box). As you do so, the audience will see the inner box lowered through the windows. The audience will now believe the two boxes to be empty.

4 Grasp the top edges of all the boxes. Then remove them together, up and away from the stand, to reveal the tiger cub (*see* Fig 5.4). Bow to the audience's thunderous applause!

Fig 5.4 All the boxes are removed to reveal the tiger cub.

PERFORMANCE ALTERNATIVES

Of course, you may not wish to produce a soft toy tiger in your illusion. If so, use an item of your choice, but only use something that is visually effective and suits your style of magic show.

You may wish to produce many items from the Magic Box, such as silk handkerchiefs, sweets, etc. If so, perform the trick in the manner described above up to the point of removing all the boxes from the stand. Instead, leave them in place and show the audience that you have nothing in your hands. Then take the items out of the box one by one. If you intend to produce sweets, it is fun to grasp handfuls and toss them (carefully!) into your audience.

A humorous and interesting variation of the tiger production illusion is described below.

Tiger production illusion 2

Equipment

The same, but with the addition of some items of food ranging in size, such as a small sweet, a biscuit, a chocolate bar, an apple, etc. All these items must clearly have teethmarks or a bite taken from them.

Preparation

The same, except that the items of food are placed carefully around the tiger.

Performance

Perform steps 1, 2 and 3 as before. Instead of undertaking step 4, put your obviously empty hand into the boxes, and remove the smallest of the foodstuffs, such as a sweet. Show your audience (who may well be laughing at the anticlimax of the small item being produced from the relatively large box) your consternation at what, or who, has eaten half your sweet.

Carry on producing the half-eaten items in ascending size order, while conveying your increasing puzzlement to the audience. As you produce the last item of food you tell the audience in exasperation that you have had enough and will get to the bottom of the problem. Repeat steps 1, 2 and 3, but this time making a great show of checking that absolutely no one or nothing could be hiding in your Magic Box, eating your food.

Next, carry out step 4 of the original illusion, with the exception that you apologize to the audience and say you do not know what or who has eaten the food and spoilt your trick. You go on to say that you will clear away the boxes and move along to the next trick. Now casually remove all the boxes and there, sitting cheekily on the stand, is the culprit – the tiger cub!

PERFORMANCE NOTES

It is intended that the audience should view this illusion from at least a few feet away. Ideally, it should be performed on a stage or dais. However, we expect that most children will show this illusion to their friends in their own homes. In this case, it may well prove prudent to cover the prepared boxes with a colourful piece of fabric, or handkerchief, until the illusion is to be performed. This is to stop the audience seeing into the top of the boxes, thus discovering the contents.

During the performance it is *vital* to the success of the illusion that the eye level of the audience is lower than, or the same as, the height of the top of the outer box.

CUTTING LIST

Outer box

Front and back (2):	210 x 180 x 6mm (8¼ x 7 3/32 x ¼in) birch plywood
Sides (2):	180 x 138 x 6mm (7 3/32 x 5 7/16 x ¼in) birch plywood

Inner box

Front and back (2):	188 x 180 x 6mm (7 13/32 x 7 3/32 x ¼in) birch plywood
Sides (2):	116 x 180 x 6mm (4 9/16 x 7 3/32 x ¼in) birch plywood

Secret box

Front and back (2):	166 x 160 x 3mm (6 9/16 x 6 5/16 x ⅛in) birch plywood
Sides (2):	160 x 100 x 3mm (6 5/16 x 4 x ⅛in) birch plywood

Stand

Base:	240 x 180 x 12mm (9 7/16 x 7 3/32 x ½in) birch plywood
Feet (4):	Wooden clock finials

Miscellaneous

Soft toy tiger cub

CONSTRUCTION

Outer box

Cut out the front, back and side pieces (*see* Fig 5.5). Mark out the 'window' shapes on the front piece (*see* Fig 5.6), and cut them out using a fretsaw. Clean up any unevenness with sanding sticks. Assemble the box using moulding pins and glue, and clean up the edges with a combination of block plane and abrasive paper.

Inner box

Cut out the front, back and side pieces and assemble using moulding pins and glue (*see* Fig 5.7).

Secret box

Cut out the front, back and side pieces (*see* Fig 5.8). As this box is constructed from 3mm (⅛in) birch plywood we do not recommend using moulding pins to assemble it. Glued, butt joints should be sufficient as this box is handled less than the others.

Stand

This is constructed from a piece of 12mm (½in) birch plywood, with four feet attached to the underside.

The feet we used were made from wooden clock finials. The top and neck sections are cut off using a fine-toothed saw, such as a dovetail (*see* Fig 5.9). The remaining base

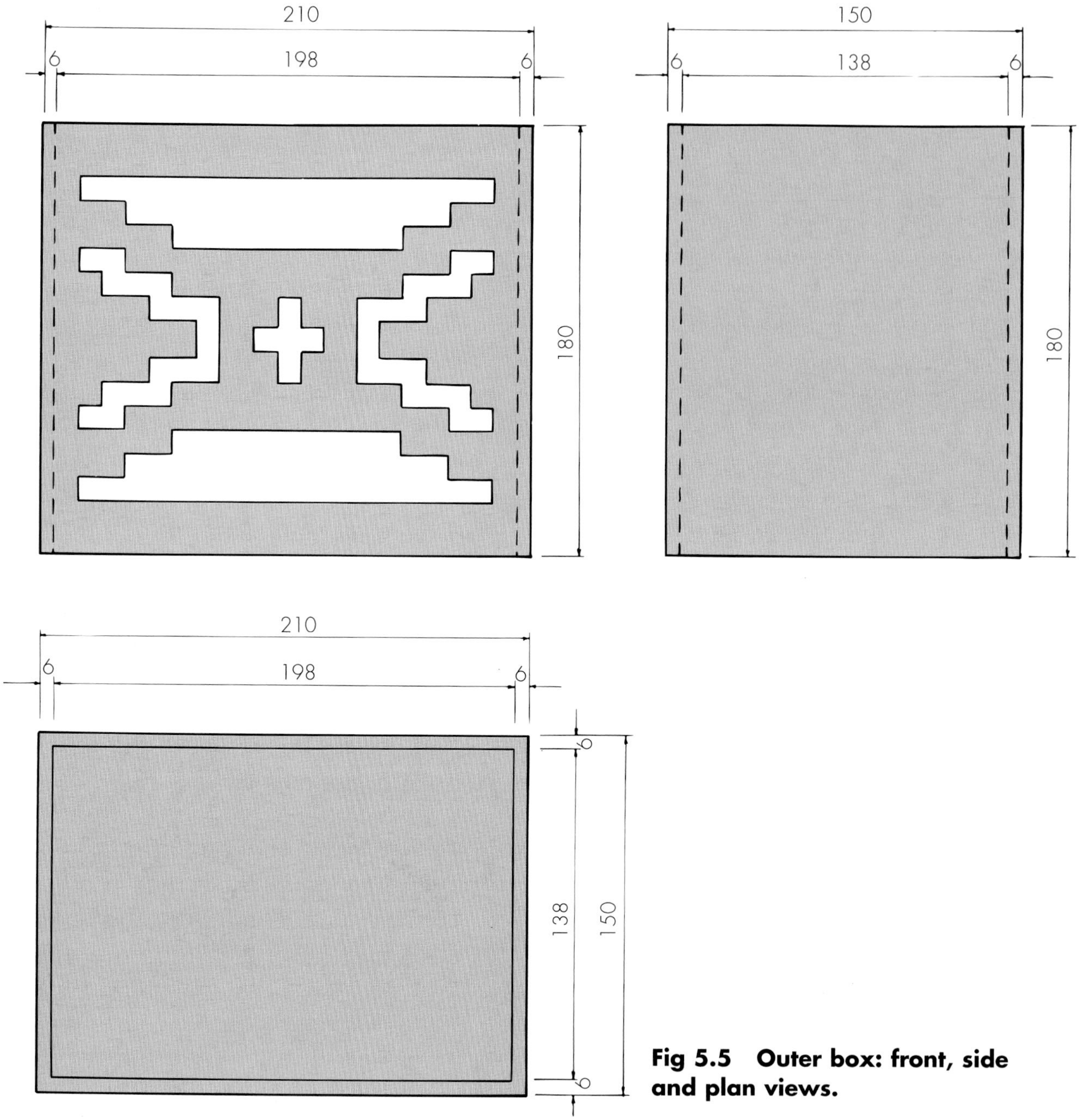

Fig 5.5 Outer box: front, side and plan views.

part, complete with lug, is then sanded smooth. Check that all the finials are the same height (not including the joining lugs). Any variation will result in the stand not being stable. Attach the finials to the stand using their lugs. Drill four stopped holes, one at each corner of the stand, to a depth and diameter to fit the lugs. Glue the lugs into these holes.

As an alternative to using wooden clock finials you could use wooden balls: 25mm (1in) would be an appropriate size. Either screw or dowel them to the stand.

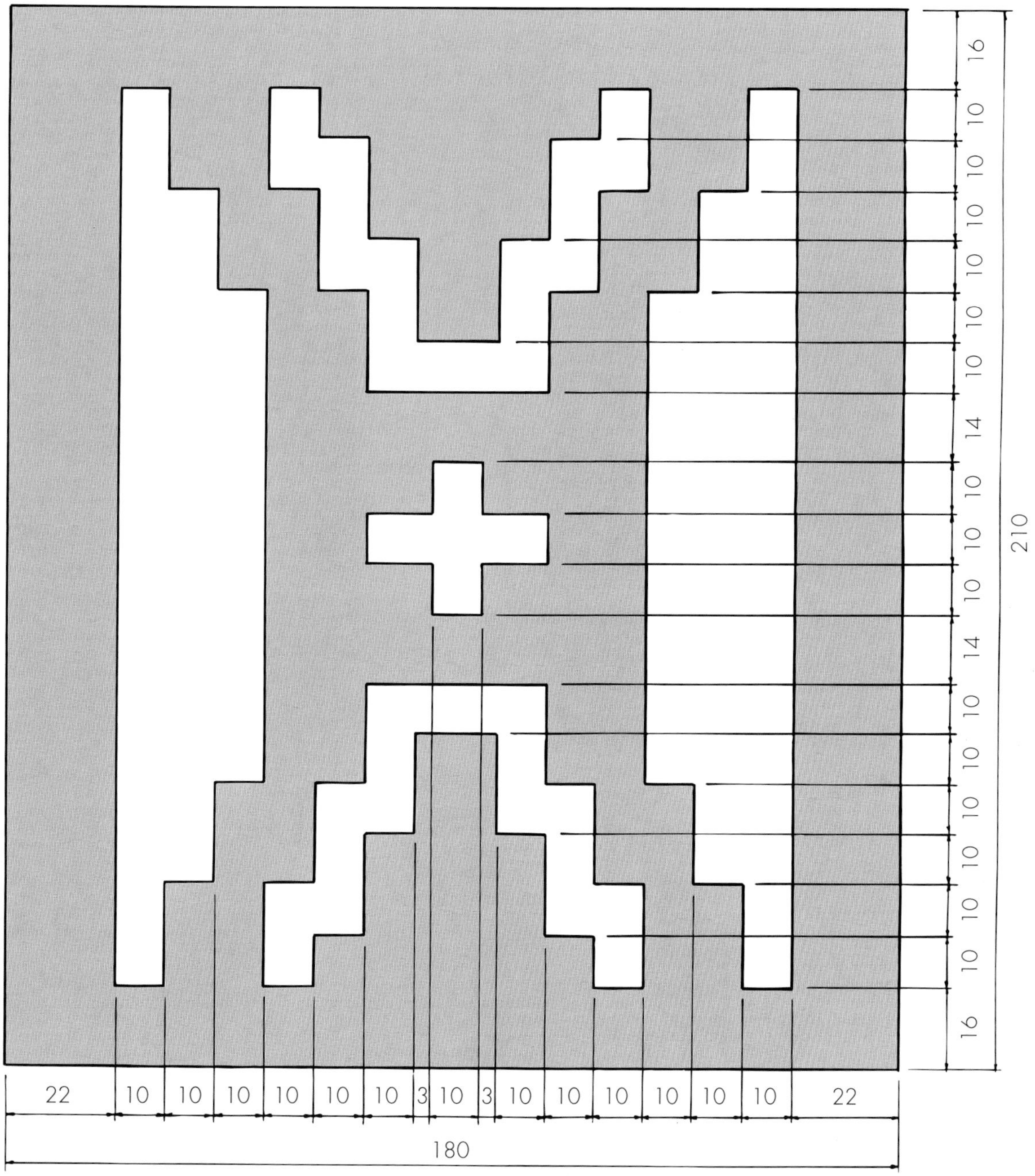

Fig 5.6 Front of outer box.

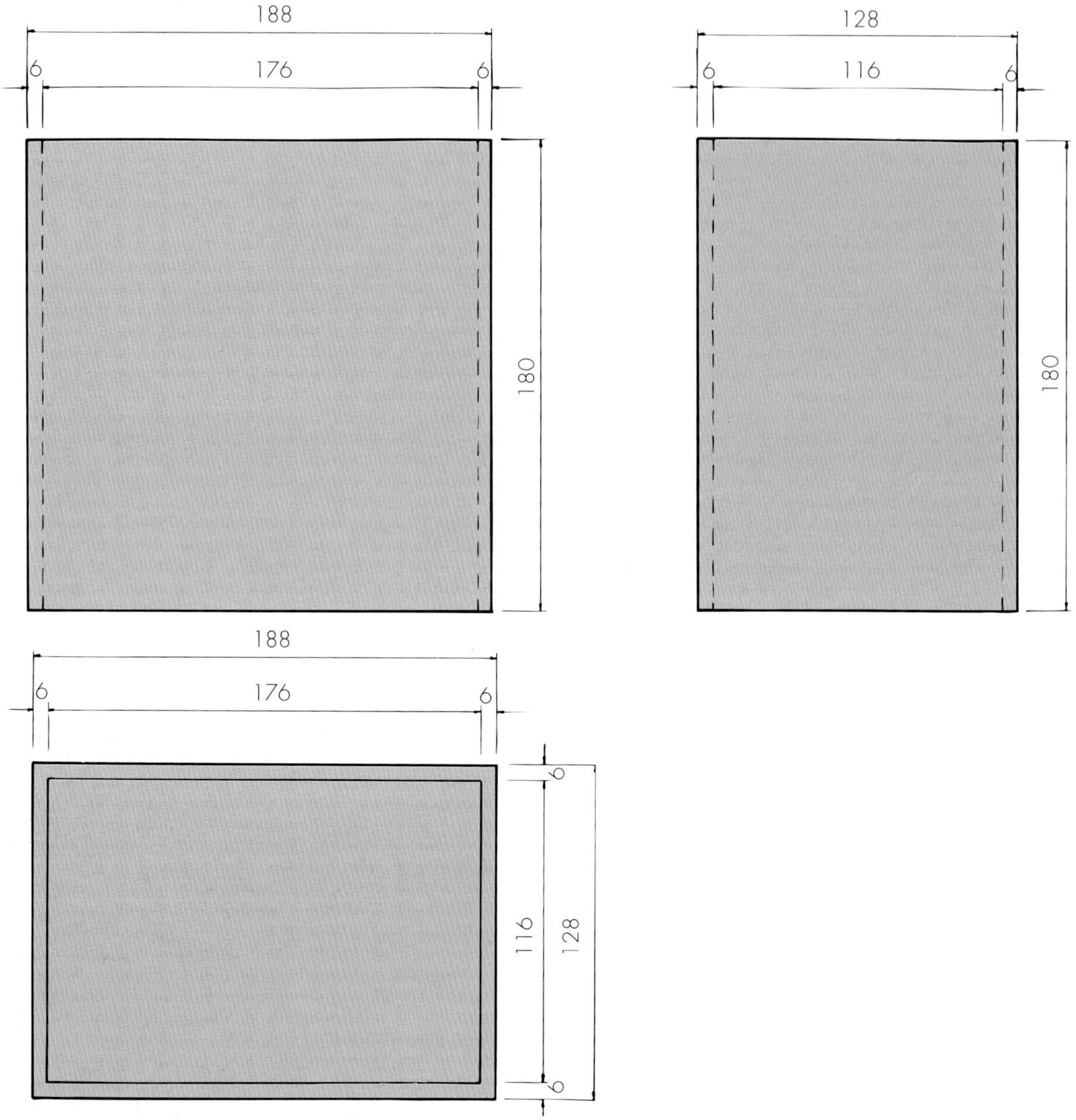

Fig 5.7 Inner box: front, side and plan views.

FINISHING

It is of paramount importance to the success of the illusion that the correct areas of the boxes are painted matt black. These areas are:

- Outer box – interior and edges
- Inner box – interior and edges
- Secret box – the entire interior, exterior and edges
- Stand – the top surface (or this could be covered in black velour).

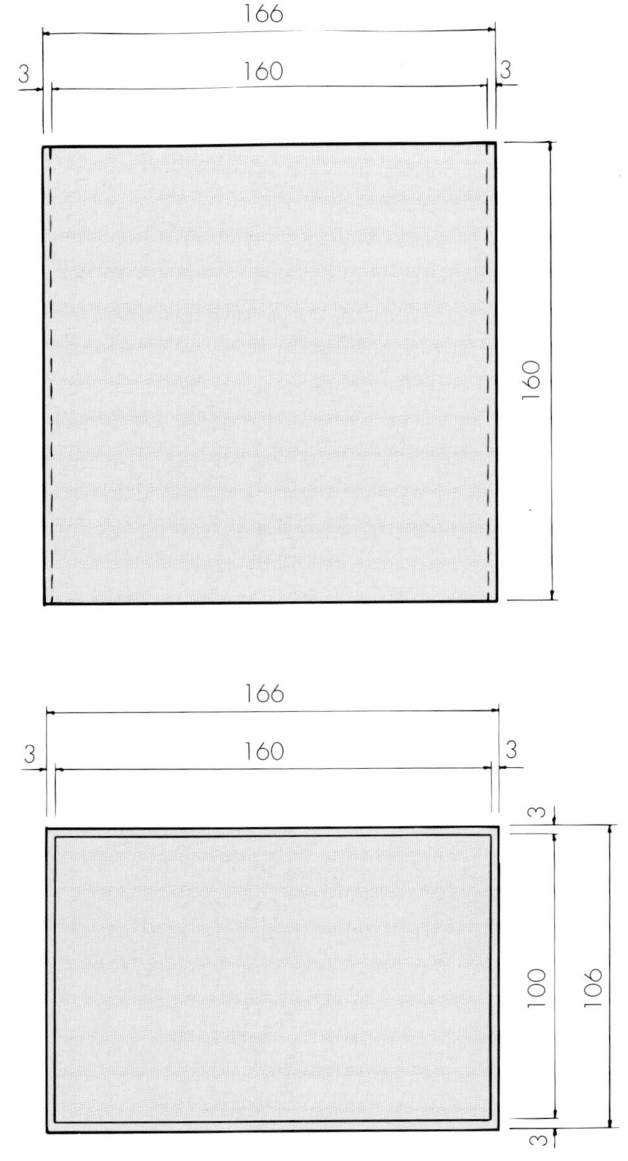

Fig 5.8 Secret box: front, side and plan views.

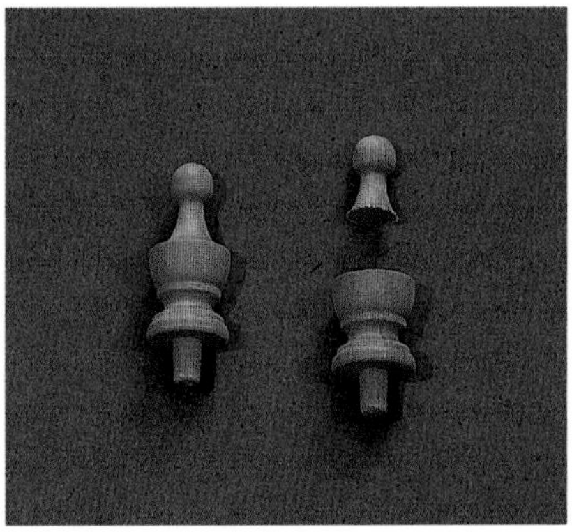

Fig 5.9 Clock finial used as feet for the stand, showing position of cut.

For visual effectiveness the outer and inner boxes should be finished in contrasting colours. The inner box shown in the photographs has been covered with a patterned self-adhesive covering. The stand should complement the outer box.

CHAPTER 6

Fishing Set

★

This project is a progression from the traditional version, which usually consists of cardboard fish, with paperclips over their mouths, and a small dowel rod. A short length of string is attached to the rod and the other end of the string is tied to a magnet (which serves as the hook). To catch a fish, you simply lower the 'hook' to its mouth. The paperclip is attracted by the magnet, and so the fish is caught.

In this wooden version the rod is more substantial, and a reel has been added for realism and extra play value. A large brass hook has been substituted for the traditional magnet. The fish are cut from birch plywood, with an eyelet screwed to the mouth of each one. A fish is caught by guiding the hook through the eyelet. Not only is this giant version great fun, it also helps to encourage good hand and eye co-ordination.

CUTTING LIST

Rod
762 x 18mm (30 x ¾in) diameter dowel

Reel
50mm (2in) diameter x 6mm (¼in) birch plywood discs (2)
20mm (25/32in) x 18mm (¾in) diameter dowel
40mm (1 9/16in) x 6mm (¼in) diameter dowel

Hook weight
32mm (1¼in) x 12mm (½in) diameter dowel

Fish (each)
170 x 62 x 12mm (6¾ x 2½ x ½in) birch plywood

Miscellaneous
Eyelets (the type used for hanging net curtain wire) (8)
38mm (1½in) no. 8 round-headed screw
Ping-pong ball
50mm (2in) brass cup hook
Length of string

CONSTRUCTION

Rod
Sand a sufficient length of 18mm (¾in) dowel. Then cut a 762mm (30in) length. About 160mm (6 5/16in) from one end, screw in a 38mm (1½in) no. 8 round-headed screw to a depth no more than three-quarters of the rod diameter. Approximately 85mm (3⅜in) further along from this, screw in an eyelet (the type used for hanging net curtains). If the user of the rod is right handed you will need to hold the rod so that the round-headed screw is horizontal on the right-hand side of the rod (this is where the reel will be fitted later). Looking down at the rod in this position it will become clear which is the underside. On the underside, screw in a further four eyelets, ensuring that they are spaced an equal distance apart.

Remove the eyelets and paint and decorate the rod. Leave the round-headed screw in position, as this will aid you in holding the rod when applying the paint. When finished, rescrew the eyelets to the rod.

Reel
Using a compass, draw two 50mm (2in) diameter circles on to 6mm (¼in) plywood.

TIP

When using a brace and expansive bit, always test on a scrap piece of plywood first. Drill the centres first with a small drill bit, approximately 1.5mm (1/16in). This will help the lead screw of the expansive bit to centre itself when you start boring. When the lead screw has broken through the back of the workpiece, remove the bit and continue boring from the back face. This will help to avoid any 'split out' from along the grain.

At the centre of each circle drill or bore a hole to accept an 18mm (3/4in) diameter dowel. I used a brace and expansive bit.

On one of the circles you will need to drill a 6mm (1/4in) hole 8mm (5/16in) in from the circumference to the hole's centre (*see* Fig 6.1).

To join the two circles together, cut a 20mm (25/32in) length of 18mm (3/4in) hardwood dowel. Glue one circle to each end. When the glue has set, sand away any unevenness.

Cut a 40mm (1 9/16in) length of 6mm (1/4in) dowel. Glue this into the hole in the reel's disc. Ensure that the dowel's end is flush with the inside face of the disc.

Drill a hole, the size of which will allow the reel to turn freely around the round-head screw, through the centre of the reel.

The reel can now be painted and decorated.

Fish hook

A 50mm (2in) brass cup hook is used for the hook. Screw this into the end of a 32mm (1¼in) length of 12mm (½in) dowel. Screw an eyelet to the other end. Ensure that you drill adequate pilot holes for the hook and eyelet, or the dowel will probably split!

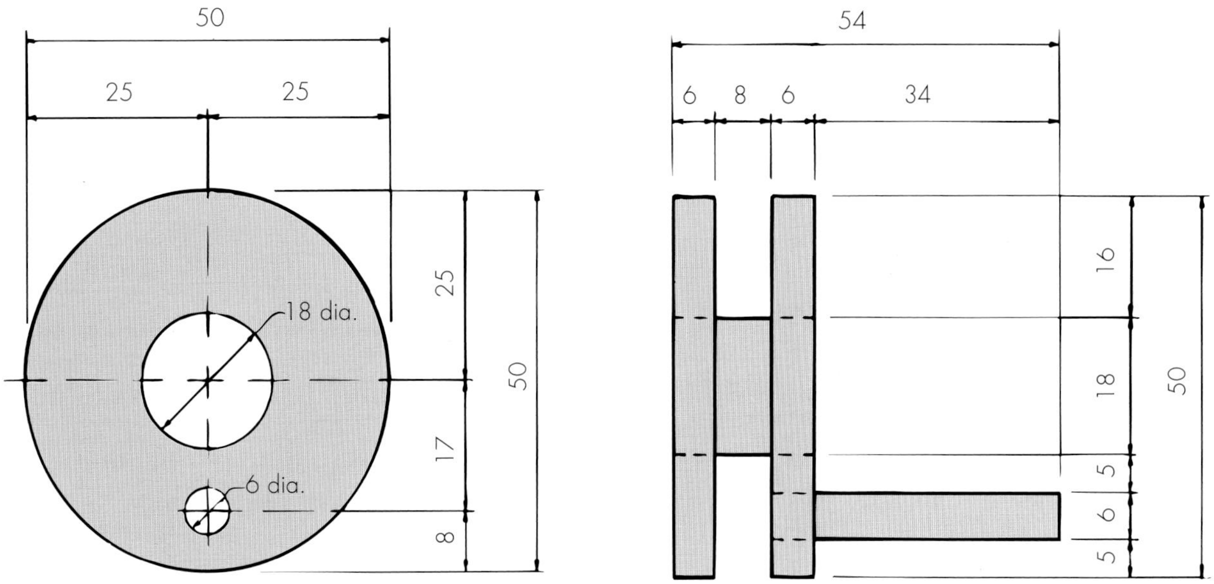

Fig 6.1 Measurements for the reel.

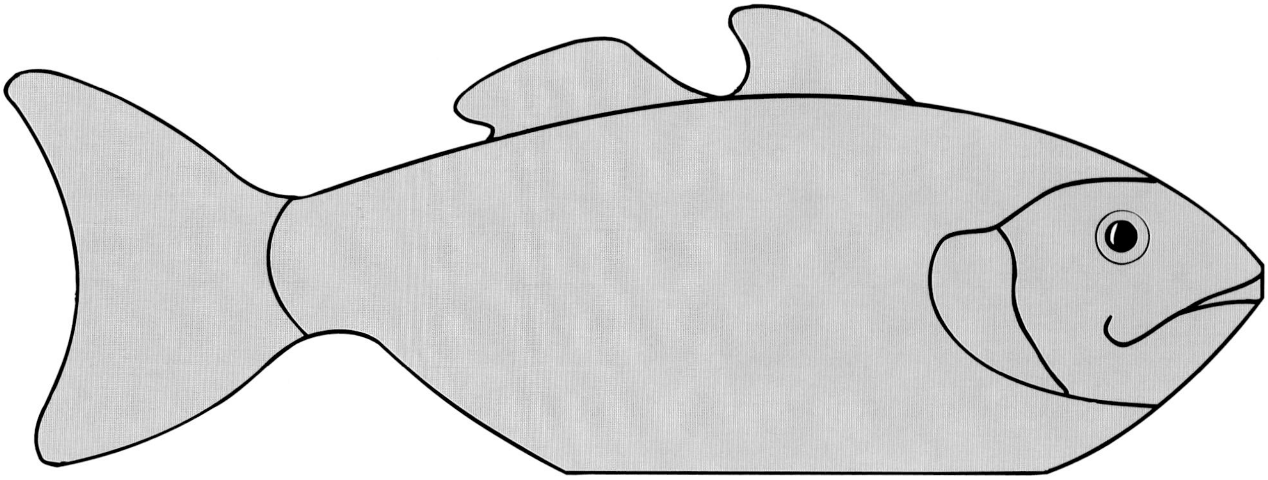

Fig 6.2 Design for the fish.

The dowel not only acts as a medium to join the two, it also acts as a weight. This aids the reeling of the line before catching a fish. The weight is stained black and matt varnished.

Fishing float

This is a painted ping-pong ball with two holes drilled or pierced at opposite sides.

Fish

Transfer the outline of the fish on to 12mm (½in) plywood (*see* Fig 6.2). Repeat this process for as many fish as you require. Cut them out using a fretsaw.

Paint and decorate the fish in a style of your choosing. Then screw an eyelet to the mouth of each fish.

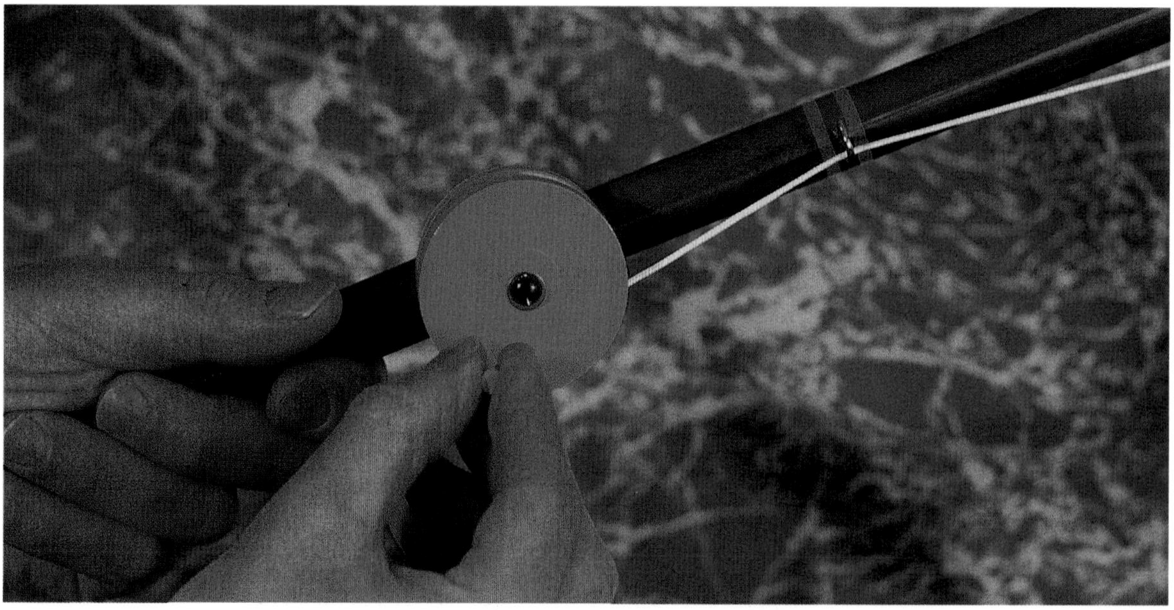

Fig 6.3 The reel in position on the rod and being operated.

ASSEMBLY

Unscrew the round-head screw from the rod. Place it through the reel's centre hole and screw it back into position on the rod (*see* Fig 6.3).

Choose a suitable type of cord for the fishing line, and cut it to the length you require. Attach one end to the central spindle of the reel – tie it in such a way that it will not slip when in use.

Thread the line through the eyelets on the rod.

Thread the float on to the line (you may need a large needle to aid you), and

Fig 6.4 Fish caught!

Fig 6.5 Note the key-ring attached to one of the fish. This makes it easier to catch.

position it as required. Tie a knot below the base hole of the float large enough to prevent the float from slipping down the line.

Tie the line to the eyelet at the top of the hook and weight arrangement.

You are now ready to go fishing!

FISHING

Place the fish base down on the ground. Stand above them holding the rod. Lower the line to the fish and try to manoeuvre the hook to catch a fish by its eyelet (*see* Fig 6.4).

For younger fishermen, attach a round key-ring clip (*see* Fig 6.5) to the eyelets. This will make it easier to catch the fish.

Happy fishing and keep your feet dry!

STOP
33

CHAPTER 7

Play Roadway

Most children like playing with small toy cars and this roadway system has been designed with these in mind. We conceived the idea while watching our son and his friends constructing a toy railway layout. Most of their fun came from the design and building of the layout. Certainly, they spent more time on this than actually playing with the trains, so we decided to design this project for their imaginative constructional skills.

The system consists of various sections of road: T-junctions, crossroads, curves, long and short straights, connected in a similar way to jigsaw puzzles. When packed away even a relatively large layout will fit into a drawer or box. It is economical to make as all the road sections are cut from 6mm (¼in) MDF. In fact, the main restrictions are how many road sections you wish to make and the size of the playroom floor!

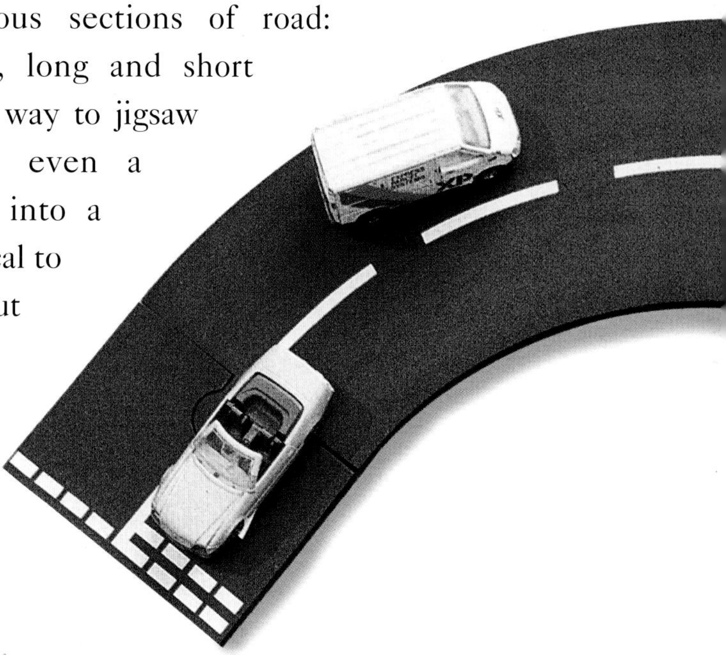

CUTTING LIST

A quantity of 6mm ($\frac{1}{4}$in) MDF, the amount of which is dependent on the number of road sections you wish to make. As a guide, the amount of material for each road section is as follows:

Long straight:	550 x 104 x 6mm ($21\frac{21}{32}$ x $4\frac{3}{32}$ x $\frac{1}{4}$in) MDF
Short straight:	275 x 104 x 6mm ($10\frac{7}{8}$ x $4\frac{3}{32}$ x $\frac{1}{4}$in) MDF
90° corner:	275 x 250 x 6mm ($10\frac{7}{8}$ x $9\frac{7}{8}$ x $\frac{1}{4}$in) MDF
T-junction:	275 x 250 x 6mm ($10\frac{7}{8}$ x $9\frac{7}{8}$ x $\frac{1}{4}$in) MDF
Crossroads:	275 x 275 x 6mm ($10\frac{7}{8}$ x $10\frac{7}{8}$ x $\frac{1}{4}$in) MDF

Miscellaneous

A roll of white sticky-back plastic for the road markings

CONSTRUCTION

Prepare the sheet of MDF by sanding it smooth.

Draw on it the road sections you require. You will probably need a large compass fitted with an extension bar for this.

To save you setting-out time, you could make templates (the first of each road section type you make could be used as such), but it is imperative that these are made perfectly. Otherwise, you will have little chance of the road sections being fully interchangeable.

The straight edges of the long and short sections (*see* Figs 7.1, 7.4), T-junctions (*see* Figs 7.2, 7.5) and crossroad sections (*see* Figs 7.3, 7.6) are straightforward to cut out. The corner road sections' outer and inner

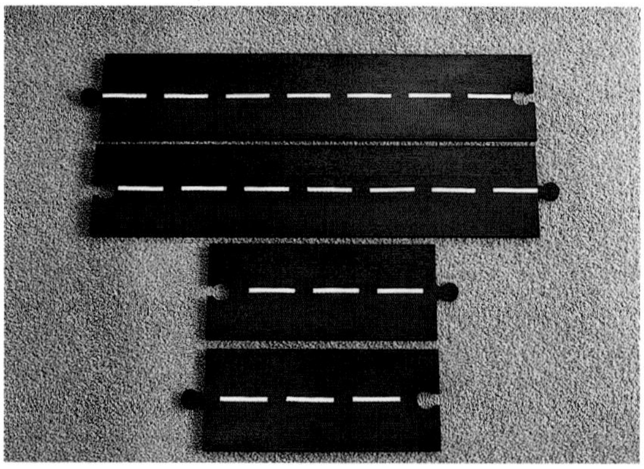

Fig 7.1 Long and short straight road sections.

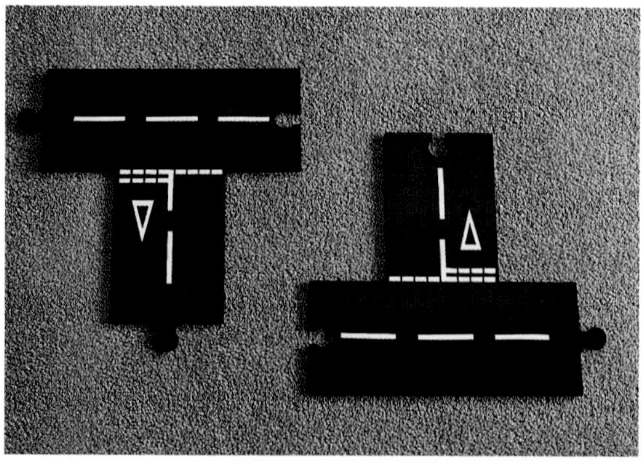

Fig 7.2 T-junctions.

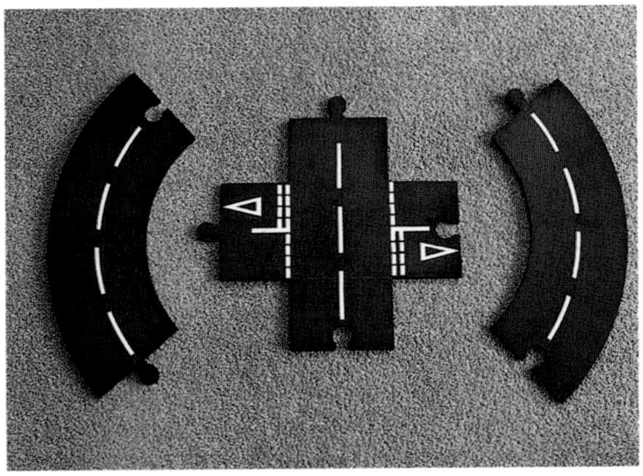

Fig 7.3 **Corner pieces and crossroads.**

The long straight section is 525mm long.

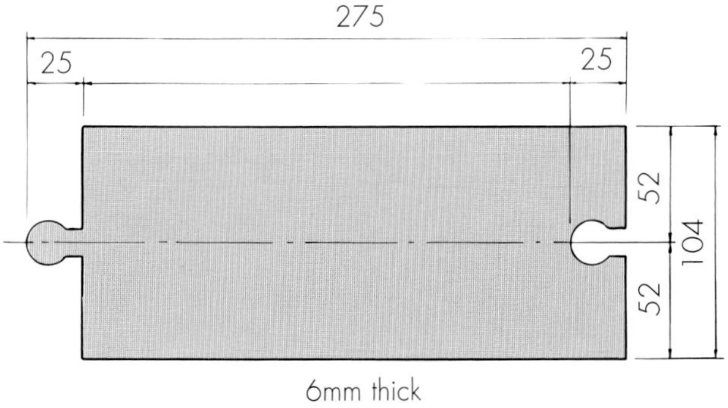

Fig 7.4 **Short straight section.**

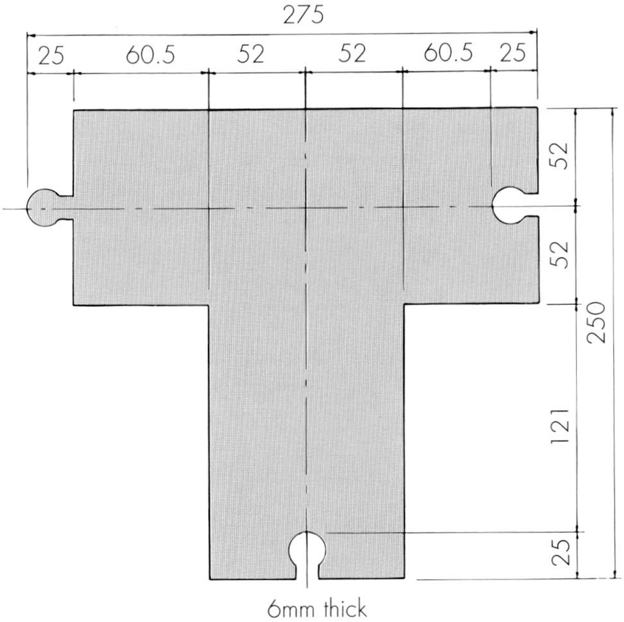

Fig 7.5 **T-junction section.**

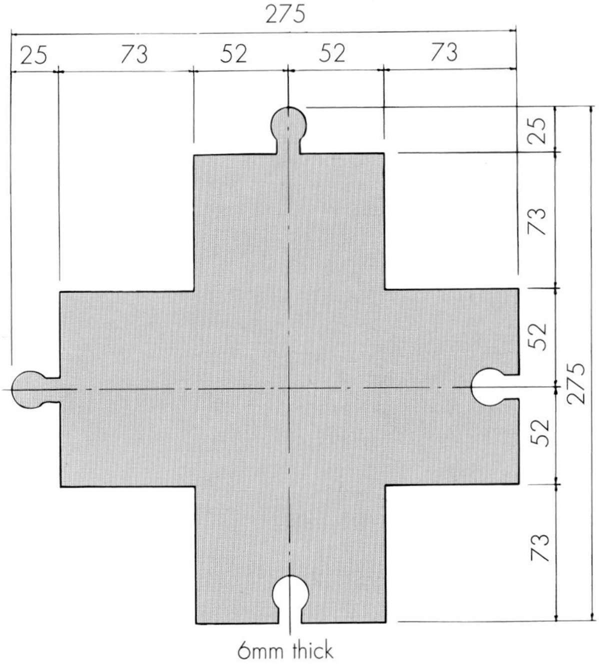

Fig 7.6 **Crossroad section.**

curves can be cut out with either a powered jigsaw, fretsaw or bandsaw (*see* Figs 7.3, 7.7). If doing this task by hand, use a coping saw or fretsaw.

Use a fretsaw (preferably a powered one) to cut out the 'male' and 'female' connecting shapes on each road section (*see* Figs 7.8, 7.9). Use as large a thickness of blade as will allow you to cut the shapes (we suggest a no. 5 or no. 6 blade). Cut exactly on the line, not the waste side as you would normally, as this should give you adequate tolerance when fitting the sections together.

An alternative to fretsawing the 'female' shape is to drill it out. A 20mm flat bit will

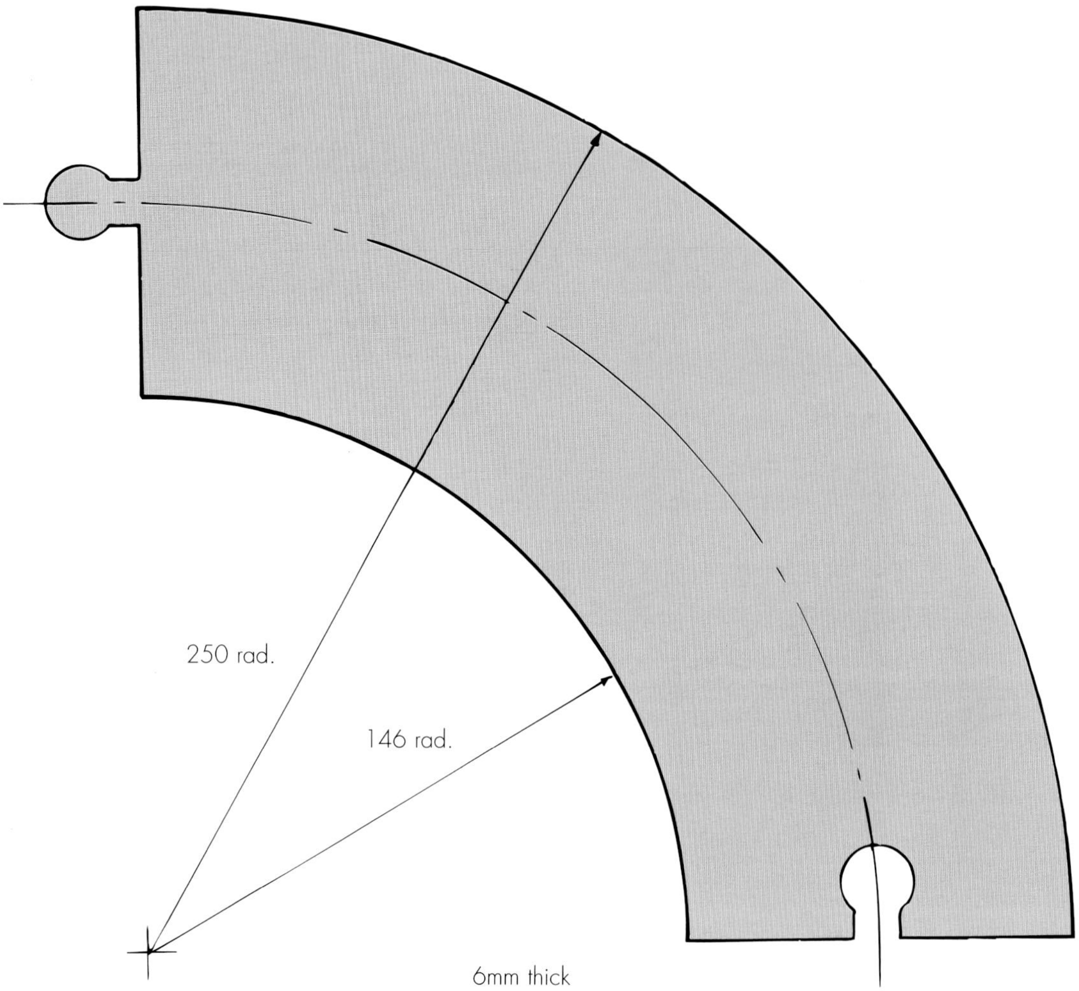

Fig 7.7 Curved section.

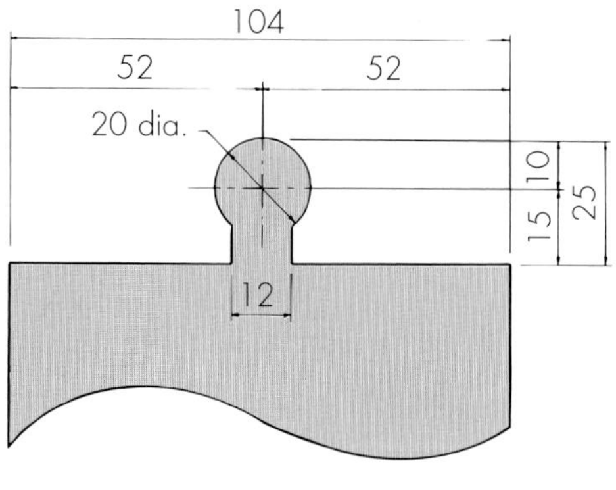

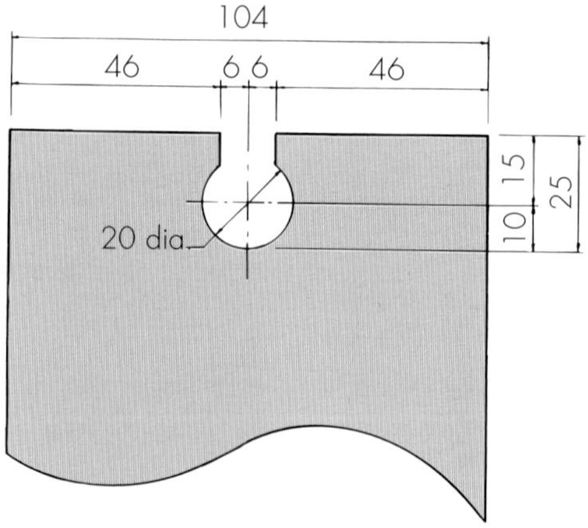

Fig 7.8 Dimensions for 'male' connector for all sections.

Fig 7.9 Dimensions for 'female' connector for all sections.

suffice, but ensure first that it is exactly the right size.

When you have cut all the sections out, any uneven edges can be smoothed to shape with sanding sticks.

It is inevitable that one or two road sections will be incompatible with the others. This can usually be rectified by some extra sanding with sanding sticks.

FINISHING

MDF's natural colour is already a suitable 'road' colour. If you wish, you could give it a couple of coats of matt varnish to seal it.

We coloured our sections black, using matt acrylic paint. The first coat raised the grain nicely, giving the road a textured effect. The second coat was applied straight on top of this without sanding between coats. When the paint had thoroughly dried, the surface of each road section was sanded, lengthways, with 000 grade steel wool. This had the pleasing effect of making the road surface surprisingly realistic.

The road markings were cut from white sticky-back plastic (*see* Fig 7.10).

ACCESSORIES

Many accessories can either be bought or made to help bring your roadway to life. As well as shop-bought road signs, you could make bridges, zebra crossings, car parks, garages and buildings. In fact, you will find that children, with guidance, will love to make cardboard buildings and accessories of their own.

Fig 7.10 Placing road markings on a T-junction section.

CHAPTER 8

Chris Clown's Tricky Trike

★★

You may be familiar with Chris the Clown from our previous book, *Making Wooden Toys and Games* (GMC Publications Ltd, 1995). Chris still likes driving his crazy car, but he has now been bitten by the keep-fit bug and can often be seen pedalling around on this tricycle!

CUTTING LIST

Small pieces of birch plywood:	3mm (⅛in), 6mm (¼in), 9mm (⅜in), 12mm (½in) and 18mm (¾in) thick
Shaped wood turnings (2):	18mm (¾in), the type often used as hub caps
Wood ball:	25mm (1in) diameter
Wood bead:	9mm (⅜in) diameter
Ramin dowel:	6mm (¼in) diameter
Ramin dowel:	3mm (⅛in) diameter
Hardwood wheels (2):	50mm (2in)

Miscellaneous

Rivets (6)

Brass washers

CONSTRUCTION

Chris Clown

Transfer all the profiles of the body parts to the appropriate thicknesses of plywood, and drill out all the relevant rivet holes (*see* Fig 8.1). The diameters of the holes will depend on the size of rivets you use (see later in these instructions for suggested sizes). The hands and boots each have a 3mm (⅛in) diameter hole drilled through them to accept either the handlebars or the pedals. Cut out the body parts with a fretsaw.

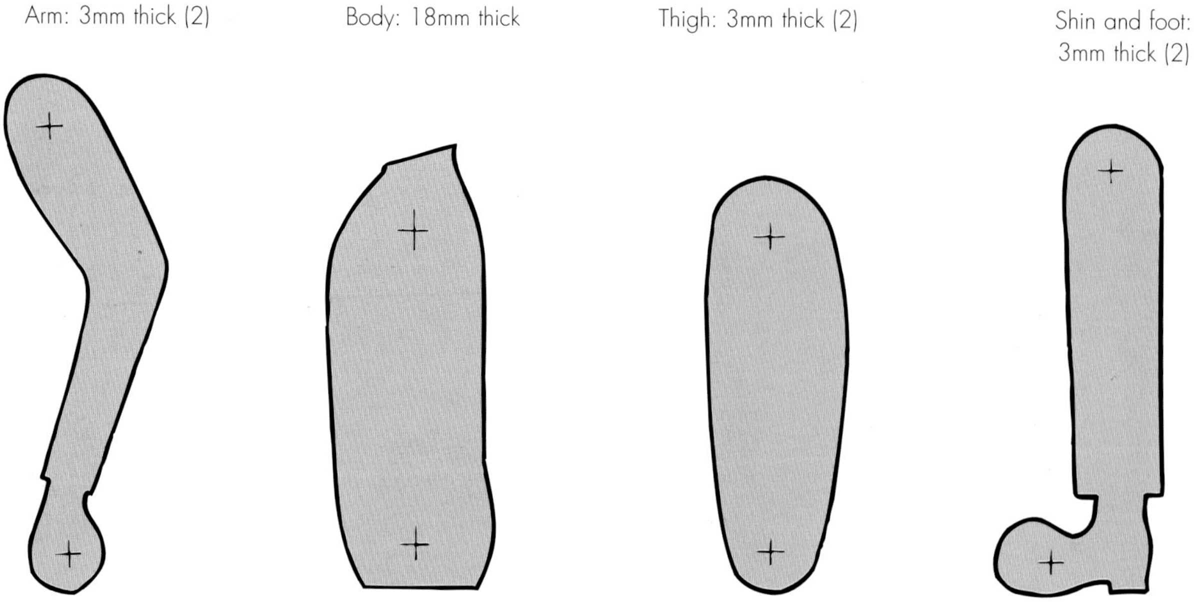

Fig 8.1 Chris Clown's body parts.

Neck holes

Mark the centre point of the top of the body torso and drill a 6mm (¼in) diameter hole to a depth of 6mm (¼in). Drill a similar hole in the head ball.

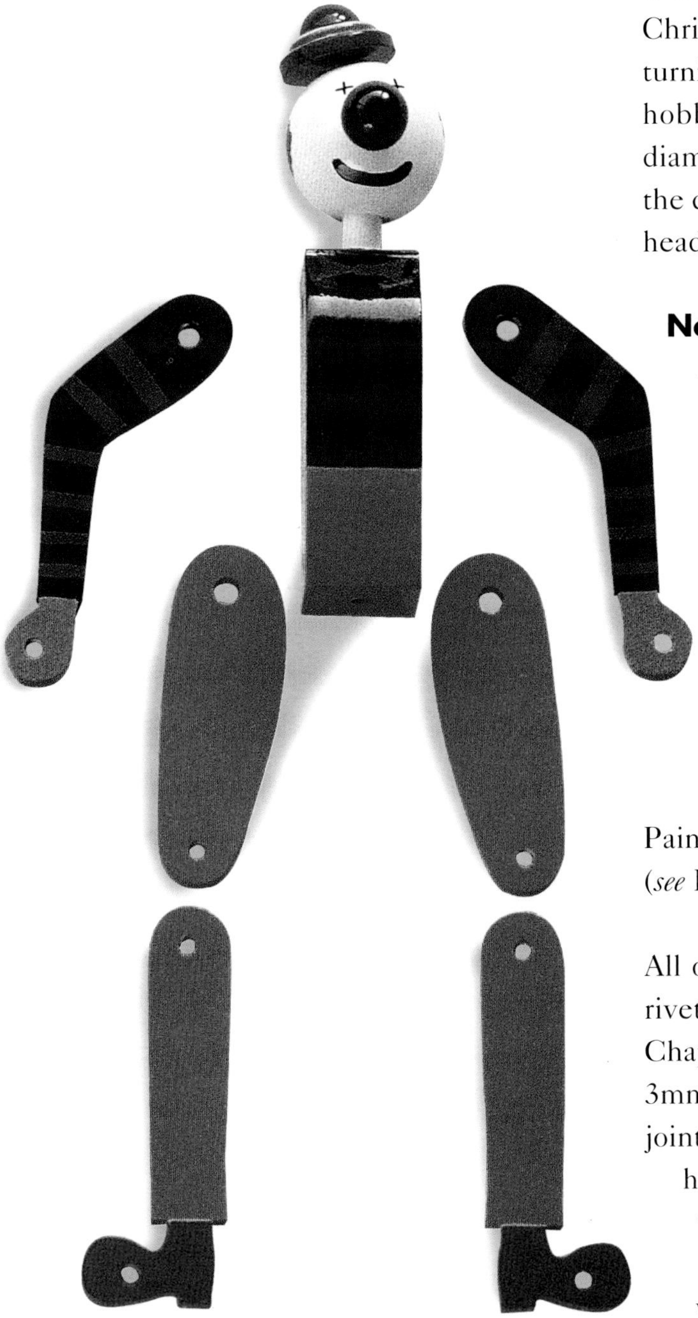

Fig 8.2 Chris Clown's body parts painted before assembly.

Saddle hole

Mark the centre point of the bottom of the body torso and drill a 3mm (⅛in) diameter hole to a depth of 6mm (¼in). The saddle peg must fit firmly into the hole.

Hat

Chris's hat is an 18mm (¾in) shaped wood turning (the type often sold as a hubcap by hobby suppliers). Drill a 3mm (⅛in) diameter hole to a depth of 6mm (¼in) in the centre bottom of the hat and also in the head ball at the required position.

Nose

A 9mm (⅜in) wooden bead is used as the nose. Fill the open end of the bead with wood filler. Drill a 3mm (⅛in) diameter hole to a depth of 6mm (¼in) at the appropriate position in the head ball.

Join the hat and nose to the head, and then the head to the torso using dowel joints (*see* Chapter 3).

Paint Chris's body parts before assembly (*see* Fig 8.2).

All of Chris's arms and leg joints are loose riveted, using the technique explained in Chapter 3 (*see* Fig 8.3). Use 2.4mm (3/32in) or 3mm (⅛in) diameter rivets for his knee joints, and 4mm (5/32in) diameter rivets for his hip and shoulder joints. Fit a brass washer between the body and all shoulder and hip joints, as well as a washer between each knee joint.

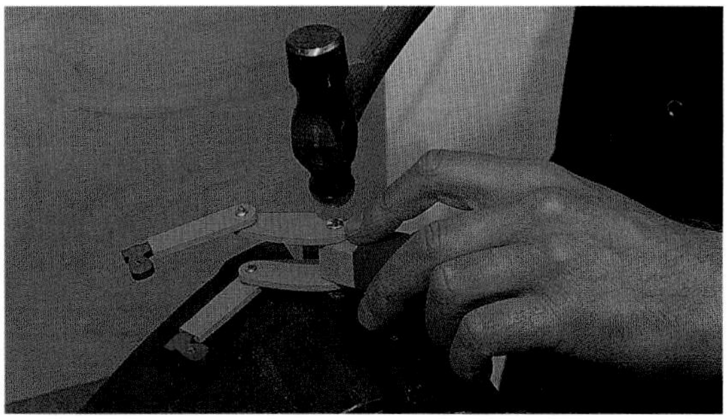

Fig 8.3 Riveting Chris's leg into position.

Trike

Transfer all the relevant cycle part profiles on to the appropriate thicknesses of plywood. Drill the holes marked before cutting out the components with a fretsaw (*see* Fig 8.4).

Drill the 3mm (⅛in) saddle peg hole and glue an appropriate length of 3mm (⅛in) dowel into it.

Glue the front forks into position (for the front fork arrangement, *see* Fig 8.5).

Next glue the rear wheel arches into position.

> **TIP**
> Pass a scrap piece of dowel through the rear axle hole. Next, spread glue on the relevant areas on the inside of the wheel arches. Then slide a wheel arch on to the dowel at each side of the trike. If necessary, pin into position and remove the scrap length of dowel.

Cut a 50mm (2in) length of 3mm (⅛in) diameter dowel. This will serve as the handlebars. Fit the handlebars through the

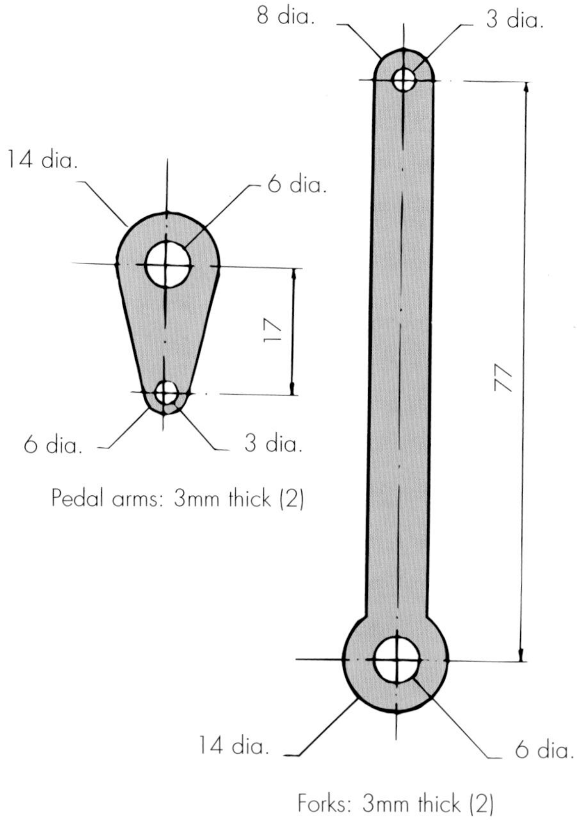

Fig 8.4 Trike parts.

trike's top fork holes. Do not glue them into position, as it is useful to be able to remove them (*see* the section on assembly, page 63). Colour them as required. We suggest a matt black – too many coats of paint will make them difficult to refit.

The headlight is made from the same type and size of wood turning as Chris's hat. Sand the outer rim away, using a sanding stick, and glue it into position.

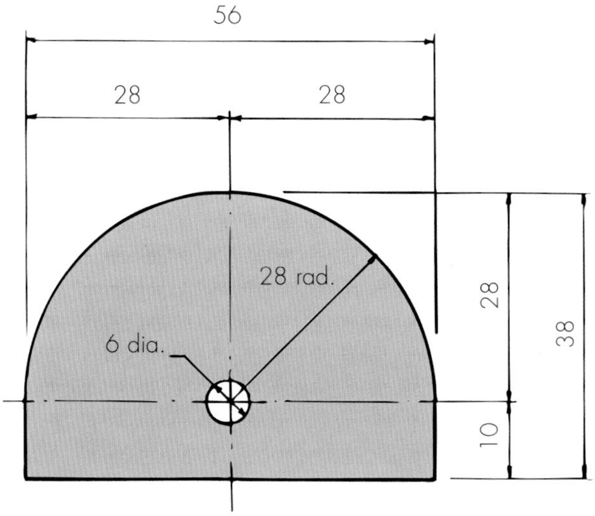

Wheel arch: 12mm thick (2)

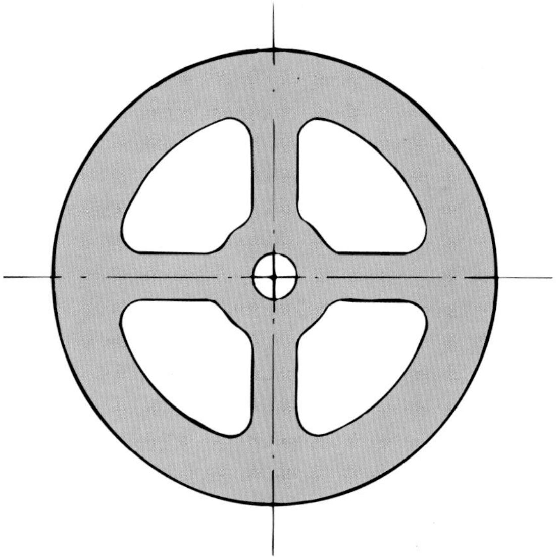

Front wheel: 6mm thick
Axle hole: 6mm dia.
Hub: 16mm dia.
Spoke/rim web: 3mm rad.
Rim: 44mm dia.
Overall dia. of wheel: 60mm

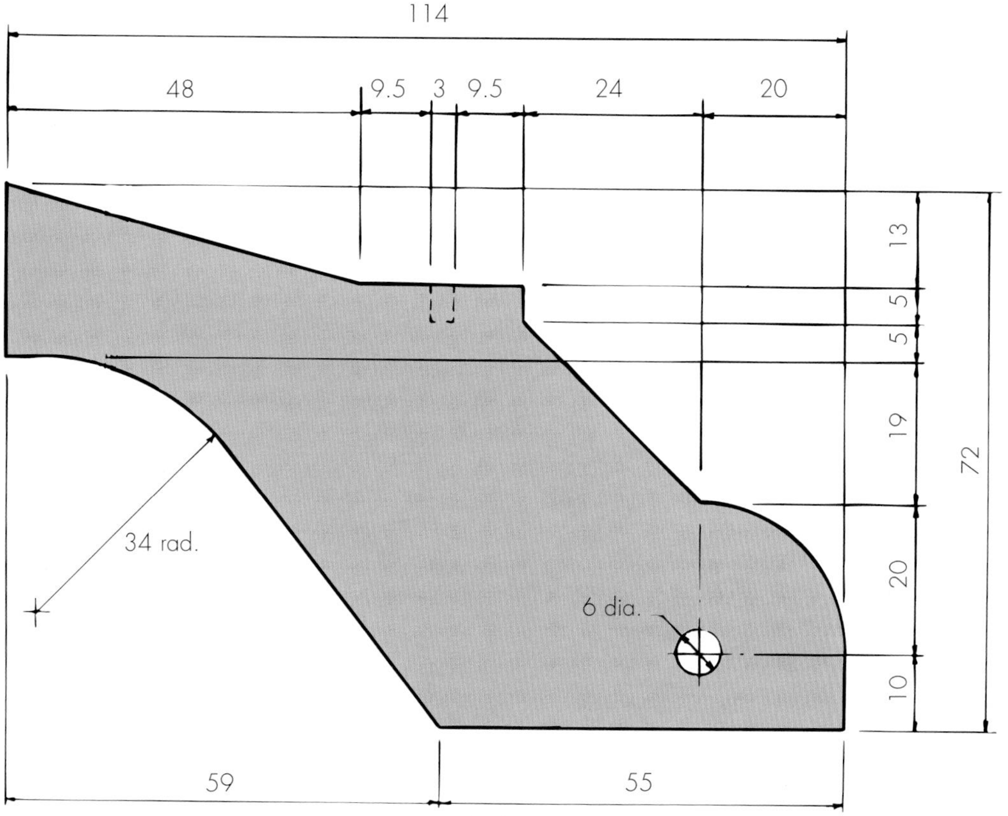

Frame: 9mm thick

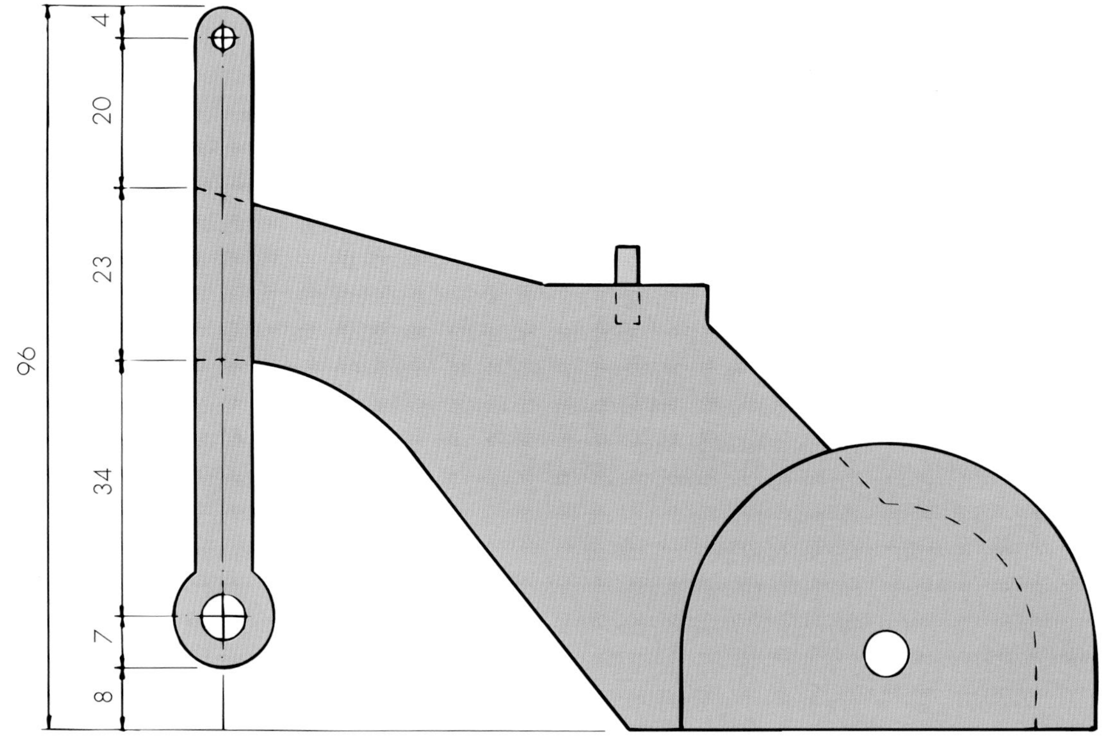

Fig 8.5 Front fork arrangement.

Cut two 15mm (19/32in) lengths of 3mm (1/8in) ramin dowel for the pedals. Glue them into position on the pedal arms. Glue a 28mm (1 1/8in) length of 6mm (1/4in) dowel into the relevant hole on one pedal arm.

The rear wheels are ready made 50mm (2in) hardwood wheels.

To fit the wheels, follow these straightforward steps.

1. Square off the sanded length of 6mm (1/4in) dowel.
2. Drill out the centres of the wheels to a diameter size that allows the axle to fit positively and firmly. Ensure that each wheel is held securely, by a vice or cramping device, during drilling.
3. Thread a wheel on to the axle so that the squared end is flush with the outside of the wheel.
4. Thread a washer on to the axle – this ensures that the wheel will turn freely and not rub against the side of the vehicle.
5. Pass the axle assembly through the axle hole in the trike.
6. Fit a washer and a wheel on to the axle at the other side of the toy.
7. Allow a small gap of about 1mm (1/32in) each side of the wheel, the washer and the toy. These gaps will ensure that the wheels will turn freely.
8. With a pencil, mark the axle at the point where it needs to be cut to be flush with the outside of the wheel.
9. Disassemble the axle.

10 Cut the axle rod squarely to length.

11 Reassemble, this time gluing the wheels into position.

TIP
It is advisable to paint all the necessary components before final assembly.

The front wheel and pedals are straightforward to fit if care is taken. First, you will need to ensure that the wheel will have a firm glue joint to the axle. To do this, score a few shallow channels, no more than 6mm (¼in) in length, along the centre of the axle. These will help to retain the glue when sliding the wheel on to the axle. Score the channels with a sharp point (either a knife or an awl).

Place a washer on the front axle and slide it against the pedal arm. Spread glue around the centre of the axle. Place the wheel into the forks so that the wheel and fork axle holes are in line. Then slide the axle through the fork and wheel arrangement. Ensure that the wheel is positioned correctly in the centre of the forks. Place a washer on the open end of the axle and then glue the remaining pedal on to the axle. Touch in the exposed ends with paint.

Fig 8.6 Hand and finger position recommended when operating the toy.

ASSEMBLY AND OPERATION

Place Chris Clown into position on the saddle and peg. Fit each foot on to a pedal. Hold his hands next to the fork handlebar holes, and slide the handlebars in place.

Hold the trike behind the saddle with your fingertips and gently propel Chris Clown forward to see him pedal away (*see* Fig 8.6).

As the handlebars are removable, Chris may be easily taken off his trike, so that he can dance or perform acrobatics for his audience.

About Chris's knee joint

For straightforward construction Chris's knee joint has been kept in its basic form. If you hold the toy as in Fig 8.6 with a finger and thumb holding the trike under Chris's lower thighs, he will cycle merrily along.

If you don't hold him in this way Chris's knees may sometimes bend the wrong way. Although we adults wince at this sight (a human leg would definitely be broken in this position), we have found that children think it very funny! The buckled leg can easily be 're-set'.

Another advantage of Chris's wonky knee joints is that, when Chris is removed from his trike for play, he is able to perform a variety of splits, contortions and tumbles.

CHAPTER 9

Chinese Acrobat

★★

The purpose of this exotic toy is both decorative and functional. Its construction offers a challenge to the fretworker, and when completed it will enhance any room. The acrobat is activated by turning a handle behind the stage. This makes him rotate on his bar, performing a series of spectacular somersaults. As a result of his loose-riveted shoulder and hip joints, and by varying the rotation rate of the handle, a multitude of effects can be achieved.

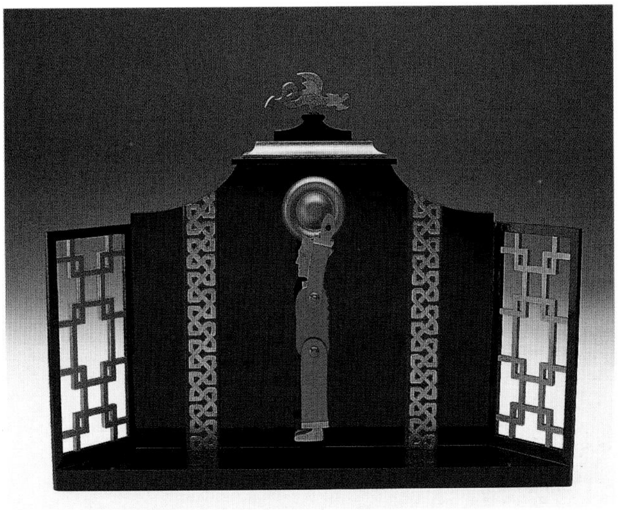

CUTTING LIST

Acrobat:	Various scraps of 3mm (⅛in) birch plywood
Stage floor:	290 x 40 x 12mm (11 7/16 x 1 9/16 x ½in) birch plywood
Backdrop:	210 x 175 x 6mm (8¼ x 6⅞ x ¼in) birch plywood
Side screen (2):	142 x 60 x 3mm (5⅝ x 2⅜ x ⅛in) birch plywood
Back box back:	175 x 70 x 6mm (6⅞ x 2¾ x ¼in) birch plywood
Back box side (2):	175 x 30 x 12mm (6⅞ x 1 3/16 x ½in) birch plywood
Decorative top base piece:	94 x 45 x 3mm (3 11/16 x 1¾ x ⅛in) birch plywood
Decorative top:	82 x 9mm (3¼ x ⅜in) hardwood scotia (2)
	33 x 9mm (1 5/16 x ⅜in) hardwood scotia (2)
Decorative top upper piece:	46 x 15 x 10mm (1 13/16 x ⅝ x ⅜in) birch plywood
Dragon:	53 x 28 x 1.5mm (2 1/16 x 1⅛ x 1/16in) brass sheet

Miscellaneous

38mm (1½in) diameter x 9mm (⅜in) ready-made hardwood wheel
60mm (2⅜in) diameter x 9mm (⅜in) ready-made hardwood wheel
6mm (¼in) dowel rod
3mm (⅛in) dowel rod
Washers (2) to fit on to 6mm (¼in) dowel rod
Snap rivets (4) – shank not to exceed 3mm (⅛in)

CONSTRUCTION

Acrobat

Transfer the body parts of the acrobat on to 3mm (⅛in) birch plywood (*see* Fig 9.1).

Drill the rivet holes. The diameter of these will depend upon the diameter of the rivet shank. However, do not use rivets with shanks in excess of 3mm (⅛in) in diameter. Therefore, if you use 2.5mm diameter rivets drill 3mm (⅛in) holes. For 3mm diameter rivets drill 3.25 or 3.5mm holes.

Cut out the body parts with a fretsaw. A no. 2 size blade is a good grade to use.

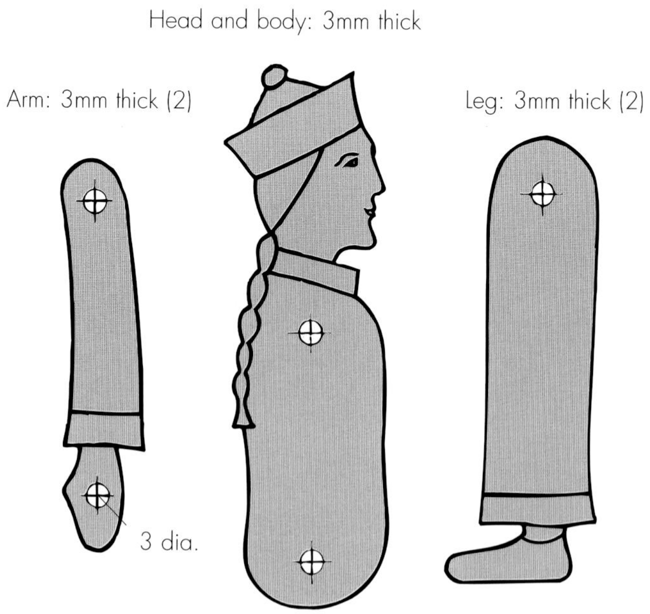

The diameters of the other holes depend upon rivet size.

Fig 9.1 The acrobat's body parts.

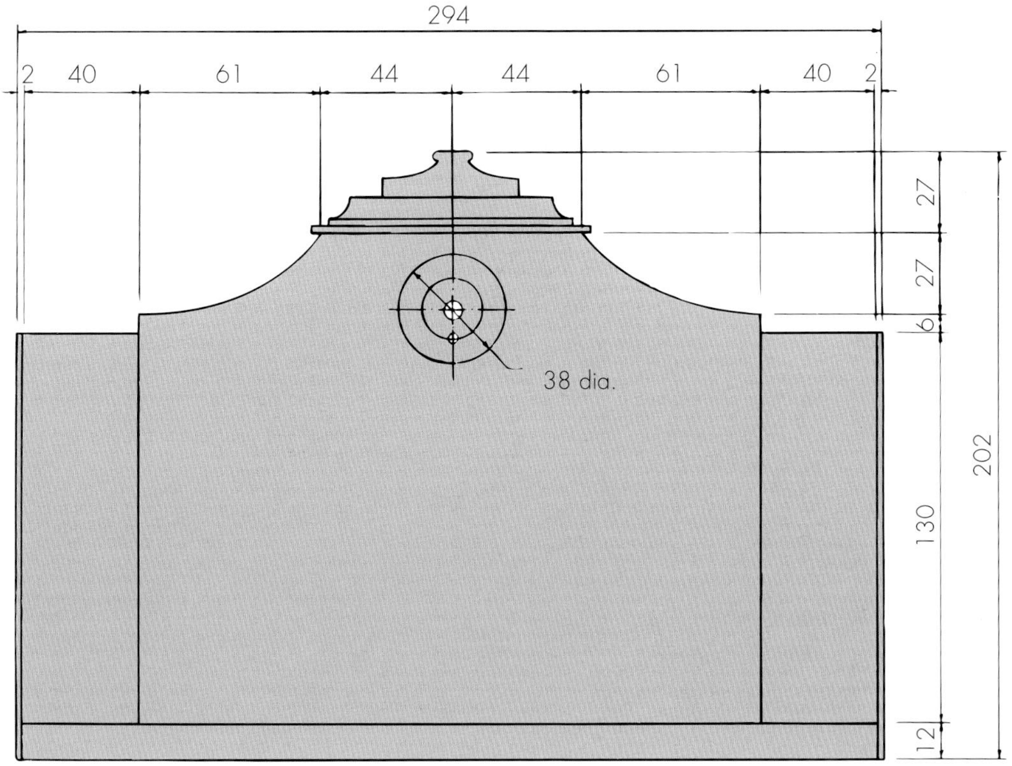

For reasons of clarity, the fretted panels, the acrobat and the dragon are not shown.

Fig 9.2 Stage: front view.

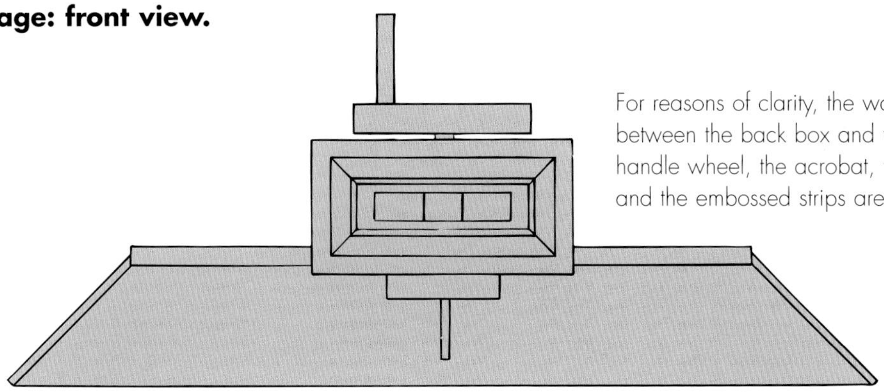

For reasons of clarity, the washer between the back box and the rear handle wheel, the acrobat, the dragon and the embossed strips are not shown.

Fig 9.3 Stage: plan view.

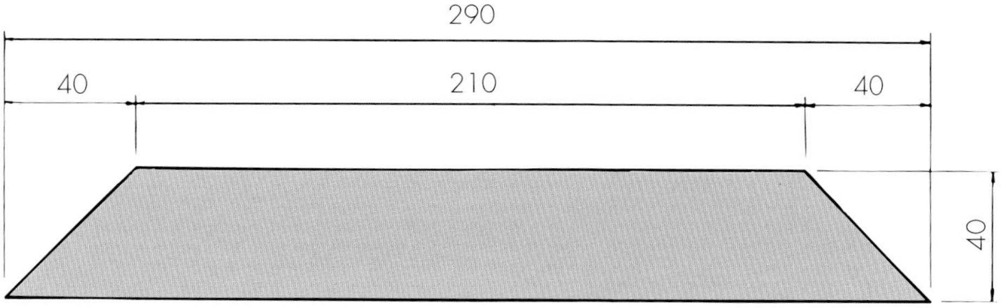

12mm thick

Fig 9.4 Stage floor.

The curves on the backdrop of the stage were marked out with French curves. You could alternatively trace curve 'A' and transfer it to both top corners of your backdrop

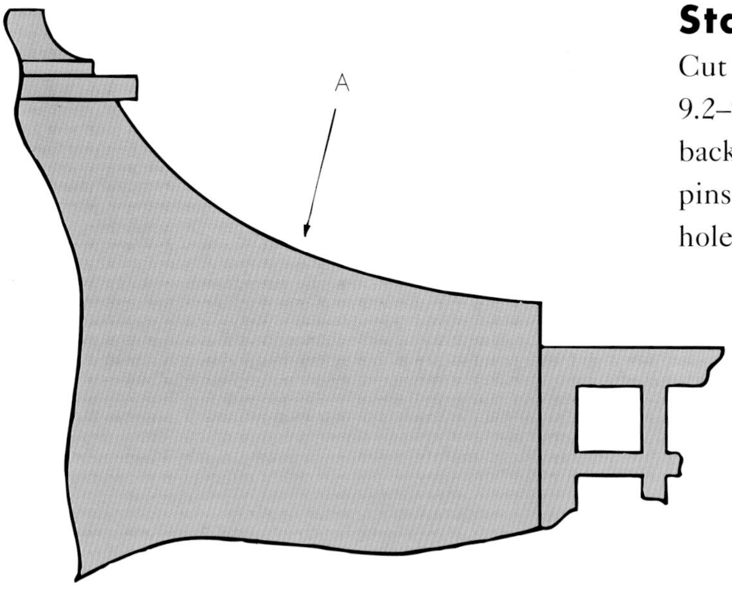

Fig 9.5 The top curve of the stage backdrop.

Clean up the body parts and paint before assembling them with rivets (*see* Chapter 3).

Stage

Cut out all the component parts (*see* Figs 9.2–9.6). Drill the top axle hole into the backdrop before fixing it, using moulding pins and glue, to the stage floor. The axle hole is 6mm (¼in) in diameter and located centrally, 150mm (6in) from the bottom edge of the backdrop.

Drill the axle hole into the back piece of the stage back box before pinning and gluing on its sides (*see* Fig 9.7).

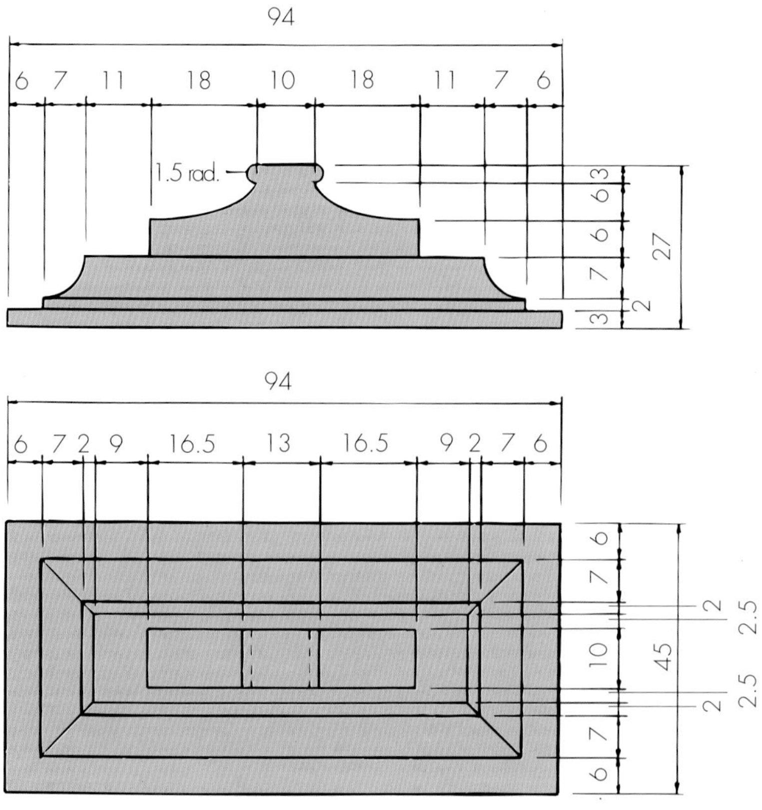

Fig 9.6 The decorative top of the stage.

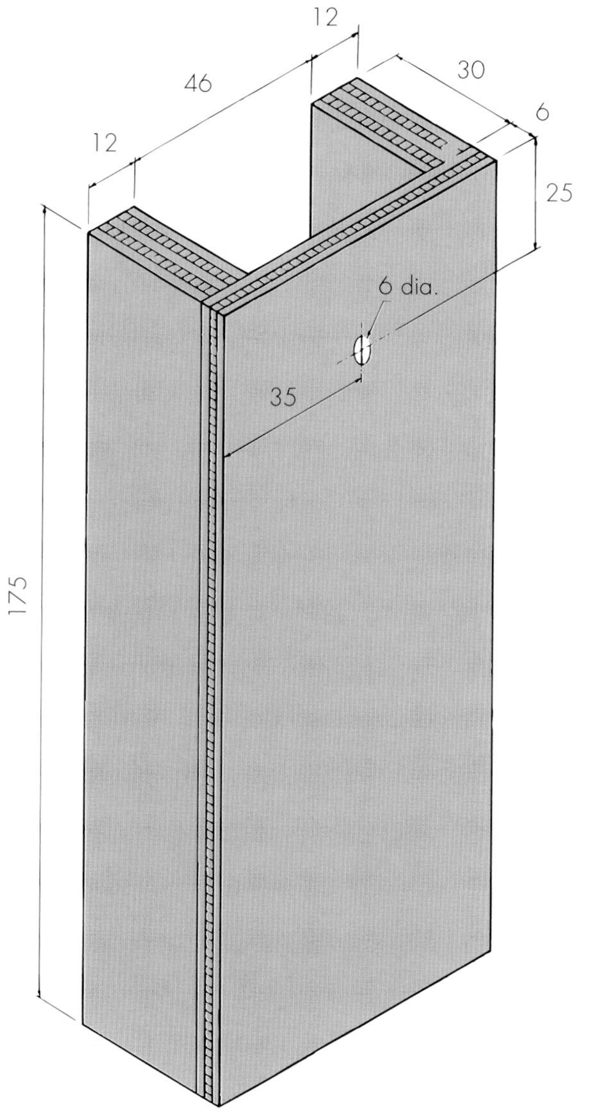

Fig 9.7 Stage back box.

With pins and glue, attach the back box to the rear of the stage backdrop. Ensure that the axle holes are in alignment.

The fretted side panels are mitred (angled at 45°) on the edges which meet the stage backdrop side edges (*see* Fig 9.8). Use a block plane to create the mitred edge. To mark out each area that requires removal, set a marking gauge to the thickness of the side panel. Then mark a line, resting the gauge on the edge to be mitred, along the face side. Regularly check for accuracy with a mitre square when planing the mitres.

Mark the fretted design on the face side of each panel (*see* Fig 9.9). Cut out each pattern carefully using a no. 1 or no. 2 size blade. Any unevenness can be rectified by using sanding sticks and needle files (*see* Fig 9.10).

Fix each side panel into position with pins and glue, but do not try to pin the mitred edge. Hold this joint together with masking tape until the glue has set.

Glue and pin the 3mm (⅛in) thick top stage piece into place on top of the stage's backdrop and back box.

The top moulding is 9 x 9mm (⅜ x ⅜in) scotia. Mitre the four lengths and glue them to the top piece (*see* Fig 9.6).

Fig 9.8 Checking the mitred edge of a screen before fretsawing the decorative pattern.

The 3mm wide vertical strip on the left denotes the mitred edge. For the other screen, the mitred edge is on the opposite side.

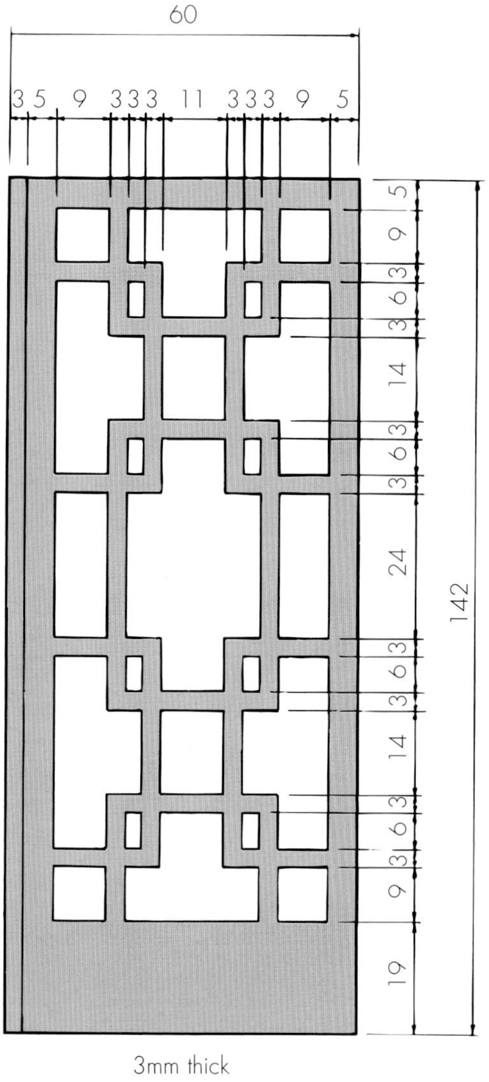

Fig 9.9 Fretted screen – right-hand side of the stage.

Using a fretsaw, cut out the decorative top piece of the stage (*see* Fig 9.11). If you wish to fit the dragon to it you must cut the dragon's retaining slot in the top. I cheated and instead of cutting a retaining slot I drilled a hole, the diameter of which was slightly smaller than the dragon's retaining tenon (approximately 3.25mm). This produces an interference fit. Glue the top piece into place.

The dragon is made from 1.5mm ($\frac{1}{16}$in) thick brass sheet (*see* Figs 9.12, 9.13). Transfer the dragon profile on to paper, cut round it and glue the paper on to the brass sheet. Cut the dragon out with a powered or hand fretsaw, ensuring that you use a metal-cutting fretsaw blade. Generally, a hand fretsaw is more suitable for cutting such a small component. Use needle files to smooth away any unevenness after cutting out.

The dragon's features were created with a combination of scriber, a cup-ended pin punch and a centre punch.

The dragon may be cleaned with 1200 grade wet and dry paper and polished with a suitable brass polish. Finally, give the

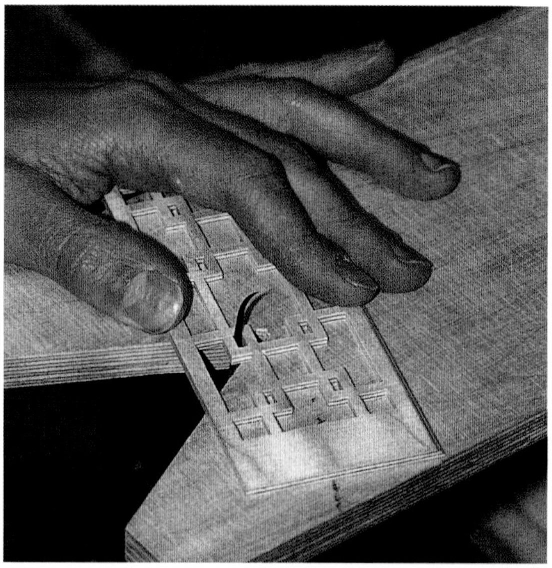

Fig 9.10 Using a needle file to clean up the screen's pattern after fretsawing. Sanding sticks should be used for the larger sections.

The two curves are drawn with the aid of an isometric ellipse template (35mm/25°).

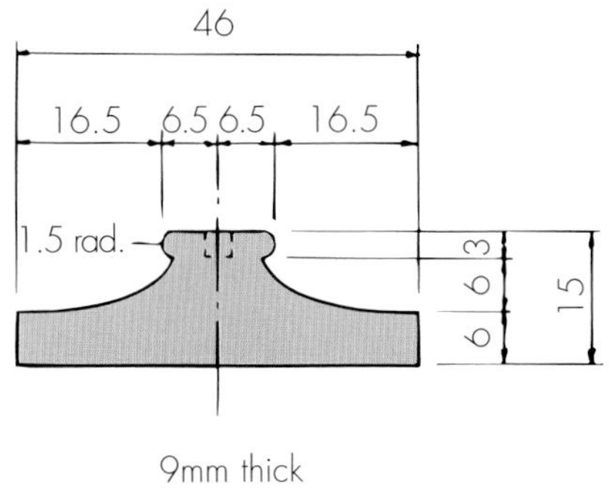

Fig 9.11 The stage's decorative top piece.

Fig 9.12 The dragon.

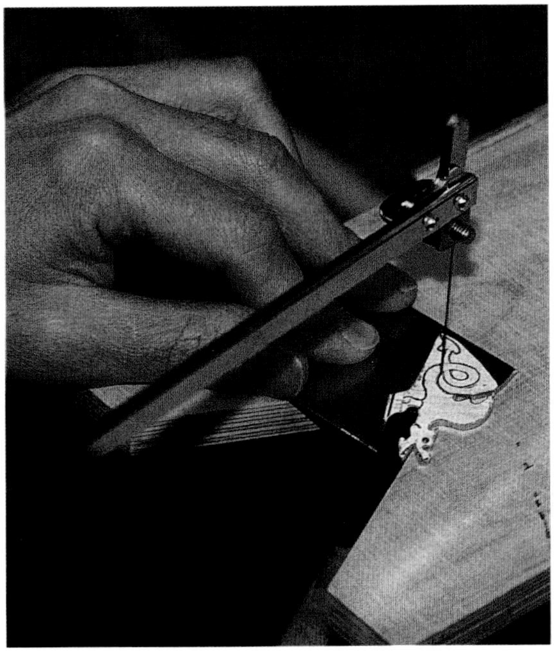

Fig 9.13 Fretsawing the decorative dragon from sheet brass.

dragon a couple of coats of clear metal lacquer, the type which prevents metal from tarnishing.

I would suggest that you do not fix the dragon to the top piece with adhesive, so that it may be easily removed. It may prove unwise to leave the dragon in place (due to the acute points of its shape) if younger children operate the toy.

The mechanism that enables the acrobat to perform is basically two wheels attached to an axle. Both wheels are ready-made from hardwood. The rear one (the handle) is 60mm (2⅜in) in diameter and the front one is 38mm (1½in) in diameter.

Drill two 6mm (¼in) diameter holes, one centrally and the other offset into the rear wheel (*see* Fig 9.14). Prepare the 6mm (¼in) diameter dowel handle and glue into position.

Drill out the centre of the front wheel, using a 6mm (¼in) drill bit. The offset hole is 3mm (⅛in) in diameter (*see* Fig 9.15). Prepare the 3mm (⅛in) diameter dowel for the acrobat's bar and glue into position.

For the axle, cut a piece of 6mm (¼in) dowel to a suitable length that will allow both wheels to turn freely when assembled. Allow adequate room for a washer to be fitted behind each wheel. Paint the wheels before assembling. However, do not paint the acrobat's bar as this may impede assembly later.

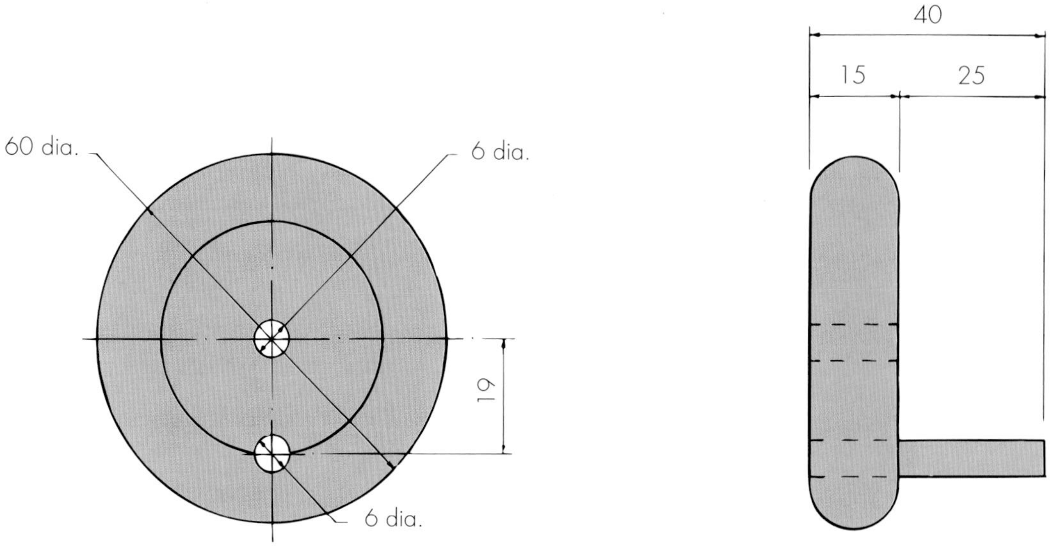

Fig 9.14 The rear wheel and handle.

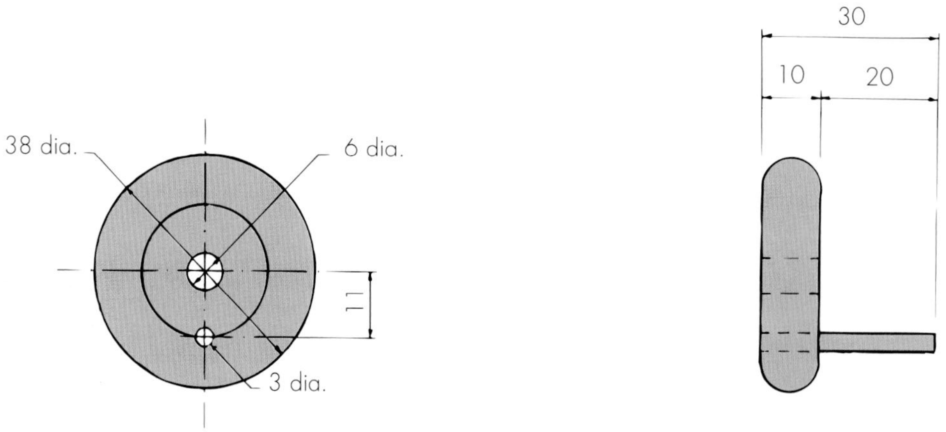

Fig 9.15 The front wheel of the acrobat's bar.

As the stage backdrop looked rather bare I glued two pieces of 20 x 5mm ($\frac{3}{4}$ x $\frac{3}{16}$in) embossed moulding to it, cutting the tops with a fretsaw to match the top curves of the backdrop. These are purely decorative (*see* Fig 9.16). Instead of applying these you could paint some Chinese letters or symbols or, if you are feeling very artistic, a pair of golden flying dragons.

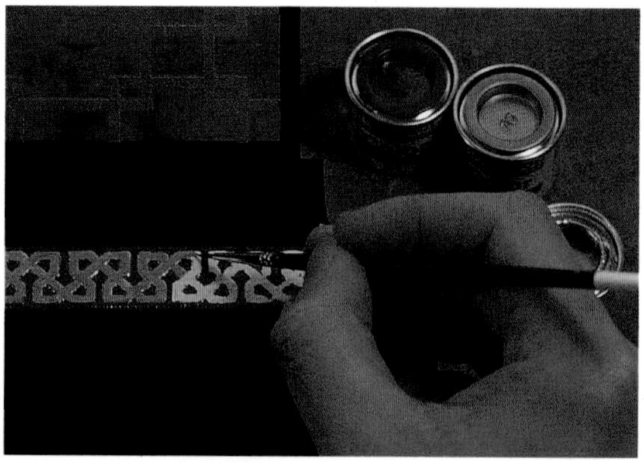

Fig 9.16 Painting one of the decorative strips on the stage backdrop.

Fig 9.17 The completed toy before finishing.

FINAL ASSEMBLY AND OPERATION

Assemble the axle and wheel arrangement to the stage. Fix the wheels on to the axle with glue, remembering to fit a washer behind each wheel. Pass the acrobat's hands on to the bar and fix with two spots of glue (*see* Figs 9.17, 9.18). The axle ends and bar may now be painted.

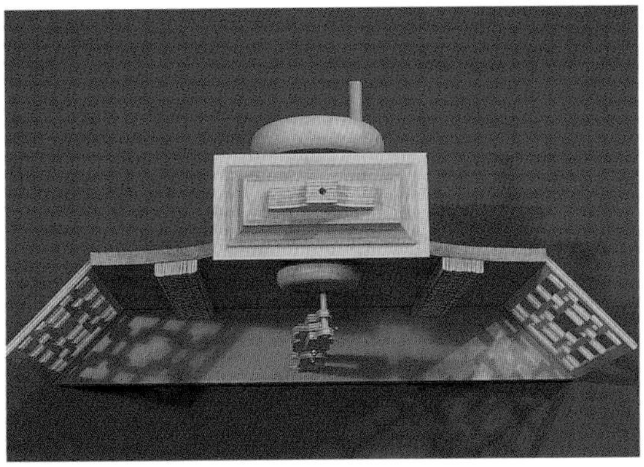

Fig 9.18 Top view of the completed toy before finishing.

Fix some velour or felt to the underside of the stage.

Turn the rear handle to operate the acrobat. By varying the handle rotation rate, a variety of effects can be achieved.

CONSTRUCTION ALTERNATIVES

If you are not a practised fretsaw user I recommend that you omit the brass dragon decoration from the project.

Should the fretted side panels prove a problem to cut, you could simply fit solid panels instead. These can be painted and finished in an exciting style which complements the project.

CHAPTER 10

Acorn Farm

★★

Animal figures were undoubtedly one of the earliest purpose-made wooden toys, and it is reassuring to note that they are as popular now as they were so many years ago.

A common fault with traditional, often carved, wooden animals is that their legs tend to break easily. Our animals are made from birch plywood which makes them stronger and less prone to this problem. The buildings and walls have been designed to be compatible with standard-size animals as well as our own.

THE FARM

We have designed the animals to be of a larger scale than that of standard shop-bought plastic ones, and to have a 'chunky' quality in both feel and appearance. This is so that children, particularly young children, will find them easy to stand up and generally manipulate during play.

The body of each animal is basically made up from three sections of plywood. The central section usually constitutes the head, middle body and tail. The two outer sections constitute the sides of the head (except in the case of the sheep and hens), body sides and legs.

CUTTING LIST

Farm building

Side wall (2):	163 x 150 x 12mm (6 7/16 x 5 15/16 x 1/2in) birch plywood
Partition wall:	163 x 138 x 12mm (6 7/16 x 5 7/16 x 1/2in) birch plywood
Back wall:	280 x 113 x 12mm (11 x 4 7/16 x 1/2in) birch plywood
Roof (2):	286 x 100 x 3mm (11 1/4 x 4 x 1/8in) birch plywood

Pigsty

Front wall:	76 x 60 x 6mm (3 x 2 3/8 x 1/4in) birch plywood
Back wall:	51 x 76 x 6mm (2 x 3 x 1/4in) birch plywood
Side wall (2):	130 x 60 x 6mm (5 1/8 x 2 3/8 x 1/4in) birch plywood
Roof:	137 x 94 x 3mm (5 7/16 x 3 11/16 x 1/8in) birch plywood

Gate	120 x 48 x 6mm (4 3/4 x 1 7/8 x 1/4in) birch plywood
Gatepost (2):	50 x 8 x 6mm (2 x 5/16 x 1/4in) birch plywood
Walls	Any quantity, any length x 38mm (1 1/2in) x 18mm (3/4in) MDF
Animals	Off-cuts of 3mm (1/8in), 6mm (1/4in), and 12mm (1/2in) birch plywood

Miscellaneous

25mm (1in) brass butt hinges per gate (2)
9mm (3/8in) brass countersunk screws per gate (4)
Short length of cord

The largest building is intended to be multi-functional. It may be used as a cowshed, lambing shed, barn, stable, workshop or tractor shed. By omitting doors, windows and other distinguishing features, we have left its purpose entirely to the creative imaginations of the children who will play with it.

We made two of these large buildings. In one, we have omitted the central partition wall. This is to create more space and distinguish its function from the other.

One often frustrating aspect of children's play farms is that there are rarely enough hedges or walls to create fields. Our walls are straightforward and economic to produce. They can be made in a variety of lengths and sizes – the quantity made is up to you.

Those of you who are familiar with our toys will notice once again that we have not used a baseboard to mount the farm. This is because we feel that play farms with baseboards prove bulky to store. Free-standing buildings and walls also allow children to change the layout of the farm as and when they wish.

CONSTRUCTION

Animals

As previously stated, the animals are made up from three sections. The following is a list of the animals and the relevant thicknesses of birch plywood required for each section:

Animal	Centre section (x1)	Outer sections (x2)
Cow	12mm (½in)	6mm (¼in)
Pig	12mm (½in)	3mm (⅛in)
Sheep	12mm (½in)	3mm (⅛in) + ears: 3mm (⅛in)
Dog	6mm (¼in)	3mm (⅛in)
Calf	6mm (¼in)	3mm (⅛in)
Lamb	6mm (¼in)	3mm (⅛in)
Hen	3mm (⅛in)	3mm (⅛in)

Transfer the outer section profile of each animal (except for the hen and sheep, this is the head, body and legs) on to the relevant thickness of birch plywood (*see* Fig 10.1). Then pin these to a sheet of the same thickness of plywood (*see* Fig 10.2). Ensure that you use pins which will protrude, allowing for easy removal later.

Cut out the animal shapes with a fretsaw (*see* Fig 10.3). If you intend to use a hand-held one, make sure you do not angle the blade during cutting or the legs on one side of the animals will be of a different width to the other side.

Now transfer the centre-section profiles (head, body and tail) of each animal on to the appropriate thickness of plywood and cut out.

Unpin the outer sections.

Glue the animal sections together in the correct order. Use a woodworking PVA adhesive (white glue), as this will allow you to manipulate the sections into place.

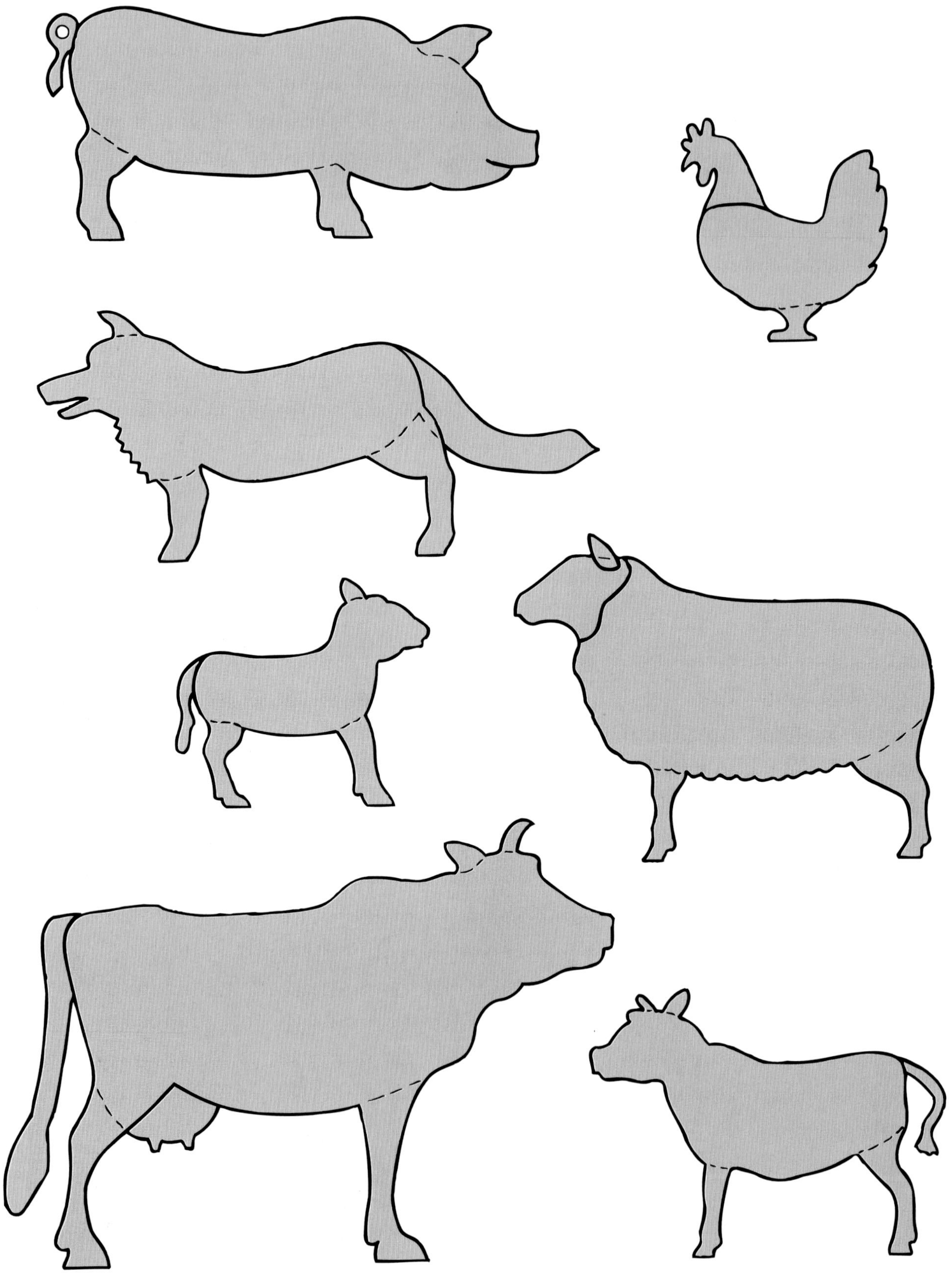

Fig 10.1 Farm animal shapes.

Clamp each animal in a vice for a few minutes, then leave them (preferably overnight) until the glue has set. The sheep's ears may be cut out and glued on before leaving the assembled sheep to dry.

When the glue has set, fill the pin holes with filler and clean up any uneven edges with a combination of sanding sticks and small files. If you have cut out the profiles and glued them together carefully this should not be too great a task. However, do not worry if the fluffy underside of your sheep and your dog's chest is uneven – it all helps to create the illusion of wool or fur!

You could go to great lengths in shaping and sculpting your animals. If you wish to do this we suggest that you make the animals using thicker plywood for the outer sections. This will provide you with more material to shape, particularly useful when doing the legs.

The animals are now ready to be primed and painted (*see* Fig 10.4). We finished ours with a very basic and simplistic colour scheme. If you wish, you could test your artistic abilities by painting them with lifelike details and colours.

Pigsty

Cut out all the walls and the roof (*see* Fig 10.5).

Fix the side walls to the front and back walls with pins and glue. Shape the protruding top edge of the front and back wall to match the slope of the side wall top edges. Use a block plane for this.

Glue and pin the roof in place.

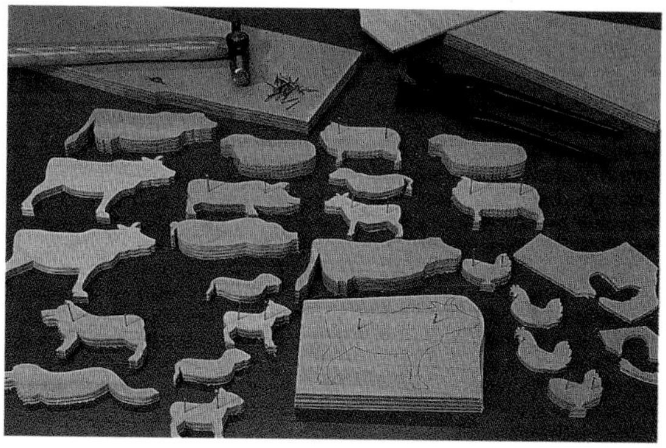

Fig 10.2 Farm animals. Note those pinned together for multiple cutting. On the left, the multi-cut side profiles of the cow have been unpinned ready to be joined with the middle section shown above them.

Fig 10.3 Multiple cutting of a cow.

Fig 10.4 Farm animals ready for painting.

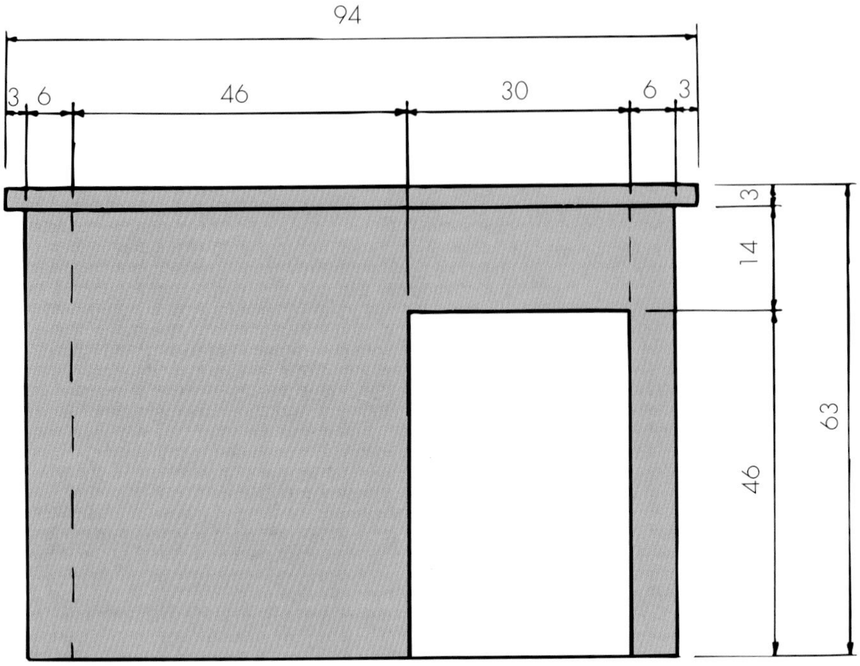

Fig 10.5 Pigsty dimensions showing front, side and roof.

Large farm building

Cut out all the wall and roof sections (*see* Figs 10.6, 10.7).

Glue and pin the side (end) walls to the back wall. The partition wall is the same shape as the side walls except that it has 12mm (½in) taken off its width to allow for the thickness of the back wall. Glue and pin the partition wall into position.

Fit one of the roof sections, with glue and pins, to the top slopes of the side and partition walls.

Using a block plane, shape its top edge to allow the other roof section to fit correctly (*see* Fig 10.8). Then fit the other roof section (*see* Fig 10.9).

Of course, the dimensions of this building may be altered to suit your requirements (though we suggest that our dimensions are probably the minimum for a building of this sort).

Walls

The walls can be constructed from almost any timber. We chose 18mm (¾in) MDF because it is relatively inexpensive.

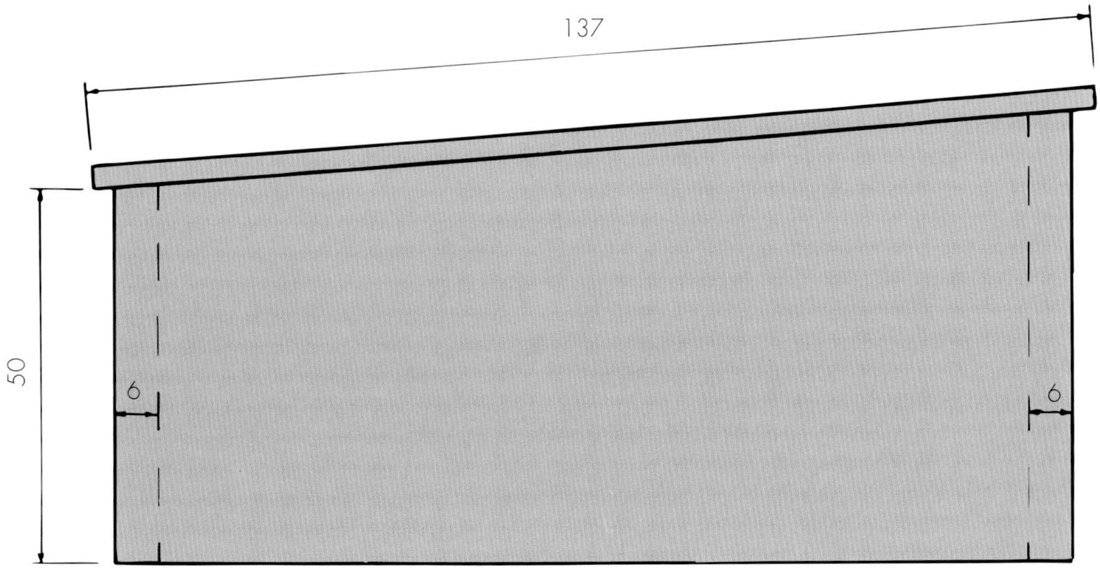
137
50
6
6

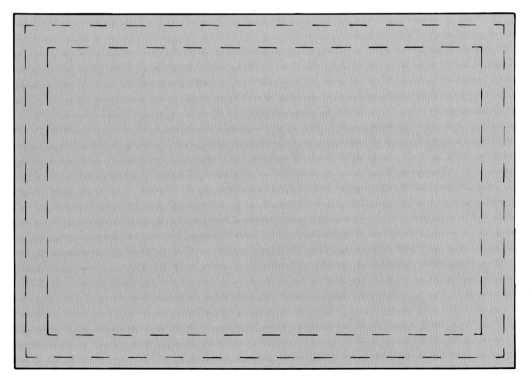

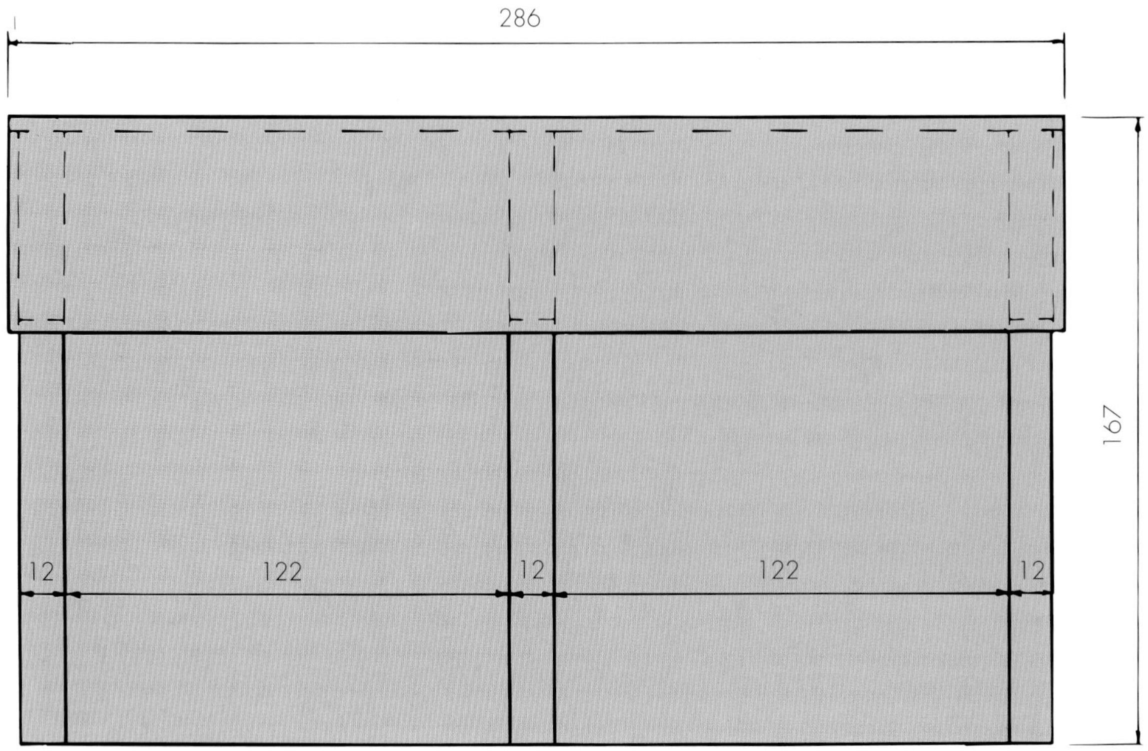

The central wall may be omitted to create more space.

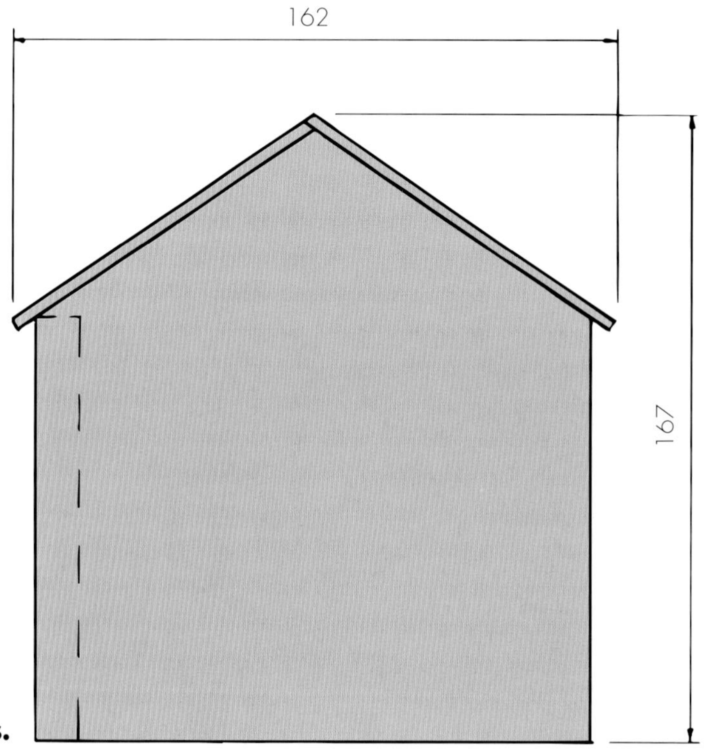

Fig 10.6 Farm building dimensions.

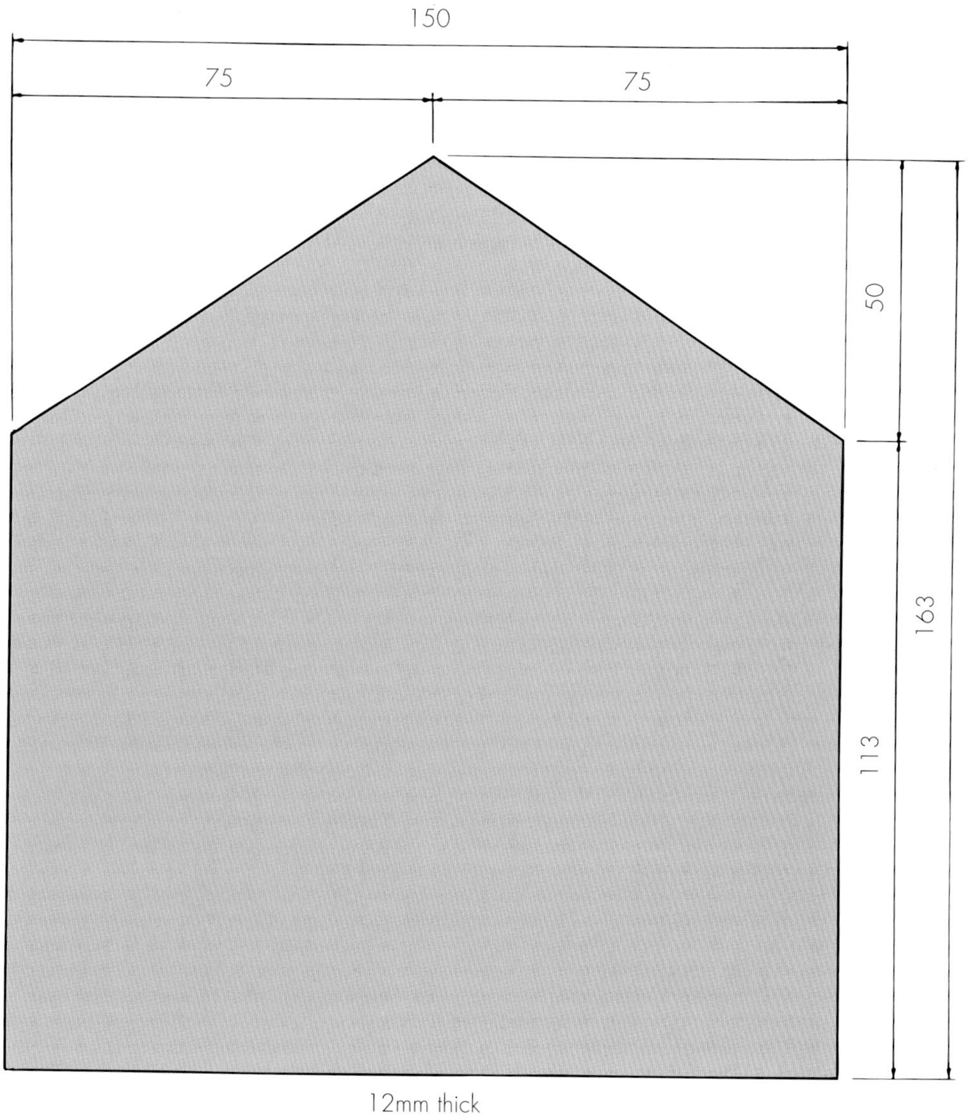

Fig 10.7 Farm building side wall.

Fig 10.8 Planing the top edge of a roof section so that the other roof section will fit correctly.

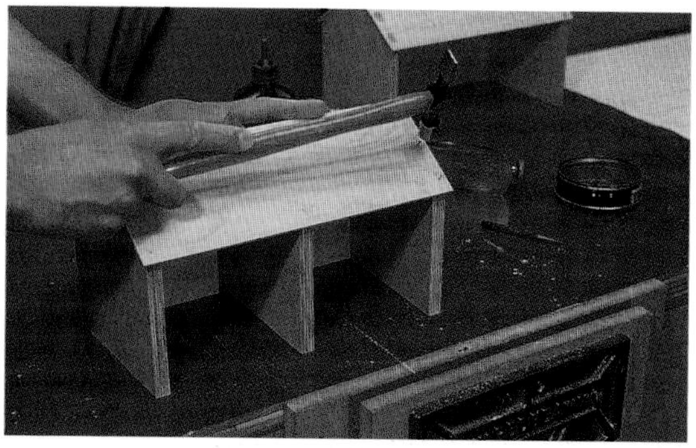

Fig 10.9 Fixing down the roof of a farm building with moulding pins and glue.

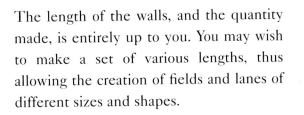

The length of the walls, and the quantity made, is entirely up to you. You may wish to make a set of various lengths, thus allowing the creation of fields and lanes of different sizes and shapes.

Hedges can also be made. Use timber slightly taller than the walls and shape the sections accordingly.

Gate and gateposts

Draw the gate on 6mm (¼in) birch plywood and cut out (*see* Fig 10.10).

Cut the gateposts from an 8mm (5/16in) wide strip of 6mm (¼in) birch plywood. Round the tops using sanding sticks.

In one, drill a hole to accommodate the cord 'catch'. Ours is 2mm in diameter. Drill yours to a size suitable for the cord you intend to use.

After they have been finished, glue and pin each gatepost to a wall end.

Hinge the gate to the gatepost that doesn't have the cord hole. Note that the hinge is simply laid on and not set into the edges, and that it is fitted on the gate stile with the completely rounded top.

Tie a cord loop through the appropriate gatepost, ensuring that it is long enough to loop over the gate's half-rounded stile. This loop should secure the gate when closed. You must always follow the country code and close gates behind you!

Omit the 2mm dia. hole from the other post.

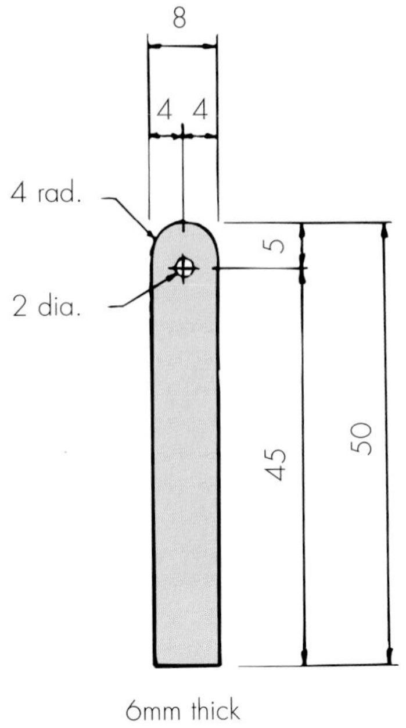

Fig 10.10 Gatepost and gate.

FINISHING

We covered our farm buildings and walls with the type of decorative finishing paper used for toy castles and dolls' houses. We chose a stone effect for the walls and red tiles for the roof (*see* Fig 10.11). Use wallpaper paste as an adhesive.

When the buildings have been covered any surplus paper can be trimmed using a very sharp, small craft knife or scalpel. Only trim the paper when the adhesive has set.

The gate and gatepost can be painted or stained. We stained ours with a wood dye and finished it with a couple of coats of matt varnish.

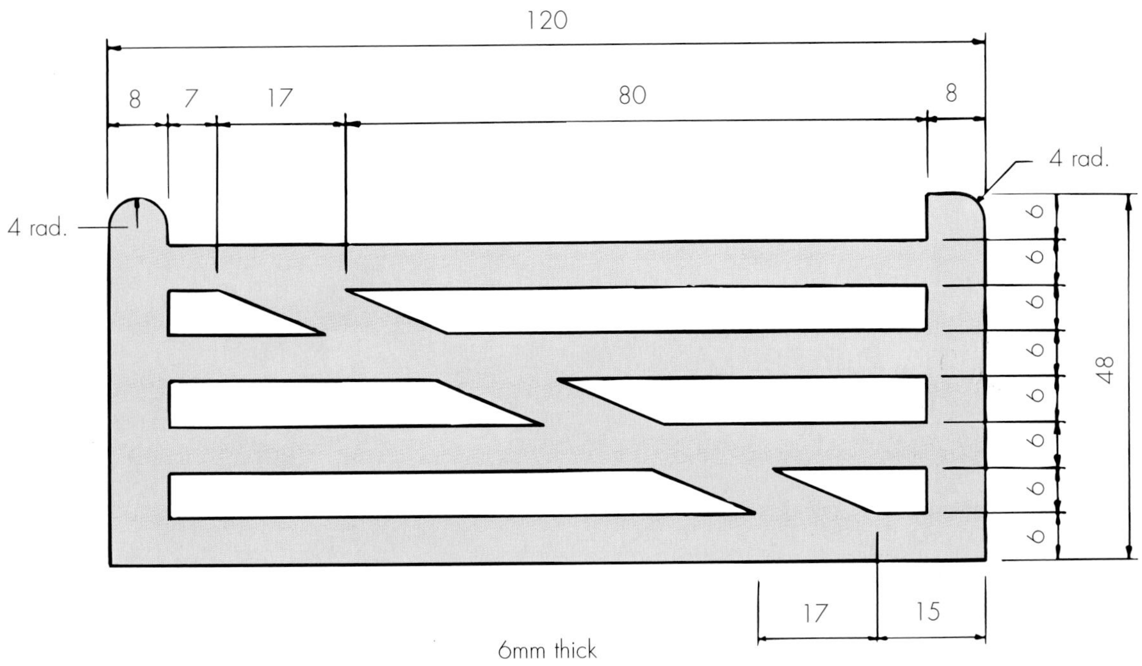

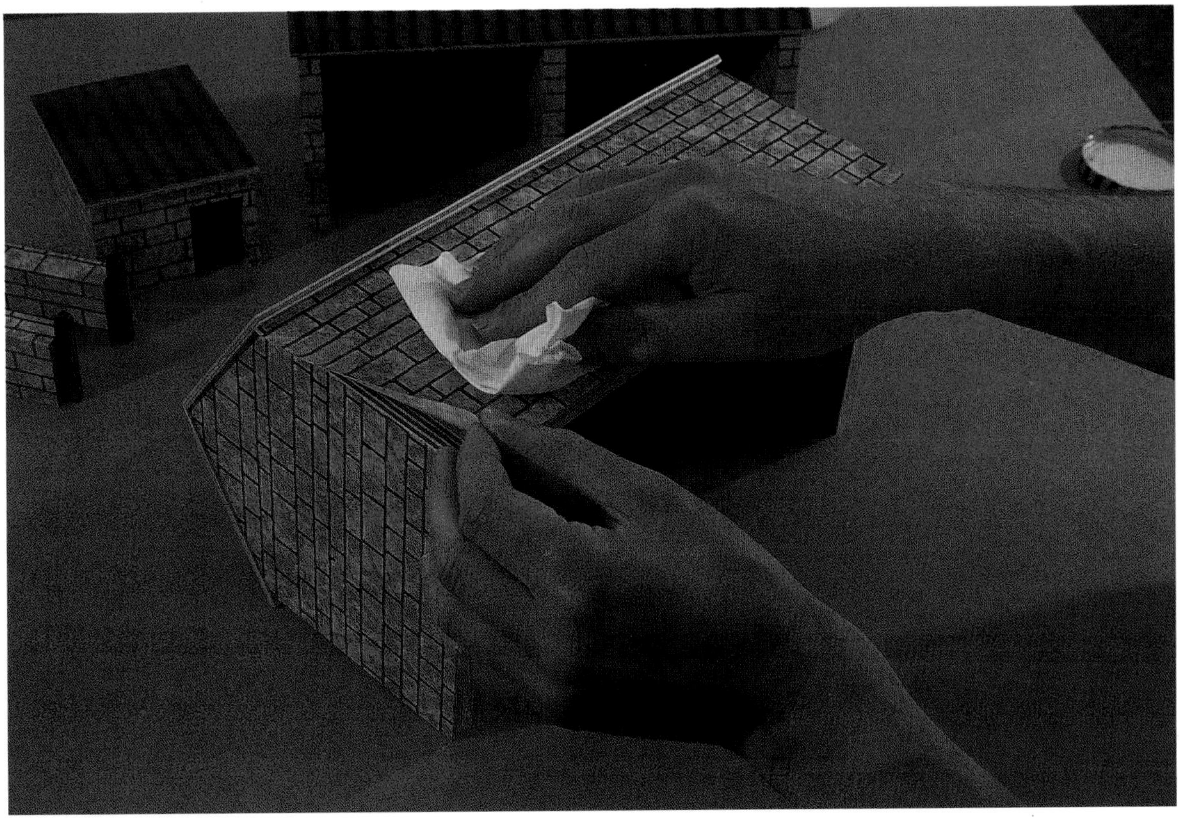

Fig 10.11 Applying the paper. Smooth away air bubbles with a soft cloth.

12
FLASH
ZAP
18
ZIPPY
9
SPEEDY
4
ZAP
18
FLASH
12
SPEEDY
4

CHAPTER 11

Snail Racing

★★

Snail racing is a family game that incorporates careful reckoning and calculated risks.

The game consists of a pre-agreed number of races. Each snail has a speed rating: for example, 'Lightning', the fastest snail, has a rating of 3 and 'Zap', the slowest, is rated at 18. Each player must guess which snail will win a race. If they are correct they win the number of points equal to the speed rating of the winning snail. The snails are made to race (or should that be slither?) by the central disc being spun. The section of track which comes to rest by the chequered flag arrow wins the race. The winner of the game is the player who accumulates the highest number of points after all the races have been run.

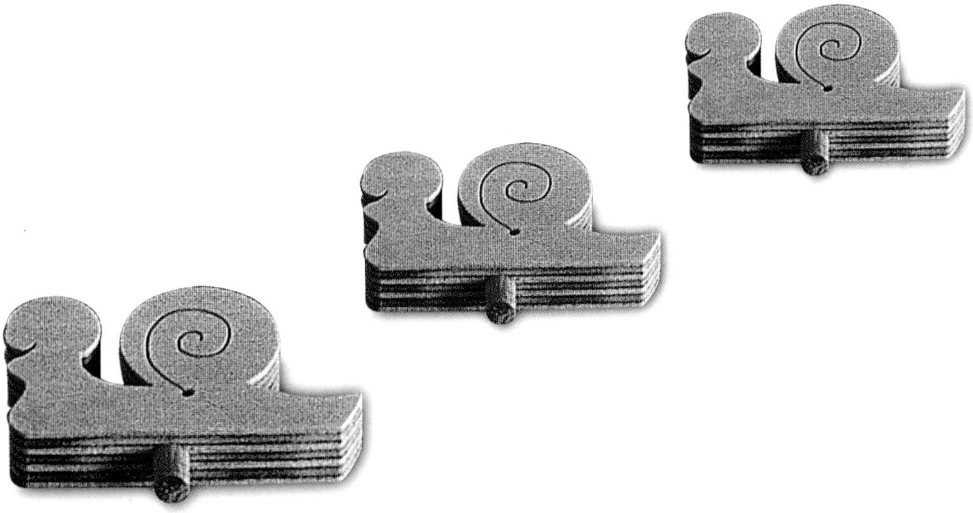

CUTTING LIST

Game board

Top piece:	305 x 305 x 12mm (12 x 12 x ½in) birch plywood
Bottom piece:	305 x 305 x 12mm (12 x 12 x ½in) birch plywood
Flags and arrow:	Scrap pieces of 3mm (⅛in) birch plywood
Spinning cross:	Scrap piece of 12mm (½in) birch plywood
Edging (4):	315 x 24 x 5mm (12 6/16 x 1 x 3/16in) hardwood (ramin)
Snails:	Scrap pieces of 9mm (⅜in) birch plywood

Miscellaneous

25mm (1in) wooden wheels for counters (one per player)
A length of 5mm (3/16in) axle rod
A length of 5mm (3/16in) dowel rod
Washers to fit the axle rod (2–4)
25mm (1in) diameter wooden ball or spring hubcap
Paper or card to make the scorecards

RULES OF PLAY

For two or more players.

Equipment

- 1 game board
- A different-coloured counter for each player
- A scorecard and pencil for each player

Object of the game

To be the player who has won the highest number of points on completion of a pre-agreed number of races.

Preparation

The game board should be placed on a flat and level surface.

Each player is given a counter, scorecard and pencil.

Determine how many races will be run in the game.

Play

Before the first, and every, race each player must choose the snail which he thinks will win the race. The number of that snail is recorded in the relevant 'Prediction' box on each player's scorecard. Each player places their counter on the chosen snail's space on the game board, indicated by the snails' names and numbers (*see* Fig 11.1). This signifies to the other players that all players are ready for the race to begin.

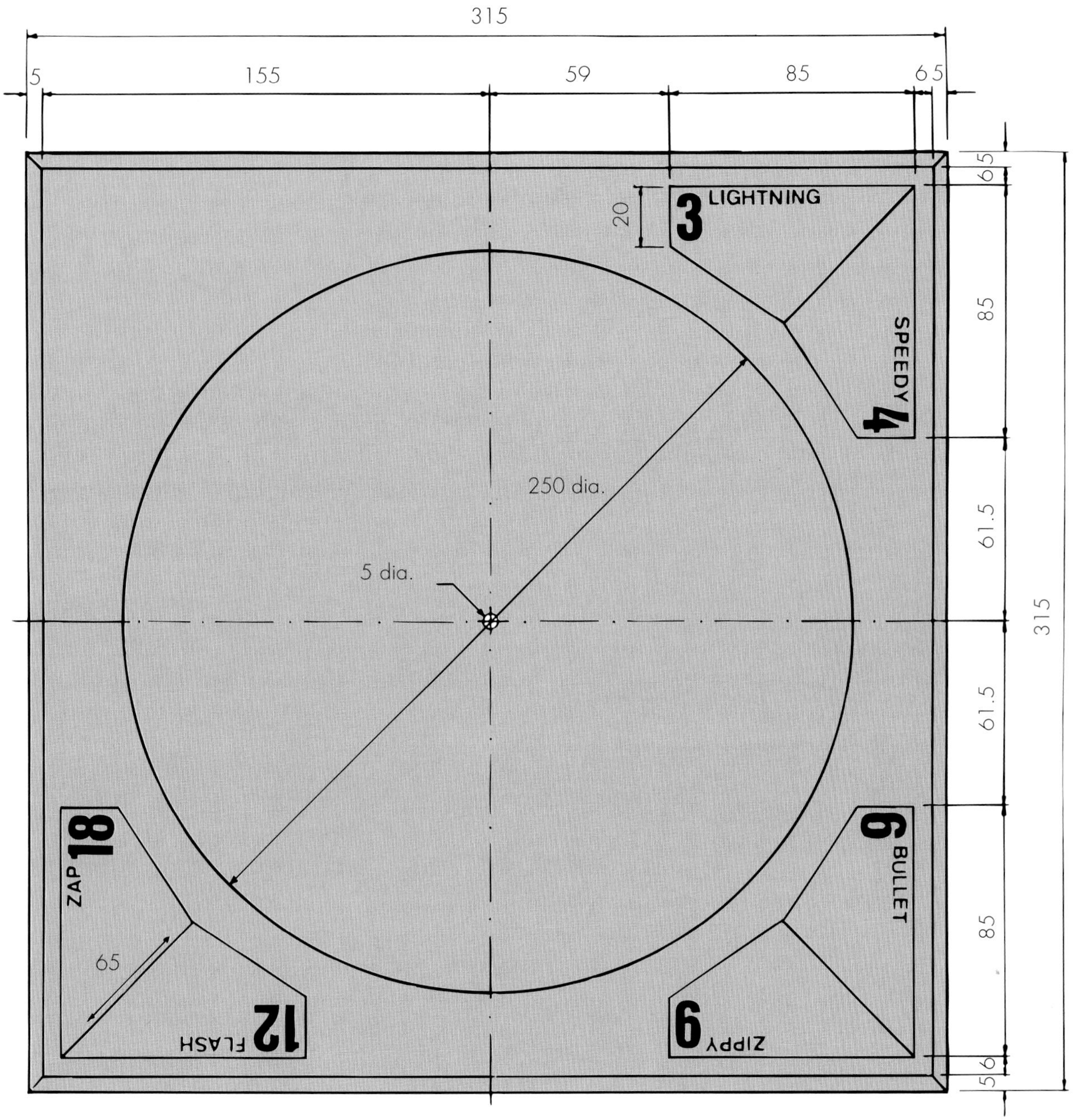

Fig 11.1 The game board.

When all the players have placed their counters on the game board the race is run. This is done by a player (take it in turns for each race) spinning the central disc (*see* Fig 11.2). The disc must complete at least six revolutions, otherwise the race is void and must be re-run.

When the disc has completely stopped turning, the snail whose section is indicated by the chequered flag arrow wins the race. If the point of the arrow is pointing exactly down the middle of a segregating line, the race must be re-run. The player, or players, who correctly guessed the winning snail score its speed points rating. This is recorded on the 'Points scored' section on the scorecard. Every player who guessed incorrectly scores nothing and must enter a zero on his scorecard for that race.

The players now remove their counters from the board. The whole process is repeated until all the races have been run.

Disc thickness: 12mm

Disc dia.: 250mm

Inner marked circle dia.: 200mm

Centre hole dia.: 5mm

Each snail's peg hole is located at the central point of their track section; each is 6mm deep x 5mm dia.

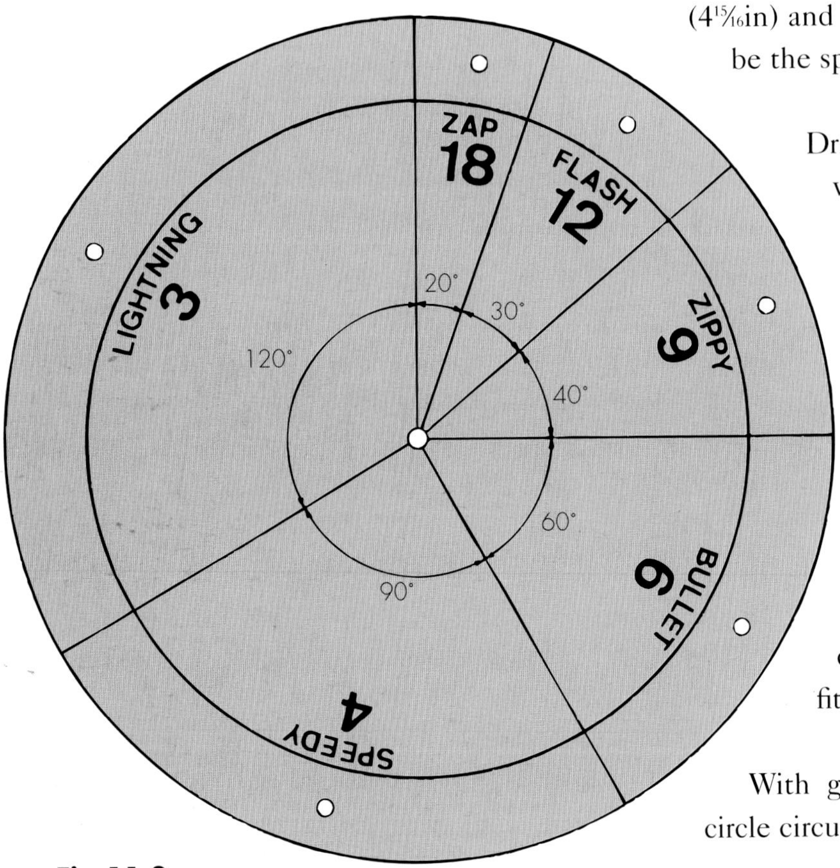

Fig 11.2
The spinning disc.

Winning the game

Upon completion of all the races, each player adds up all, if any, of the points he has scored. The total number is entered in the 'Total points' box on each scorecard (*see* Fig 11.12).

The player with the highest total points wins the game.

CONSTRUCTION

Cut out and prepare the top piece of the game board. Find and mark its centre point (*see* Fig 11.1).

Set a large compass to a radius of 125mm ($4\frac{15}{16}$in) and draw a circle. This circle will be the spinning disc.

Drill a hole, the diameter of which will just allow a fretsaw blade to pass through it, directly on the circumference of the marked circle. Thread the blade through the hole and secure it in your fretsaw (preferably machine). Use as large a grade (size) blade as you can, as a thicker blade will produce a wider kerf, thus allowing more clearance around the disc when fitted later.

With great care cut exactly on the circle circumference line.

When you have cut out the disc, place the game board top on to a flat surface. Then lower the disc into it. If you have cut the disc out correctly, you should be able to turn the disc freely.

If the disc sticks at any point, smooth any unevenness on the edge of the disc by using abrasive paper wrapped around a sanding block. Start with a coarse grade and finish with a fine one.

Prepare the game board base, cutting it slightly bigger than the game board top piece.

Glue the top piece on to the base piece. Place some evenly distributed weights on top until the glue has set.

When the glue is completely dry, trim the edges smooth and square with a plane.

You will now need to mark the layout of the game on the game board and spinning disc, so ensure that their top surfaces are smooth and even.

The 'racing track' is created by marking a 200mm (7⅞in) diameter circle on the spinning disc (*see* Fig 11.2).

Use a black ballpoint pen to mark this circle. If you have a large compass with an attachment to hold a pen, all well and good. If not, you will need to make a circular template to mark around.

If using a template, draw the circle on the spinning disc with a pencil-point compass first. This will aid you in positioning the template.

We made our template from 6mm (¼in) MDF, but you could use hardboard or plywood if preferred.

Practise marking around your template on paper or card first, as any mistakes are hard to rectify.

It will soon become obvious if your template is inaccurate. Any nicks or unevenness in the template edge will become evident as you mark around it. Smooth away any unevenness with abrasive paper wrapped around a sanding block.

The division lines separating the snail segments are now marked. Use a protractor to divide the disc accurately (*see* Fig 11.2). Again, use a black ballpoint pen to mark the segment lines.

Mark the six boxes (on which the players place their counters) on the game board. Draw them lightly with pencil first, then ink over them. Erase any pencil marks, but make sure that the ink is completely dry before you do so.

You will now need to drill the spindle hole through the centre of the spinning disc and halfway into the base of the game board. If you have a large drill press this can be done in one operation. Clamp the game board, with the spinning disc exactly in the centre, to the table of the drill press and set the depth stop (*see* Fig 11.3). Drill the hole to

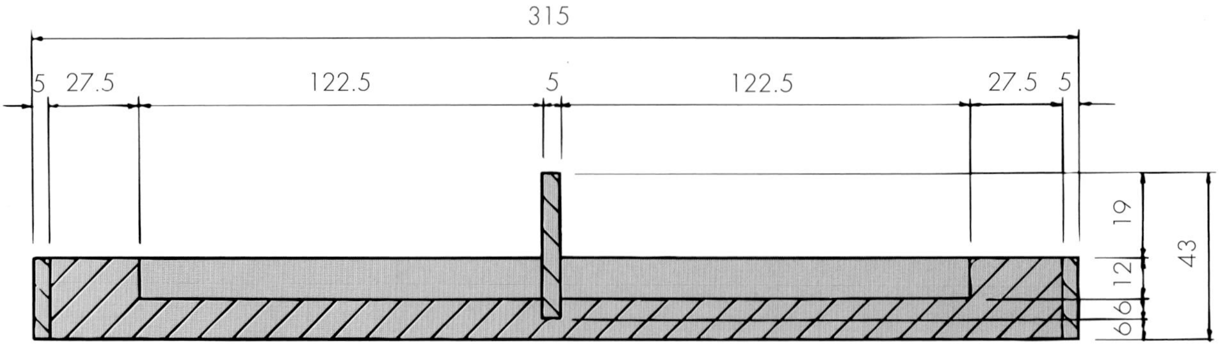

Fig 11.3 Cross-section of the game board.

the exact diameter of your spindle. Unclamp the game board, remove the disc and, with a drill bit fractionally larger in diameter, drill out the disc hole. This will ensure that the disc will spin freely around the spindle.

If the capacity of your drill press is not large enough, or you do not have one, then use a hand drill. Clamp the game board, with the spinning disc exactly in the centre, to your worktop or in your vice, if it is big enough. Drill out as described above, using sticky tape as a depth stop on your drill bit (*see* Fig 3.10 on page 23).

Fix a length of axle rod (spindle) into the central hole of the game board. Do not glue it into position yet. Thread the spinning disc on to it and drop it into the game board. Gently turn the disc. If it catches at any point, the drilled holes are not central. This can be rectified by sanding the high point/s from the edge of the disc with a sanding block.

If the disc has become jammed in the game board, remove the spindle and the disc should drop out easily.

Drill the snail peg holes in the spinning disc. These are located at the central point of the track sections. Each is 6mm (¼in) deep and 5mm (3⁄16in) in diameter (*see* Fig 11.4).

Mark out the central cross (a fingerhold for spinning the disc) on 12mm (½in) birch plywood (*see* Fig 11.5). Drill out the central hole, then cut out the cross with a fretsaw.

Transfer the chequered flags and arrow profiles on to 3mm (⅛in) birch plywood (*see* Fig 11.4). Cut them out with a fretsaw.

Transfer the snail profile six times on to 9mm (⅜in) birch plywood and fretsaw them out. Drill their peg holes, cut their pegs and glue these into place (*see* Fig 11.6).

Prepare a length of hardwood edging about 1270 x 25 x 5mm (50 x 1 x 3⁄16in), and varnish it with gloss varnish.

Varnish the snail track on the spinning disc, the game board counter boxes, the central cross and the arrow.

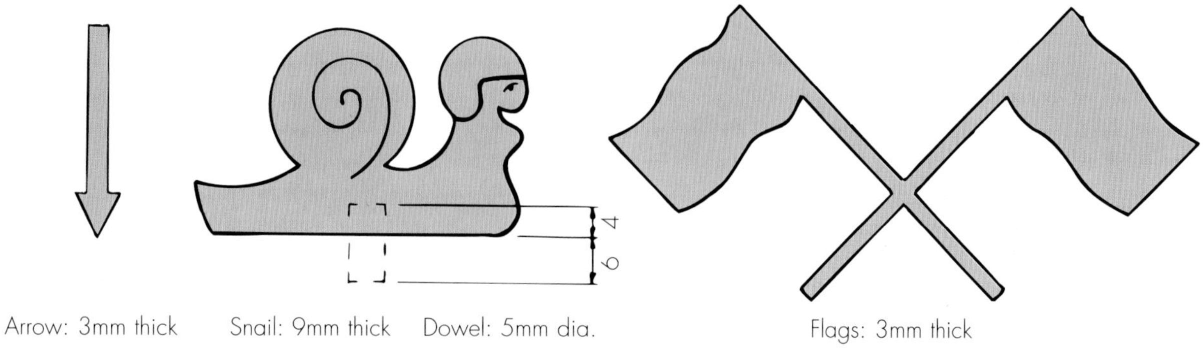

Fig 11.4 Winning post arrow, racing snail and flags.

The chequers on the flags are marked with a black ballpoint pen, given a sealing coat of gloss varnish, then filled in with black paint and finished with gloss varnish.

Paint the snails. Use different colours for their crash helmets (*see* Fig 11.7). Their identifying numbers are 2.5mm dry rub down transfers, though a permanent marker pen could be used if preferred.

Paint the green sections of the spinning disc and game board.

Re-mark the black segment division lines on the spinning disc. This is done by aligning a rule with the line on the track and the central hole of the disc.

Identify each of the disc segments and game board counter boxes, using dry rub down transfers (*see* Fig 11.8). The counter box numbers are 18mm (¾in). The numbers on the disc are 12mm (½in) and the letters 6mm (¼in).

Give the top surfaces of the disc and game board a final protective coat of gloss varnish.

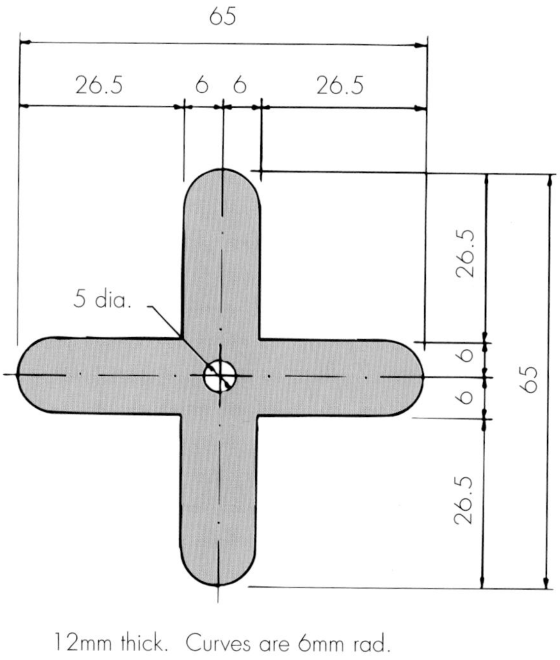

Fig 11.5 The spinning disc's central cross.

Fig 11.6 The racing snails ready for painting.

Fig 11.7 The racing snails during finishing. Note the use of a scrap piece of MDF as a painting jig.

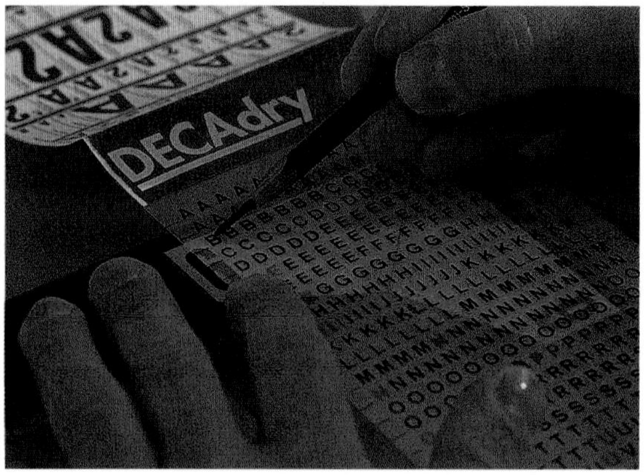

Fig 11.8 Applying dry rub down transfer lettering to the game board.

When the top surface varnish is completely dry, apply one coat of varnish to the edges and underside of the spinning disc. This will help to prevent it from warping.

Carefully glue and pin the central cross in place on the spinning disc. Ensure that the spindle hole is exactly in line with the hole in the spinning disc. Fill the pin holes and varnish.

Apply the hardwood edging to the game board, using butt mitre joints at the corners. A mitre jig (or mitre box) will aid you in cutting them (*see* Fig 11.9). Attach the edging using moulding pins and glue (*see* Fig 11.10).

Fill in the pin holes and give the edging a final coat of varnish.

Glue the flags and arrow in place on the game board.

Glue each snail into its peg hole on the spinning disc.

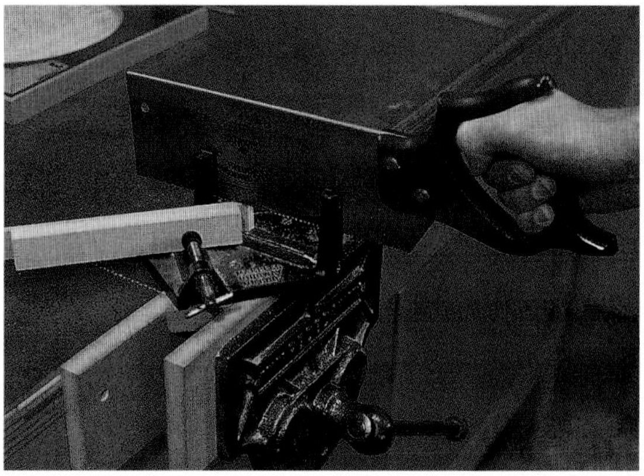

Fig 11.9 Using a mitre cutting jig to cut the mitre joints for the edging of the game board.

The spindle length is dependent upon what you cap it with. You could use a spring hubcap, though we used a varnished 25mm (1in) wooden ball with a 5mm (3/16in) hole drilled 12mm (1/2in) deep into it. You will need a washer or two, placed on the spindle, between the underside of the disc and the game board base so that the disc will spin freely. Bear this in mind when you calculate the length of spindle you require. Ours is approximately 37mm (1 1/2in) long (*see* Fig 11.3), but you may need yours to be

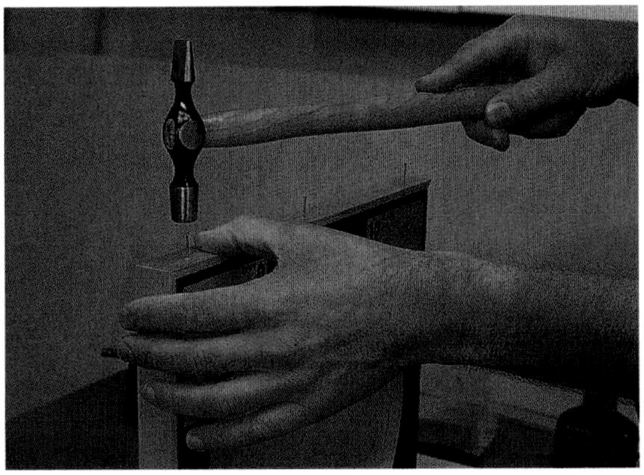

Fig 11.10 Fixing the edging to the game board with moulding pins and glue.

Fig 11.11 Colouring the centres of the wooden wheels used as counters.

slightly longer or shorter. Check before cutting your spindle from the axle rod.

Fix the spindle in place with a suitable adhesive such as epoxy resin.

Place a washer(s) over the spindle and thread the spinning disc on to it.

Our wooden ball fitted firmly on the spindle, so we did not fix it with adhesive. This is useful if you ever need to remove the disc.

We used 25mm (1in) ready-made wooden toy wheels for our player counters. Their centres were coloured and then they were varnished (*see* Fig 11.11). Buttons, tiddlywinks or the like could be used as an alternative.

Draw the players' scorecards on suitable pieces of paper or card (*see* Fig 11.12).

Let the racing begin!

Race number	Prediction	Points scored
	Total points	

Fig 11.12 Scorecard.

CHAPTER 12

Pool Players

★★

This miniature pool table allows you to play pool almost anywhere. Play a game against a friend just as you would with a full-size table, except that here you use the small players as 'rests' for your miniature cues. The upright player is used for shots near to the cushions, the crouching player for shots requiring a longer reach. The balls are 15mm (⅝in) diameter marbles. In British pool there are usually 7 red balls, 7 yellow balls, a black ball and the white, cue ball. Due to space considerations our table has 5 red balls and 5 yellow balls (actually blue patterned ones, as our local shop doesn't sell yellow marbles). This will make an uneven pyramid, so the spare ball is placed at the rear of the group when setting the table ready for play.

CUTTING LIST

Table

Cushions/pockets:	230 x 130 x 12mm ($9\frac{1}{16}$ x $5\frac{1}{8}$ x $\frac{1}{2}$in) birch plywood
Table top:	230 x 130 x 6mm ($9\frac{1}{16}$ x $5\frac{1}{8}$ x $\frac{1}{4}$in) birch plywood
Side (2):	224 x 46 x 3mm ($8\frac{13}{16}$ x $1\frac{13}{16}$ x $\frac{1}{8}$in) birch plywood
End (2):	118 x 46 x 3mm ($4\frac{21}{32}$ x $1\frac{13}{16}$ x $\frac{1}{8}$in) birch plywood
Feet (2):	118 x 12 x 6mm ($4\frac{21}{32}$ x $\frac{1}{2}$ x $\frac{1}{4}$in) birch plywood
Ball return slope:	200 x 118 x 3mm ($7\frac{7}{8}$ x $4\frac{21}{32}$ x $\frac{1}{8}$in) birch plywood
Return slope rest:	118 x 12 x 6mm ($4\frac{21}{32}$ x $\frac{1}{2}$ x $\frac{1}{4}$in) birch plywood

Players

Upright player:	162 x 126 x 12mm ($6\frac{3}{8}$ x $4\frac{15}{16}$ x $\frac{1}{2}$in) birch plywood
Bending player:	148 x 133 x 12mm ($5\frac{13}{16}$ x $5\frac{1}{4}$ x $\frac{1}{2}$in) birch plywood
Bases (2):	118 x 50 x 3mm ($4\frac{21}{32}$ x 2 x $\frac{1}{8}$in) birch plywood
Base handles (2):	50 x 30 x 3mm (2 x $1\frac{3}{16}$ x $\frac{1}{8}$in) birch plywood

Cues

Lengths of 3mm ($\frac{1}{8}$in) diameter ramin dowel
Small amount of 6mm ($\frac{1}{4}$in) diameter ramin dowel

Miscellaneous

Red 15mm ($\frac{5}{8}$in) diameter marbles (5)
Yellow 15mm ($\frac{5}{8}$in) diameter marbles (5)
Black 15mm ($\frac{5}{8}$in) diameter marble
White 15mm ($\frac{5}{8}$in) diameter marble
Quantity of green, self-adhesive velour

CONSTRUCTION

Pool table

Cut out all the components needed to construct the base of the pool table (*see* Fig 12.1). Mark out and cut the ball return aperture from one of the end panels.

Glue and pin the side panels to the bottom of the table base. Then glue the end panels into position.

The pool balls are sent to the aperture at one end of the base by means of a sloping panel. When a ball drops down a pocket hole, the slope sends the ball towards the aperture. A channel is formed by the end of the return slope panel and the lower lip of the ball return aperture. The returned balls come to rest in this channel ready for retrieval.

The slope is constructed from a 6mm (¼in) strip of birch plywood, glued to the bottom of the base, at the opposite end to the ball return aperture (*see* Fig 12.2). Before fitting this strip, lightly plane away the leading edge to allow the return slope panel to rest comfortably on it when fitted. Glue the ball return slope panel into position on the strip.

The bed (top) section of the table consists of a piece of 6mm (¼in) birch plywood on which a fretted piece of 12mm (½in) birch plywood (the cushions) is glued.

To make this section you will need to mark the entire plan view (*see* Fig 12.1) of the cushions and pocket holes on a suitable piece of plywood. Then pin this to the piece of plywood which you are using for the bed (*see* Fig 12.3). Use pins which are of sufficient length to allow their heads to protrude, so allowing easy removal later.

With a 20mm flat bit, drill the pocket holes through both pieces of plywood. Then cut away the waste part around the outside profile of the combined cushion and bed pieces.

Remove the pins with a pair of pincers and disassemble the two pieces. With a piece of abrasive paper wrapped around a short length of 6mm (¼in) or 9mm (⅜in) diameter dowel, clean up the pocket holes in the table bed. Fill the pin holes with filler.

Cut out the cushions and pockets with a fretsaw. Clean up any unevenness with a sanding stick.

The cushions/pockets section may now be glued to the bed.

TIP

Before gluing the cushions/pockets section to the bed, it is wise to make a template to assist you in cutting the velour playing surface to size. To do this, place the cushions/pockets section on some card and mark around the cushions and pockets. Cut this shape out. You now have a template. When you need to cut the velour for the bed, simply place the template on the velour, mark round it and cut out. You should then have a perfectly sized piece for fitting. Unfortunately, we neglected to make such a template and found it an incredibly fiddly job trying to fit the baize without one!

Paint and/or stain the interior of the table base before gluing the bed into position.

Prepare and glue the 6mm (¼in) plywood strips used for the feet into position.

Paint and/or stain the exterior of the table. We used a spirit-based Victorian mahogany stain. Then we applied two coats of a deep-red mahogany polyurethane varnish, finishing with a couple of coats of clear gloss varnish. This gave a really deep, rich colour.

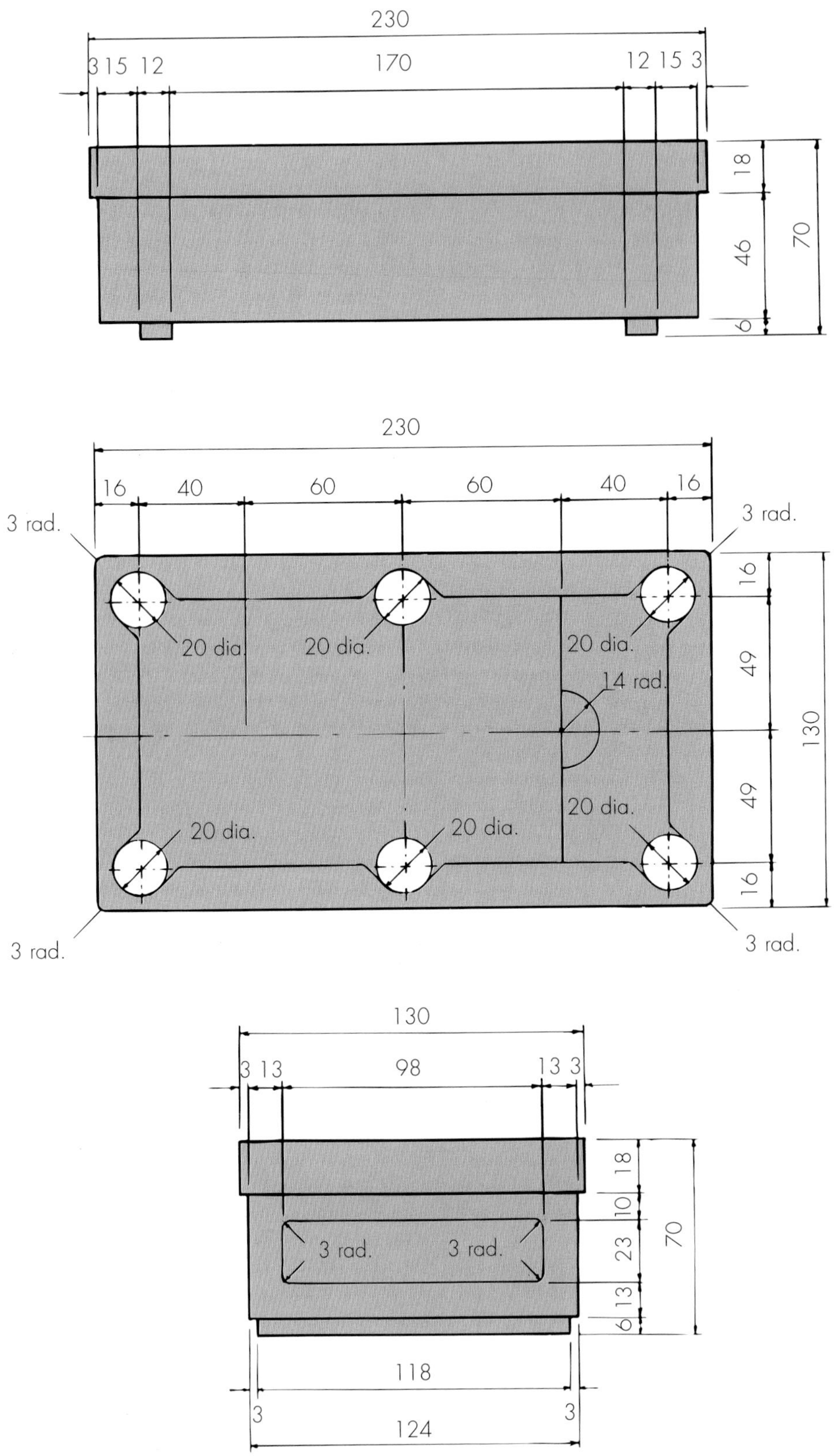

Fig 12.1 Plan, side and end elevations.

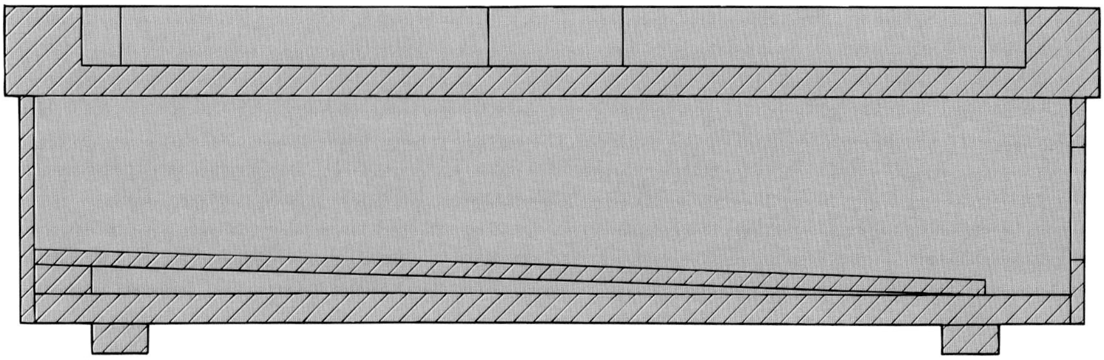

Fig 12.2 Cross-section of pool table, illustrating the ball return facility.

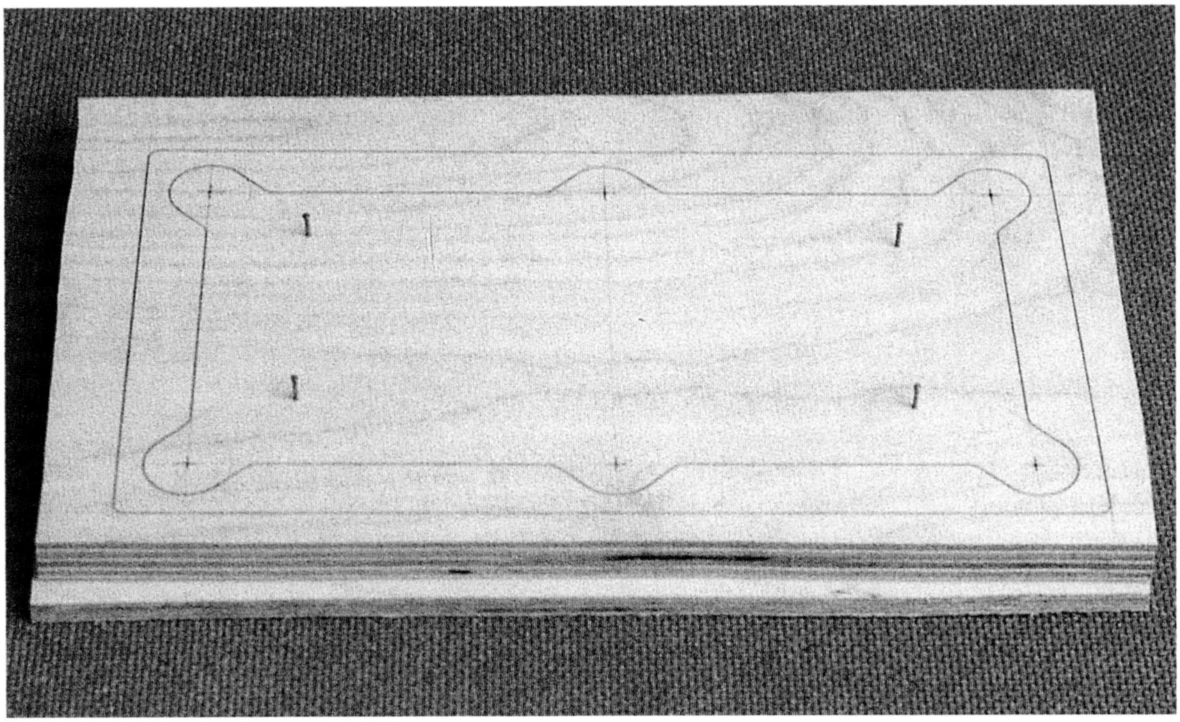

Fig 12.3 Cushion and pocket section pinned on top of the bed section before drilling out the holes.

Cut the velour to size (*see* Tip, page 99). Mark the balk line and head spot with a black ballpoint pen on the velour and then fit it on to the table top. If necessary, trim the pocket holes with a scalpel or very sharp craft knife.

Cut some 12mm (½in) strips of velour and cover the cushion sides. Cover the underside of each foot of the table with a strip of velour to avoid marking the surface the toy is placed upon during play.

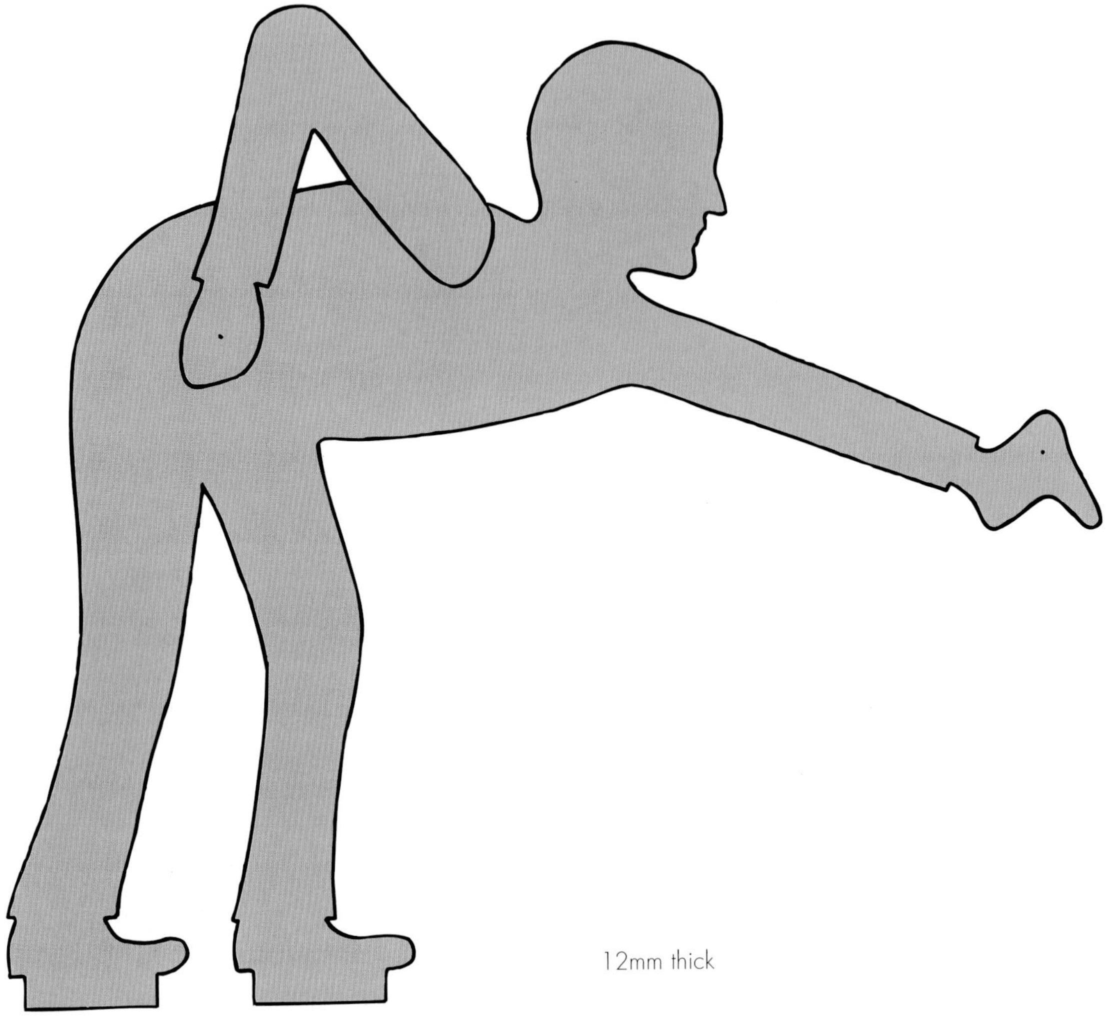

Fig 12.4 Profiles of the players.

Pool players

Transfer the profile of each player on to 12mm (½in) birch plywood and cut out (*see* Fig 12.4). Cut out the players' bases and handles (*see* Fig 12.5).

The players have a tenon below each foot. These are glued into reciprocating mortise slots on the bases. Place each player in the correct position on his base and mark around each tenon with a sharp pencil. Then cut out the mortises with a fretsaw.

Glue a player and a handle to each base. Clean up any protruding tenons and/or handles from the bottom of each base with a block plane.

The pool players are now ready to be painted and finished (*see* Fig 12.6).

After finishing, fit a 3mm (⅛in) diameter screw eyelet to the 'rest' hand of each player. Fit a larger screw eyelet to the second hand of each player.

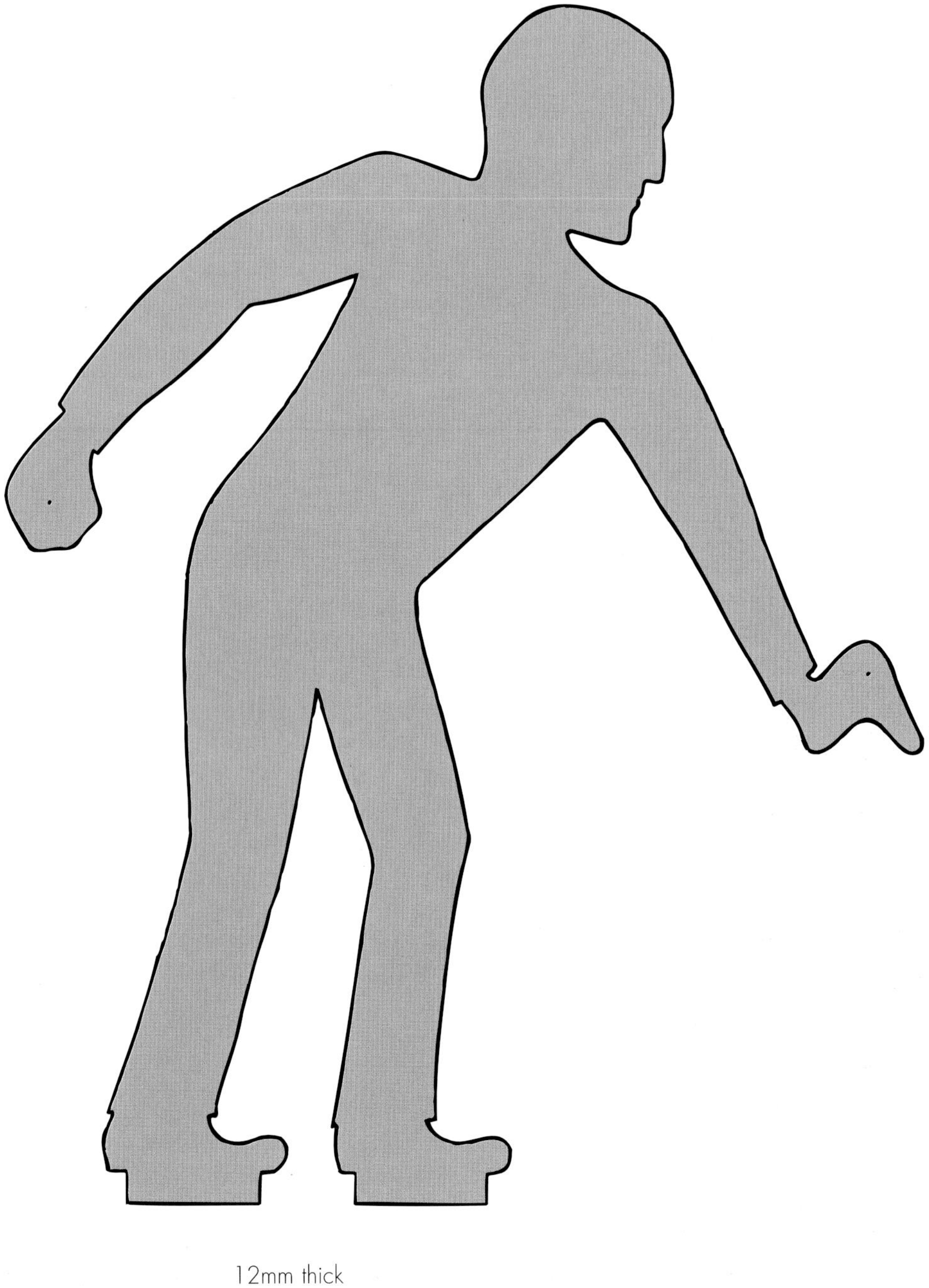

12mm thick

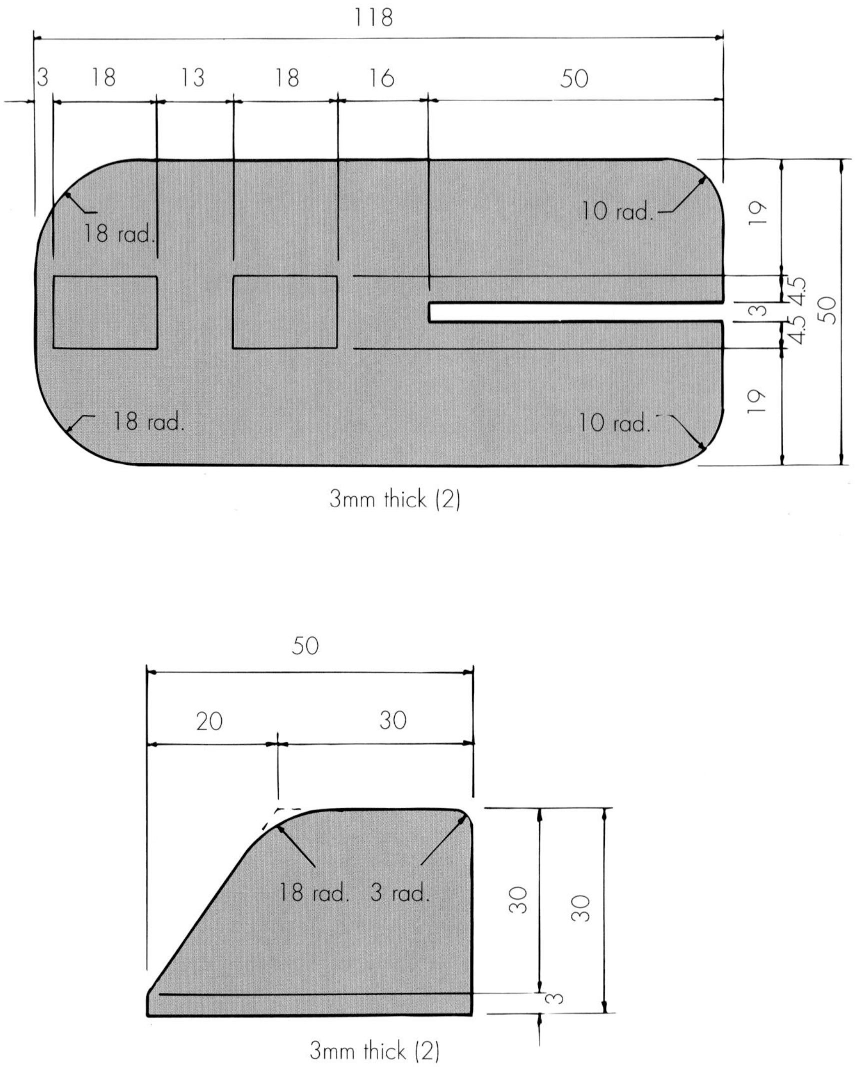

Fig 12.5 Player's base and handle.

Finally, apply velour to the underside of the base of each player.

Cues

Cut the cues from 3mm (⅛in) diameter dowel. A longer cue can be cut for when playing awkward-to-reach shots with the crouching player.

If you have difficulty in holding such fine cues, a bead or short length of 9mm (⅜in) dowel can be attached to the handle end. Drill out the 9mm (⅜in) dowel and glue the cue into it (*see* Fig 12.7).

Apply a small piece of velour to the playing end of the cues as a tip.

Players' height adjustment

If you have constructed the table and players correctly, each player's 'rest' hand should just rest on the playing surface when they are placed at the table.

Fig 12.6 The finished pool players.

If there is a small gap between the rest hand and the velour, say 1mm (1/32in), this is acceptable and will not interfere with play.

If a player is too short when the rest hand is placed on the playing surface it will cause the player to tilt backwards. Not only will this look unsightly, but it will impair his cueing action.

This fault can be rectified by increasing the thickness of the base of the faulty player. Do this by gluing a piece, or pieces, of veneer (stiff card would do as a substitute) to the underside of the player's base. In an extreme case a piece of 1.5mm (1/16in) or 3mm (1/8in) plywood could be used.

Do not apply a packing piece without first removing the velour from the base. Apply a fresh piece of velour when the adjustment is complete.

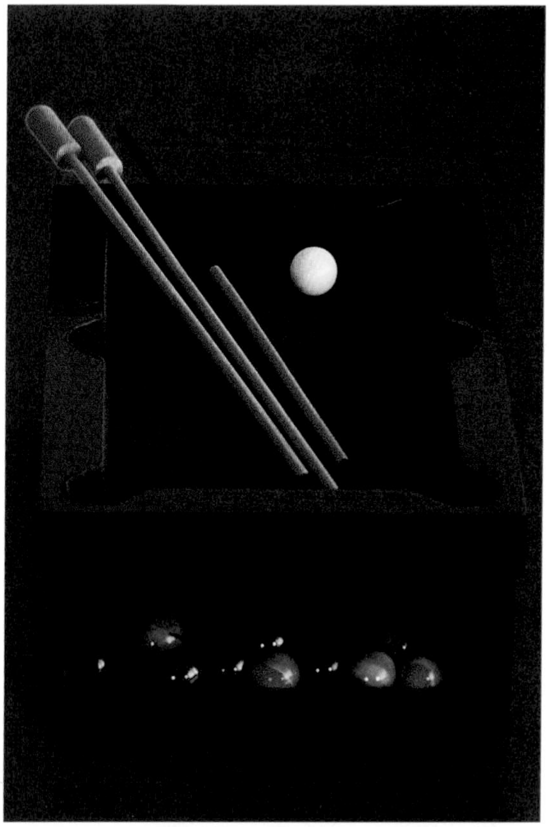

Fig 12.7 The finished pool table and cues.

3

CHAPTER 13

Snargon's Wrath

★★

Snargon's Wrath is an original three-dimensional family game which consists of a playing board, Snargon the Dragon, four knights, four castles, precious orbs (marbles) and quest-recording units.

SNARGON'S WRATH

For decades Snargon the fire-breathing dragon has been terrorizing the kingdom. Eventually, the people can bear it no more, so they besiege the royal castle and demand that the king take action.

The king orders his alchemist to toil day and night until a magic spell or potion is produced to vanquish the terrible beast.

Eventually, the alchemist declares that he can concoct such a potion. Unfortunately, he needs six precious orbs that are only to be found in the far castles of Snargon's Wrath, the dragon's lair!

The king orders his most able and bravest knights to go forth and collect these orbs. Can they succeed in their quest without being sizzled to a crisp by Snargon's fiery breath?

Each player controls a questing knight. They must travel around the game board collecting orbs from four of Snargon's castles. However, dominating the game board is the huge beast himself, Snargon.

As the knights move, Snargon spins around the board. If his fiery breath reaches a knight he is roasted! If this happens to a knight three times he is well and truly cooked and out of the game.

RULES OF PLAY

For two to four players.

Equipment

- Game board
- Snargon the Dragon
- Knights (4)
- Castles (4)
- Orbs (32)
- Quest recording units (4)
- Life pegs (12)
- Dragon die, with three sides marked with a dragon and three sides blank
- Standard die marked from one to six

Object of the game

To be the first player to collect six of Snargon's precious orbs.

Preparation

Place one castle on each of the four large corner squares on the board. Fill the base tray of each castle with eight precious orbs.

Allocate a knight to each player. Each knight is then placed on a castle platform. Each player is given a quest-recording unit, with a life peg placed in each hole under each skull.

Play

Determine who will begin the game by each player rolling the standard die. The player with the highest score starts.

Movement

The player rolls both dice. He moves his knight, in a clockwise direction, the number of squares indicated on the standard die.

CUTTING LIST

Game board:	335 x 335 x 12mm (13 3/16 x 13 3/16 x ½in) birch plywood
Edging (4):	Lengths cut from 20mm (25/32in) hardwood scotia
Dragon:	198 x 72 x 12mm (7 13/16 x 2 13/16 x ½in) birch plywood

Castles

Side wall (4):	70 x 70 x 3mm (2¾ x 2¾ x ⅛in) birch plywood
Side wall (4):	67 x 70 x 3mm (2⅝ x 2¾ x ⅛in) birch plywood
Triangular top floor (4):	67 x 67 x 6mm (2⅝ x 2⅝ x ¼in) birch plywood
Base (4):	67 x 67 x 6mm (2⅝ x 2⅝ x ¼in) birch plywood
Orb retaining strips (4):	67 x 6 x 3mm (2⅝ x ¼ x ⅛in) birch plywood
Orb retaining strips (4):	61 x 6 x 3mm (2 13/32 x ¼ x ⅛in) birch plywood

Knights

Head (4):	9 x 9mm (⅜ x ⅜in) diameter ramin dowel
Body (4):	20 x 12mm (25/32 x ½in) diameter ramin dowel
Shields and axes:	Various scraps of 1.5mm (1/16in) birch plywood

Quest-recorder unit

Top (4):	146 x 68 x 6mm (5¾ x 2 11/16 x ¼in) birch plywood
Base (4):	146 x 68 x 3mm (5¾ x 2 11/16 x ⅛in) hardboard
Skull (12):	From scraps of 3mm (⅛in) birch plywood
Life pegs (12):	25 x 3mm (1 x ⅛in) diameter ramin dowel
Dice (2):	24 x 24 x 24mm (1 x 1 x 1in) beech

Miscellaneous

3mm (⅛in) diameter bolt, approximately 40mm (1 9/16in) in length
Nuts to fit on to bolt (2)
Nut with a centre diameter larger than the bolt
Washers (4)
15mm (⅝in) diameter marbles (32)

If a dragon has been rolled on the dragon die, the player must spin Snargon. This must only be done after the player has moved his knight. Snargon may be spun clockwise or anticlockwise, but he must revolve at least three times before stopping. If he fails to do this the player must spin him again. If, when he has stopped spinning, Snargon's fiery breath points to a space on which a knight stands, that knight is deemed to be roasted. The player who controls the charred knight must remove a life peg from one of the skulls on his quest-recording unit. If a knight loses all three of his life pegs, he is deemed to be burnt to a crisp, removed from the board and takes no further part in the game. Any orbs which have been collected by that knight are also removed from play.

If a blank is rolled on the dragon die, Snargon is not spun.

A knight is protected from Snargon's fiery breath if he is on a castle.

In the event of Snargon's fiery breath coming to rest on the line dividing two spaces, he is re-spun.

If, when a knight has moved the appropriate number of spaces shown on the standard die, he lands on the space at which Snargon is pointing he is considered to be roasted and loses a life peg.

Collecting orbs

When a knight lands on a castle at the end of his move he collects one orb from that castle. This is placed in one of the holes on that player's quest-recording unit. If all the orbs have been removed from that castle he may not collect an orb.

Winning the game

The first player to collect six orbs is the winner of the game.

CONSTRUCTION

Game board

Cut out and plane the edges of the game board to ensure that it is square. Finely sand the top surface.

Using a sharp pencil and steel rule lightly mark the layout of the game on to the board (*see* Fig 13.1).

Using a good quality black ballpoint pen and steel rule, ink over the relevant lines. Do this with confident, even strokes of the pen. Use two or three strokes on the same line rather than one heavy stroke. This will help to reduce possible errors.

After completion of a line wipe the end of the pen on a piece of scrap paper to clean away any ink build-up or wood fibres. The rule may also need the occasional wipe clean.

When all the marking has been completed, erase any pencil lines still showing – but only when the ink is thoroughly dry. Any really stubborn marks can be removed by very light sanding with a fine grade of abrasive paper.

The slight indentation of the inked lines, coupled with their thickness, will help to reduce the likelihood of the green stain, when applied, from spreading along the grain on to the castle and movement squares. As a further safeguard, seal these areas with clear varnish. Apply one or, preferably, two coats of clear gloss varnish.

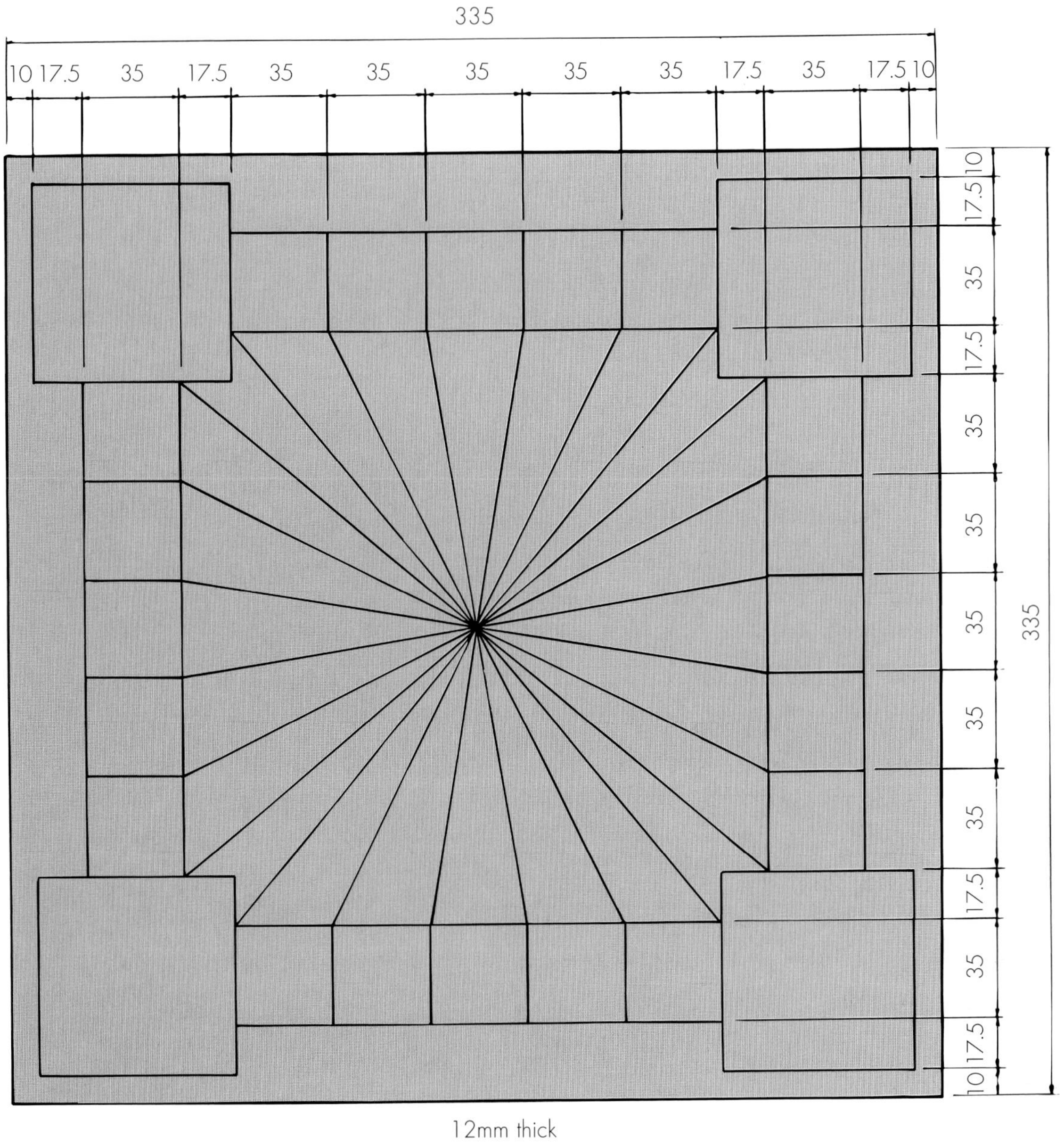

Fig 13.1 Game board.

Do not thin the varnish, as this may cause it to creep to an area which you wish to colour.

When the varnish is completely dry apply the green colour/stain to the appropriate areas. We used a thinned acrylic paint. As an alternative, you could choose a ready-made stain or varnish stain from the large range that is now available. Whatever you use, test your chosen medium on a scrap piece of birch plywood first.

When all the colouring is finished you may need to ink lightly over the black lines again.

Next, give the entire playing surface two or three coats of gloss varnish.

Fig 13.2 Game board without accessories.

The edge of the game board is 20mm (25⁄32in) hardwood scotia. Use mitre butt joints at the corners and attach it by using moulding pins and glue. We pre-drilled the moulding pin holes (in the scotia only) with a drill bit that was marginally larger than the diameter of the pin shafts, but not bigger than the pin heads. This helps to prevent the scotia from splitting when applied.

Using a pin punch, drive the moulding pins slightly below the surface of the scotia. Then apply a suitably coloured wood filler into the pin holes. Sand smooth when dry.

Finally, give the game board and edging a further three or four coats of clear gloss varnish (*see* Fig 13.2).

Snargon the Dragon

Transfer Snargon's body profile on to 12mm (½in) birch plywood, and his legs on to 3mm (⅛in) birch plywood and cut out each component with a fretsaw (*see* Fig 13.3).

Hold the body, as level as possible, in a vice and drill out the bolt hole using, preferably,

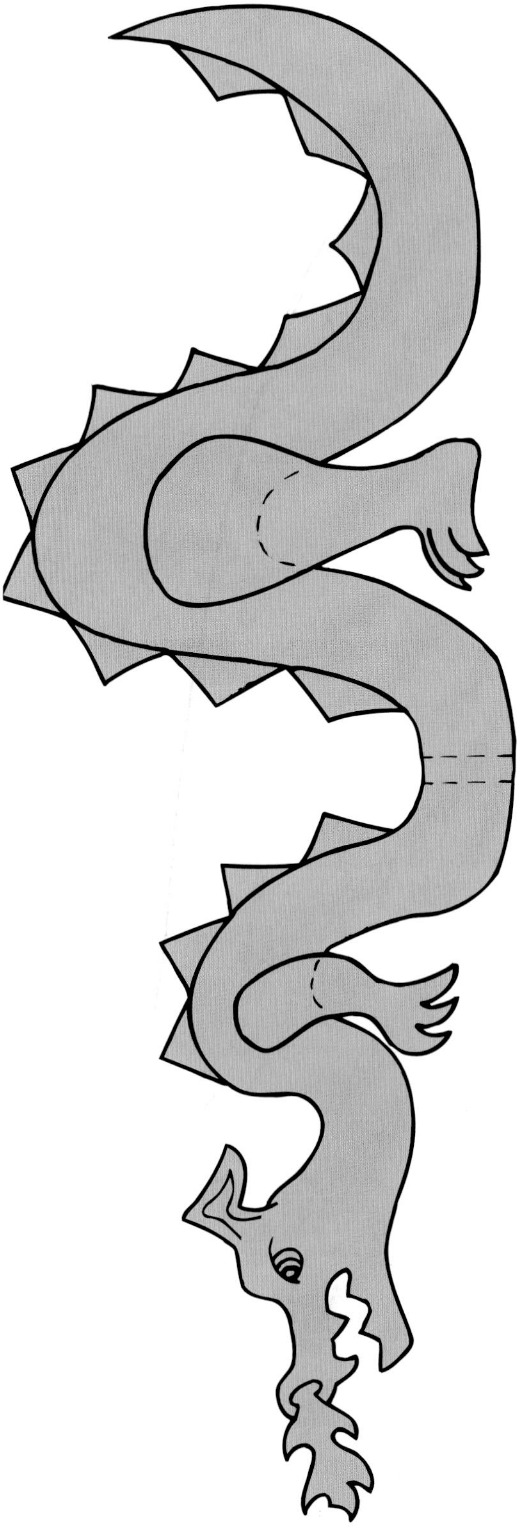

Fig 13.3 Snargon the Dragon.

Fig 13.4 Snargon's bolt/nut assembly on the underside of the game board.

a hand drill. Ideally, the bolt that you use should be 3mm (⅛in) in diameter. We used a 3.3mm diameter drill bit, to allow Snargon to spin freely around the bolt.

Glue the legs to the body. When the glue has set, paint Snargon as you wish.

To attach Snargon to the game board, place a washer on the bolt and then thread the bolt through the hole in his body. As Snargon's centre of gravity is offset, a nut (with a larger centre hole diameter than the bolt's diameter) is used as a spacer between Snargon and the playing surface of the game board. Thread a washer on to the bolt, then the spacer nut and then another washer.

Drill a hole directly into the centre of the game board to accept Snargon and the bolt assembly. Use a drill bit of a diameter size that will just allow the bolt to pass through the board. Put a washer and two nuts on the end of the bolt. The first nut should not be tightened, otherwise Snargon will be unable to turn. The second nut should be tightened against the first nut. This second nut will act as a lock and stop the first nut from unthreading itself (*see* Fig 13.4).

Note The type and size of scotia used for the edging of the game board allows the two nuts to stand proud of the bottom of the board. Make absolutely sure that the nuts and bolt are compatible with the moulding used for your edging before fitting. Otherwise you may find that the nuts will protrude below the edging.

Castles

The castellations are best cut out with a fretsaw. Clean up any unevenness with a small flat file or sanding stick.

Glue and pin the castle walls to the base. Then glue and pin the platform into place (*see* Fig 13.5).

Next, glue the orb retaining strips into position (again, *see* Fig 13.5).

The castles may be painted or covered with stone-effect paper. These papers, often used for decorating dolls' houses, are available from hobby suppliers (*see* Fig 13.6). Before papering the castles, paint the edges. Use a colour shade that is sympathetic to the stonework. Conversely, you could paint all the edges matt black for a strikingly bold effect.

Knights

After cutting the ramin dowel used for the heads and bodies to size, clean up the cut ends. This can be done by placing a sheet of fine-grade abrasive paper (about 180) on a flat, even surface. Then hold the dowel to be sanded upright on the paper. Using gentle circular sanding motions you can sand the ends smooth and level.

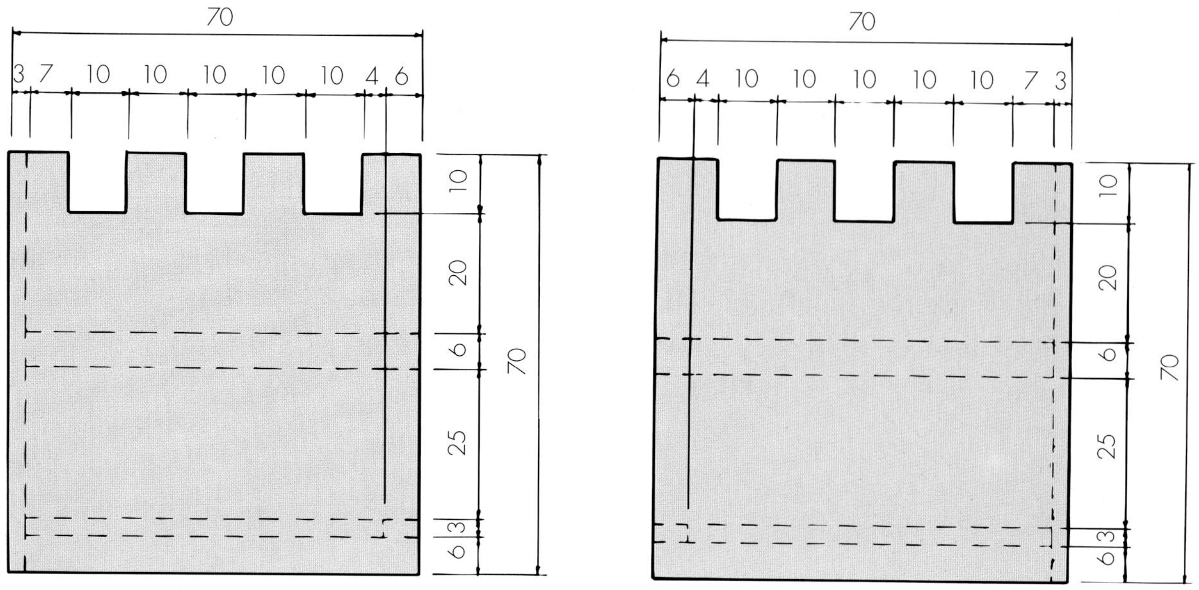

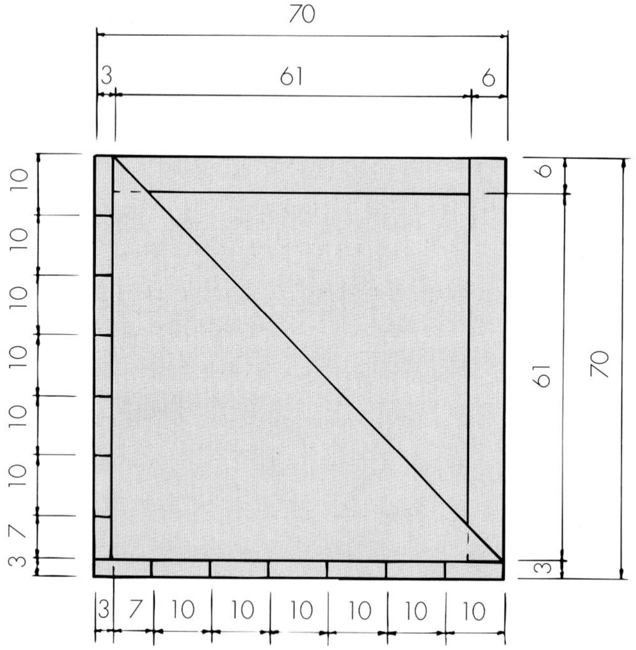

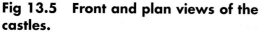

Fig 13.5 Front and plan views of the castles.

Transfer the profiles of the shields and axes on to 1.5mm (1/16in) birch plywood and cut out. We would recommend that you cut out the axes with a hand-held fretsaw.

Glue the heads, shields and axes to the bodies (*see* Fig 13.7).

The knights may be finished in any style you choose, remembering that they should be easily distinguishable from each other (*see* Fig 13.8).

Quest-recording units

Mark out the units on 6mm (¼in) birch plywood (*see* Fig 13.9). When cutting them out, allow approximately 6mm (¼in) of surplus all round – the reason for this will be made clear later.

Drill the orb holes with either a 14mm (9/16in) flat bit or wood (twist) bit. Drill the life peg holes with a bit that allows the pegs to fit easily. We used a 3.3mm bit.

Now, evenly spread wood glue on the reverse side of each unit. Place an appropriate sheet of 3mm (⅛in) hardboard, smooth face up, on a flat surface, and stick the units on it. Use something suitable to weight them down until the glue has set.

Fig 13.6 **A castle.**

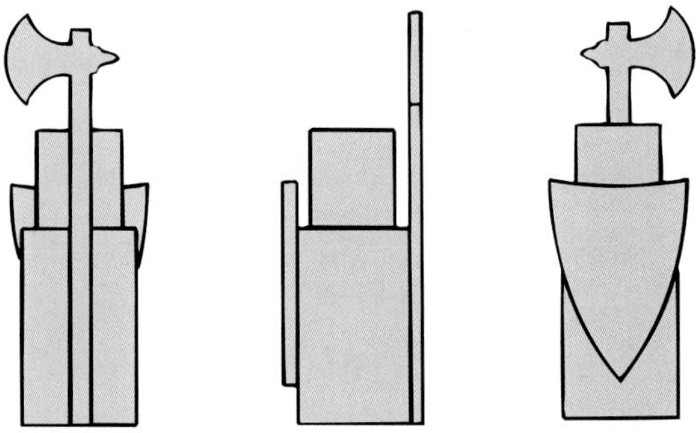

Fig 13.7 **Knight: front and side views.**

Fig 13.8 **The finished knights.**

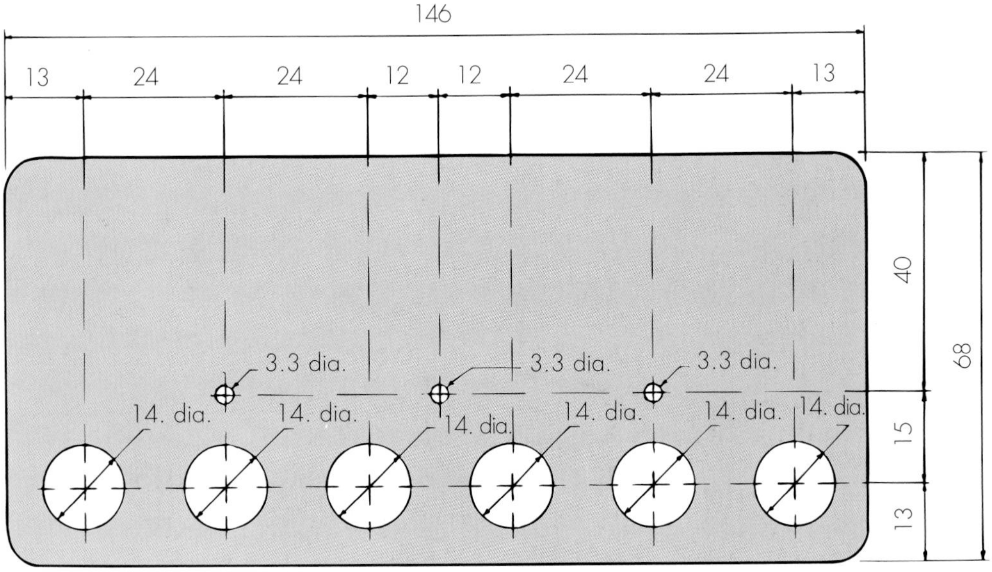

6mm thick.

Unit's top part only (hardboard base not fitted).

Fig 13.9 **Dimensions of the quest-recording units.**

TIP
To cut out the pegs, use a sharp knife to score all the way round the dowel 25mm (1in) from a square end. Then you should be able to snap the peg away from the dowel with your fingertips.

3mm thick (3)

Fig 13.10 The skull.

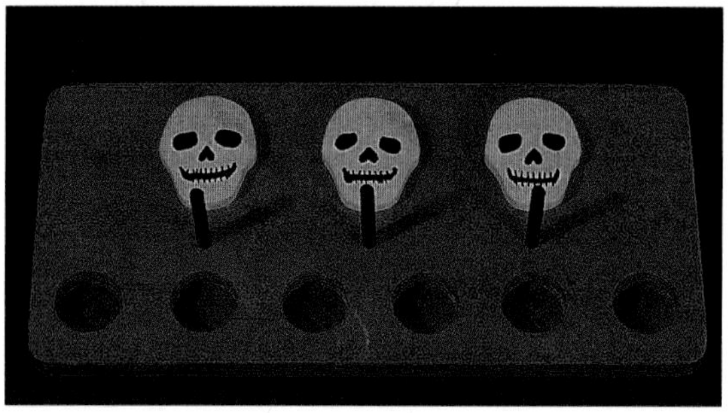

Fig 13.11 A completed quest-recording unit.

Cut each unit away from the rest. A panel or tenon saw is ideal for this purpose. Now, cut the 6mm (¼in) surplus away from the units.

Clean and true up any unevenness with a combination of block plane and abrasive paper. Then give each unit a few coats of varnish.

Transfer the skull image 12 times on to 3mm (⅛in) birch plywood (*see* Fig 13.10), and cut them out with a fretsaw. Clean them up and paint them.

Glue the skulls into position on the quest-recording units – three per unit, each placed directly behind a life peg hole (*see* Fig 13.11).

The life pegs are cut from a length of 3mm (⅛in) diameter hardwood dowel. Stain the dowel black (or any other colour you wish) before you cut the pegs.

After cutting them out, sand away any unevenness with a fine-grade abrasive paper placed flat on a level surface. The ends of the pegs will now need touching up with your chosen colour of stain.

Dice

The dice are two 25mm (1in) cubes of beech. Shop-bought dice are usually 15mm (⅝in) square. However, as they are an important component of the game, we felt standard-size dice would look insignificant alongside Snargon and the castles.

Bigger dice are also easier to decorate (a boon when replicating Snargon's silhouette!).

Use a block plane to true up the end grain faces of the cubes. However, do not run the blade of the plane over an entire surface in one pass. If you do, the grain will tend to split away – it is better to plane halfway from both sides (*see* Figs 13.12, 13.13).

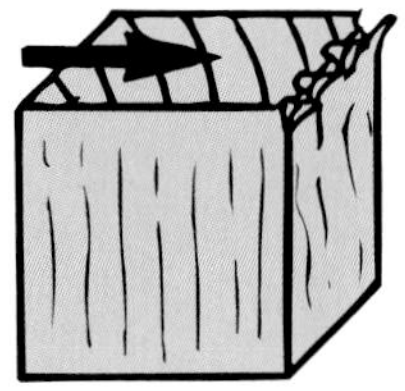

Fig 13.12 End grain splits outwards when planed in one direction.

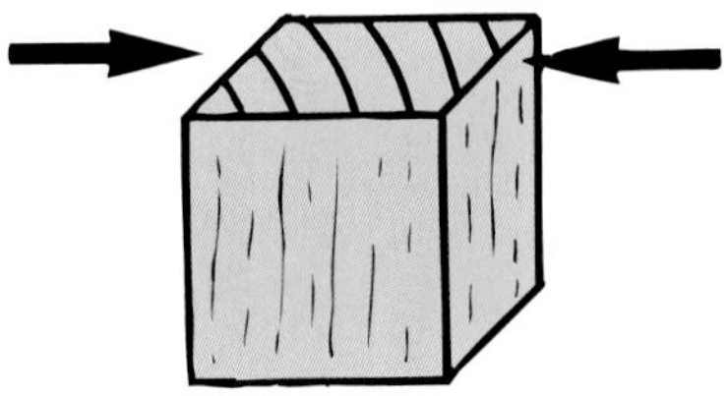

Fig 13.13 End grain will not split outwards when planed from both ends (stopping in the centre).

If you find it difficult to use a block plane on such a small piece of work, you can square the dice in the following way.

Place a sheet of abrasive paper (graded according to the amount to be removed) face up on a flat, even surface. Hold the die firmly in your hand and, using gentle circular strokes, sand as necessary. It is important to keep the pressure on the die even in order to keep it square. Periodically, check the die with a square while gradually working down the grades of abrasive paper, finishing with a very fine grade.

Once you are satisfied that all the sides of the dice are square their edges should be rounded. To do this you will need either a sanding stick or a small sanding block. Hold a die in the fingertips of one hand while rounding the edges with the sanding stick or block. The degree of roundness is entirely up to you, but it must be even on each edge.

Give each die a couple of coats of clear gloss varnish. They are now ready for decoration (*see* Fig 13.14).

Standard die

This is marked in the usual manner of 1–6. Ensure that it is numbered so that any two directly opposite faces total 7 – that is, 1 is opposite 6; 2 opposite 5; and 3 opposite 4. Gothic-type 10mm (⅜in) dry rub down transfers were used for the numbers. We drew swords and shields around the numbers with a black, fine-nibbed, permanent marker pen.

Dragon die

This die has three blank faces and three faces with the silhouette of Snargon on them. The silhouette could be either painted on or drawn with a permanent marker pen or ballpoint pen.

Finally give each die a few protective coats of varnish. Check that the varnish does not react with the marker pen used.

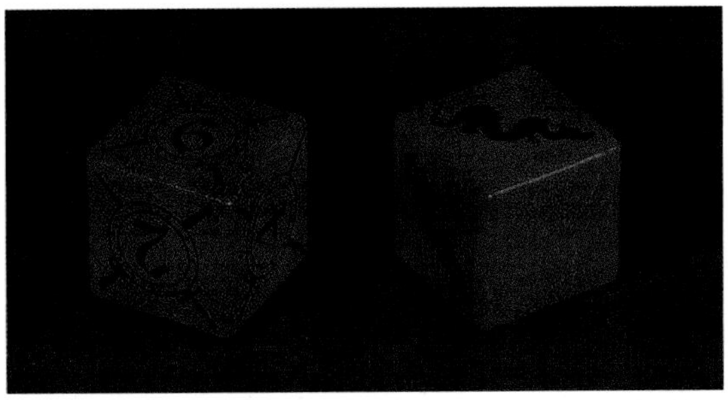

Fig 13.14 The completed dice.

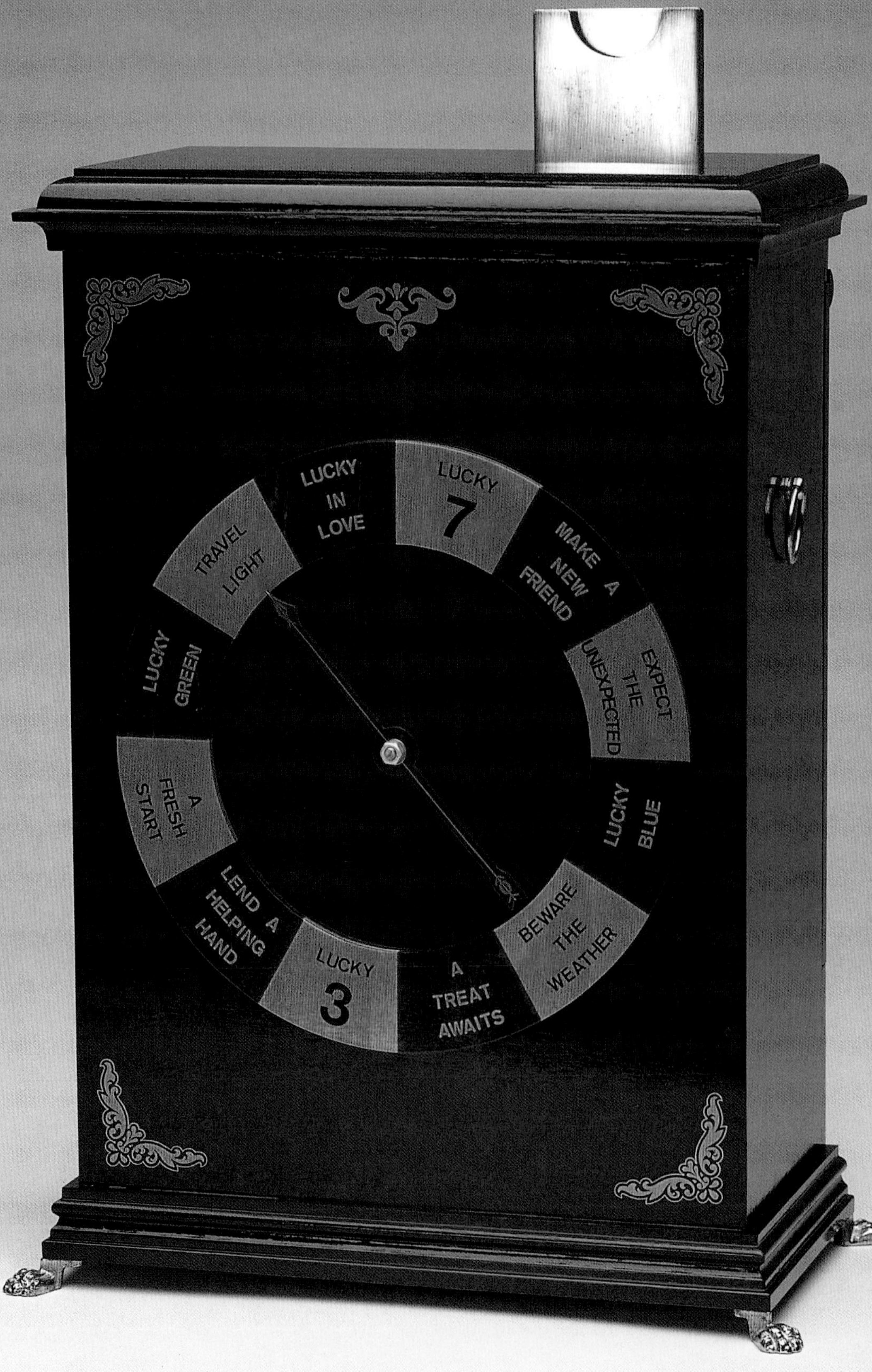
LUCKY IN LOVE
LUCKY 7
MAKE A NEW FRIEND
EXPECT THE UNEXPECTED
LUCKY BLUE
BEWARE THE WEATHER
A TREAT AWAITS
LUCKY 3
LEND A HELPING HAND
A FRESH START
LUCKY GREEN
TRAVEL LIGHT

CHAPTER 14

Fortune-telling Money Box

★★★

We have styled this money box on the coin-operated fortune-telling machines of the late Victorian period. It is hard to imagine that, in their heyday, many people believed that the predictions of these machines were true. However, it makes it more believable when you consider that the symbolic concept of a spinning wheel of fate has been deeply rooted in our psyche for centuries. The Romans introduced the idea to our isles, their goddess Fortuna possessing a wheel that represented a man's fate. Our wooden 'machine' is intended for amusement only, and is a novel way to save any spare change you may have.

THE MECHANISM

The mechanism of our Fortune-telling Money Box is simple, and consists mainly of a paddle wheel. When a coin is fed into the brass slot at the top, gravity accelerates it down the coin chute which in turn directs it on to the paddle wheel below. The coin will then strike a paddle, the force of which turns the wheel. This wheel is attached to a spindle that runs right through the case of the machine. A pointer is fixed to the spindle at the front of the case, so that, as the paddle wheel revolves, so does the pointer.

You may already have deduced that the heavier the coin the faster and longer the arrow will revolve. Thus, as in life, you get what you pay for! The coin slot and chute are designed to accommodate all UK and many foreign coins.

Coins can be retrieved by means of a door at the rear of the case which is secured with a lock and key.

CONSTRUCTION

Case

Cut out and prepare the relevant pieces for the case, but not the moulding at this stage (*see* Figs 14.1, 14.2).

Drill a 3.5mm (9/64in) diameter hole through the front piece in the position illustrated in Fig 14.1. This hole is for the spindle to pass through. Ensure that the spindle (4BA studding) can turn freely in the hole.

Using moulding pins and glue, fix the front to the sides, then the base piece, then the case's back bottom and back top pieces.

Make the coin chute from 3mm (⅛in) birch plywood (*see* Fig 14.3). The easiest way is to make a rectangular tube a little longer than shown in Fig 14.3. Use rapid-set glue to join the pieces. Then cut one end of the tube at 90° and the other, at the appropriate length, at 45°. Transfer length and width dimensions of the tube on to the case's 6mm (¼in) top piece (*see* Fig 14.4). Cut this slot out with a fretsaw. Glue the top piece to the case and then glue the coin chute into place.

After planing and sanding any unevenness of the newly joined pieces, the back door piece may be fitted. To do this, cut out and prepare to size a piece of 6mm (¼in) birch plywood. Mark the position of the 3.5mm (9/64in) diameter spindle hole (as in Fig 14.1) and drill it out.

A brass wardrobe lock is used to secure the door at its top. Place it into position on the inside face of the door and mark through its screw holes with an awl. Then measure and mark the centre of the keyhole. Cut out the keyhole (*see* Fig 14.2).

Fit the door with two fancy brass cutlery hinges. These are easy to fit as they are placed on the surface of the workpiece (instead of being set in) and attached with screws. Use either eight No. 1 x ¼in countersunk or eight No. 2 x ¼in round-head brass screws. If you use countersunk screws you may need to countersink the holes in the hinges to accommodate them.

CUTTING LIST

Case

Front:	308 x 213 x 6mm (12 1/8 x 8 3/8 x 1/4in) birch plywood
Back top piece:	213 x 14 x 6mm (8 3/8 x 9/16 x 1/4in) birch plywood
Back base piece:	213 x 77 x 6mm (8 3/8 x 3 1/16 x 1/4in) birch plywood
Back door:	213 x 205 x 6mm (8 3/8 x 8 1/16 x 1/4in) birch plywood
Back door dust cover:	213 x 12mm (8 3/8 x 1/2in) half-round ramin strip
Side (2):	308 x 100 x 12mm (12 1/8 x 4 x 1/2in) birch plywood
Base:	189 x 100 x 12mm (7 7/16 x 4 x 1/2in) birch plywood
Top piece:	213 x 112 x 6mm (8 3/8 x 4 13/32 x 1/4in) birch plywood
Uppermost top piece:	206 x 108.5 x 12mm (8 3/32 x 4 9/32 x 1/2in) birch plywood
Front base moulding:	231 x 21 x 9mm (9 1/16 x 13/16 x 3/8in) ramin base moulding
Side base moulding (2):	121 x 21 x 9mm (4 3/4 x 13/16 x 3/8in) ramin base moulding
Front decorative quadrant:	226 x 9mm (8 7/8 x 3/8in) ramin quadrant
Side decorative quadrant (2):	118.5 x 9mm (4 21/32 x 3/8in) ramin quadrant
Front decorative scotia:	237 x 12mm (9 5/16 x 1/2in) ramin scotia
Side decorative scotia (2):	124 x 12mm (4 7/8 x 1/2in) ramin scotia
Dial:	180mm (7 1/8in) diameter x 3mm (1/8in) birch plywood
Pointer:	120 x 16 x 1.5mm (4 3/4 x 5/8 x 1/16in) birch plywood
Coin chute (2):	120 x 46 x 3mm (4 3/4 x 1 13/16 x 1/8in) birch plywood
Coin chute (2):	120 x 9 x 3mm (4 3/4 x 3/8 x 1/8in) birch plywood
Coin slot (2):	50 x 50 x 1.5mm (2 x 2 x 1/16in) brass
Coin slot (2):	50 x 9 x 3mm (2 x 3/8 x 1/8in) birch plywood or brass
Paddle wheel:	160mm (6 9/32in) diameter x 1.5mm (1/16in) birch plywood
Paddles (12):	40 x 20 x 1.5mm (1 9/16 x 25/32 x 1/16in) birch plywood

Miscellaneous

Length of 4BA studding
4BA nuts
Washers with 3.5mm (9/64in) diameter hole
Brass wardrobe lock with key
Fancy brass hinges (2) and brass screws (8)
Brass claw feet (4)
Brass O/D rings (2)

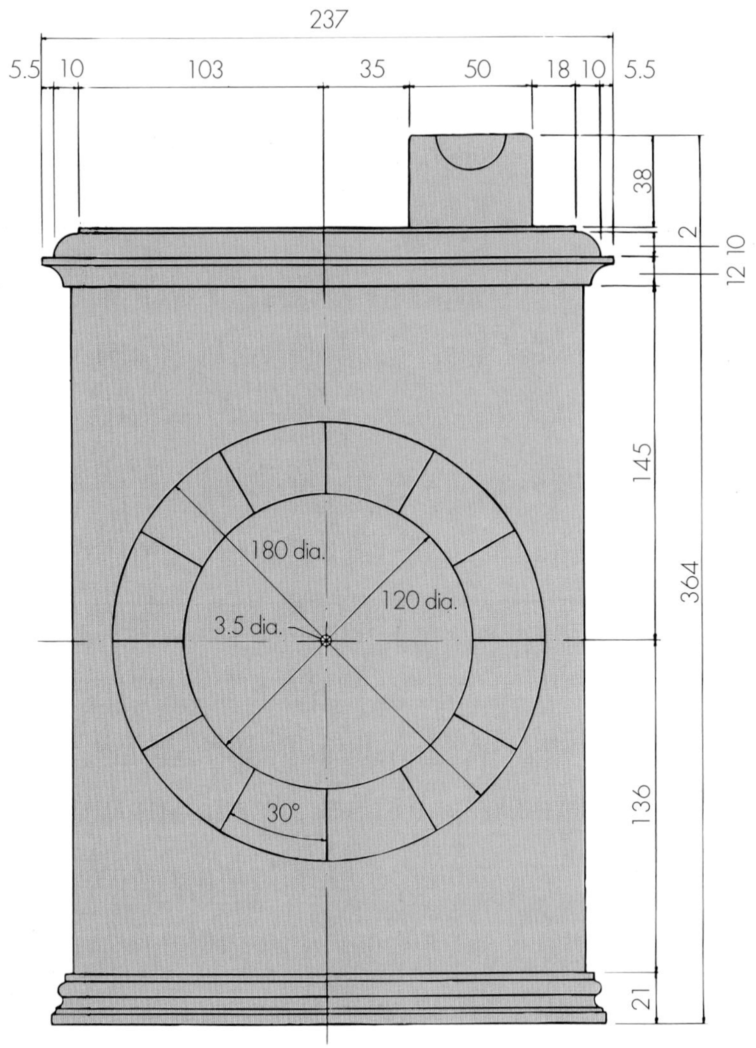

Fig 14.1 Front elevation.

Do this with an appropriate countersinking bit. Then remove the hinges and door for finishing later. You may wish to fit a dust cover to the top of the door. We used a piece of 12mm (½in) ramin strip. This was simply glued into place.

The coin slot is made from 1.5mm (1/16in) brass sheet (*see* Fig 14.5). We bought ours from a model shop. Hobby shops and some tool or hardware suppliers may also stock some.

You will need to mark out the back and front pieces of the coin slot on the brass sheet. Ideally you should coat the surface with engineers' layout blue and then use a scriber (or an awl will do) to mark them out. However, if like us you undertake little metalwork you will not wish to purchase some blue. We used a permanent black marker pen (*see* Figs 14.6, 14.7).

Hold the brass sheet securely in a vice (preferably an engineers' vice), and cut out

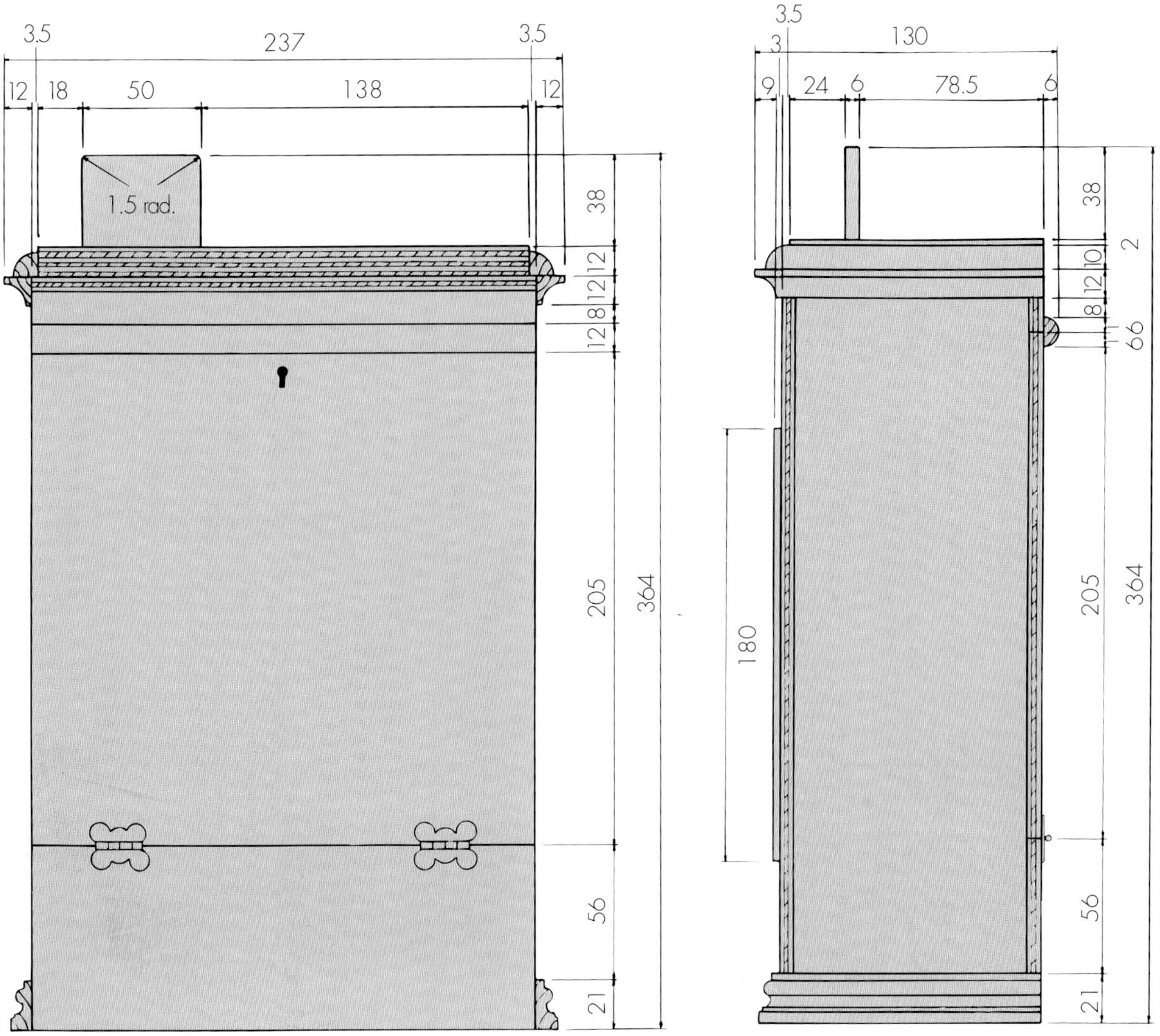

Fig 14.2 Back and side elevations.

the components with a hacksaw fitted with a fine-toothed metalworking blade.

The semicircle of the front piece can be filed out using a second-cut half-round engineers' file.

Ensure that all the brass edges are deburred.

The brass back and front of the coin slot was joined with two strips of 3mm (⅛in) birch plywood. This was for reasons of economy, as we did not think the job justified the purchase of 3mm (⅛in) brass. Of course, you could make up two strips of doubled 1.5mm (1/16in) brass, but this does seem unnecessarily fiddly.

Glue the coin slot sides together with a suitable adhesive – we found a rapid-set glue to be adequate. Stain and/or varnish the exposed plywood and polish the brass carefully.

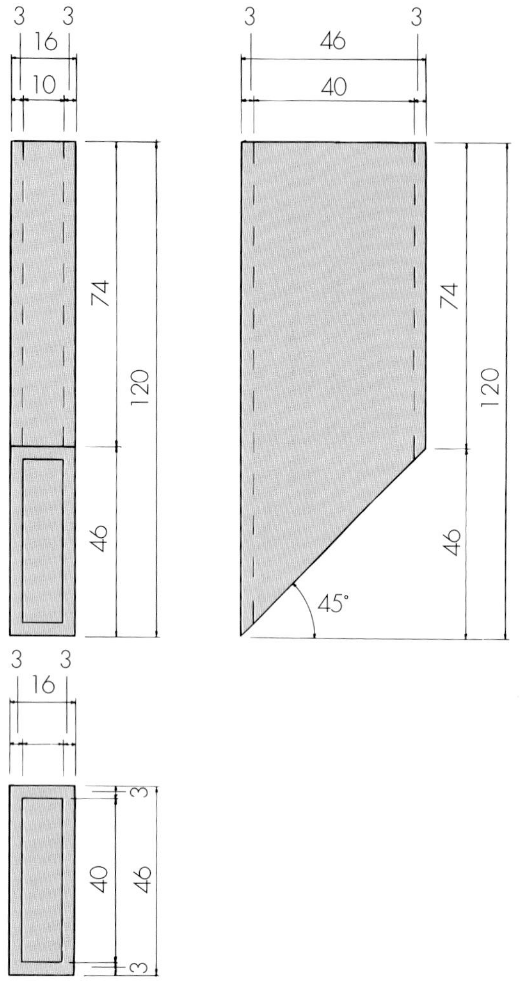

Fig 14.3 Coin chute: plan, and front and side elevations.

Prepare a piece of 12mm (½in) plywood and cut out the uppermost top piece of the case. In the appropriate place (*see* Figs 14.1, 14.4), mark the length and width dimensions of the coin slot and cut this slot out with a fretsaw. Use a flat needle file to smooth away any unevenness on the inside faces of the slot. Check that the coin slot fits snugly into place, and that it is aligned so that when the top piece is fitted to the case the coin slot is directly over the coin chute, thus allowing coins to pass right through to the paddle wheel inside the case.

Glue the top piece into position on the case but do not fit the coin slot yet. Place a suitable heavy object on the top piece to weigh it down while the glue sets.

A piece of 21 x 9mm (13/16 x ⅜in) ramin base moulding was applied to the base of the case. Mitre it at the corners and attach it with moulding pins and glue (*see* Figs 14.1, 14.2).

Attach 12mm (½in) ramin scotia flush with the case's 6mm (¼in) top. On top of this and around the case's 12mm (½in) top piece, fix some 10mm (⅜in) ramin quadrant (*see* Figs 14.1, 14.2).

Paddle wheel

Using a large compass, protractor, rule and hole template, set out the wheel onto 1.5mm (1/16in) birch plywood (*see* Fig 14.8). Drill out all the holes before cutting the wheel out with a fretsaw.

Cut the twelve paddles from 1.5mm (1/16in) birch plywood.

The paddle retaining slots can be cut out using a fretsaw, though this can be very tricky. We suggest that you cut them using a 6 TPI crosscut saw. We found our saw cut a slot of exactly the right size to receive the paddles (*see* Fig 14.9). Test the saw you use on a scrap piece of plywood first.

When cutting the slots, hold the wheel securely in a vice with a thicker scrap piece of timber behind it. The scrap piece will aid cutting and help to protect the plywood from damage.

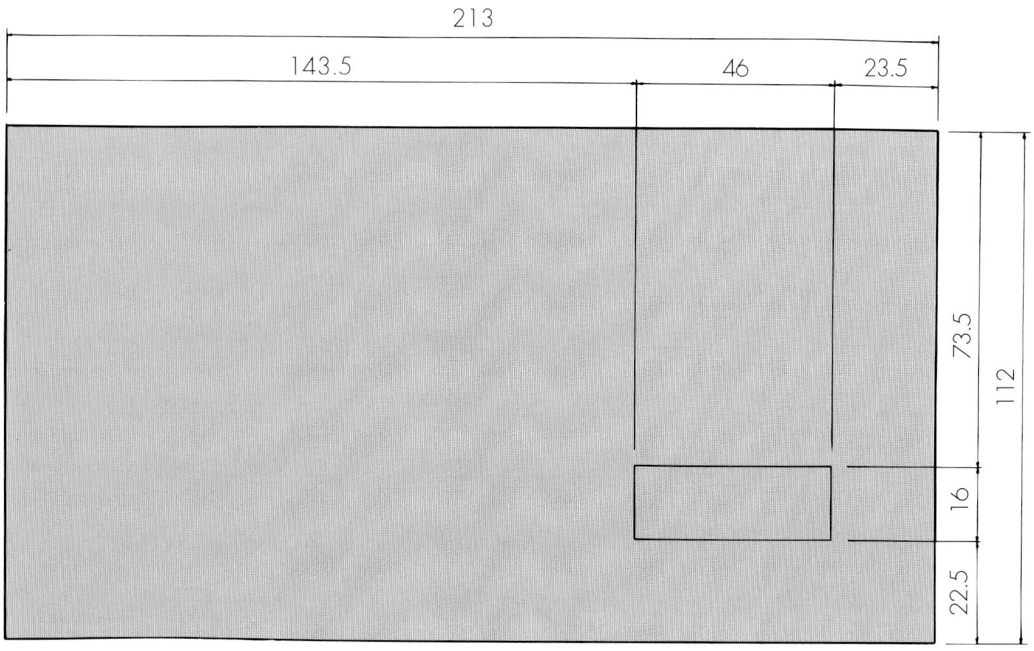

Fig 14.4 The carcass top piece that retains the coin chute.

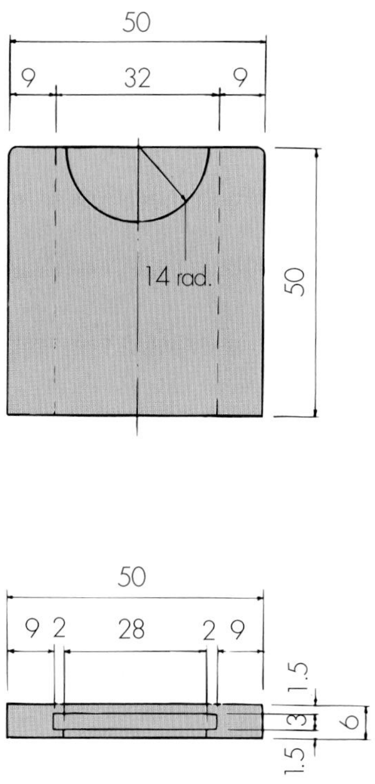

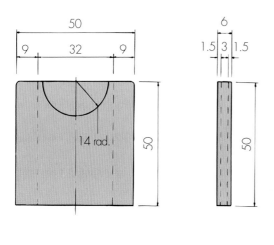

Fig 14.5 Coin slot: plan, and front and side elevations.

Fig 14.6 Using a permanent marker pen to colour the brass sheet before marking out.

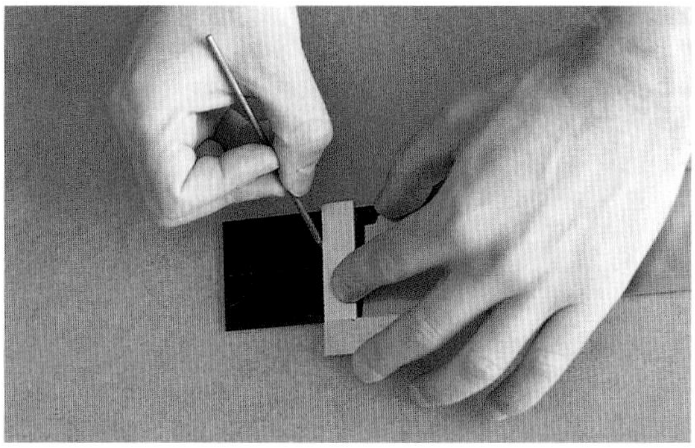

Fig 14.7 Marking out the coin slot, using a scriber and an engineer's try square.

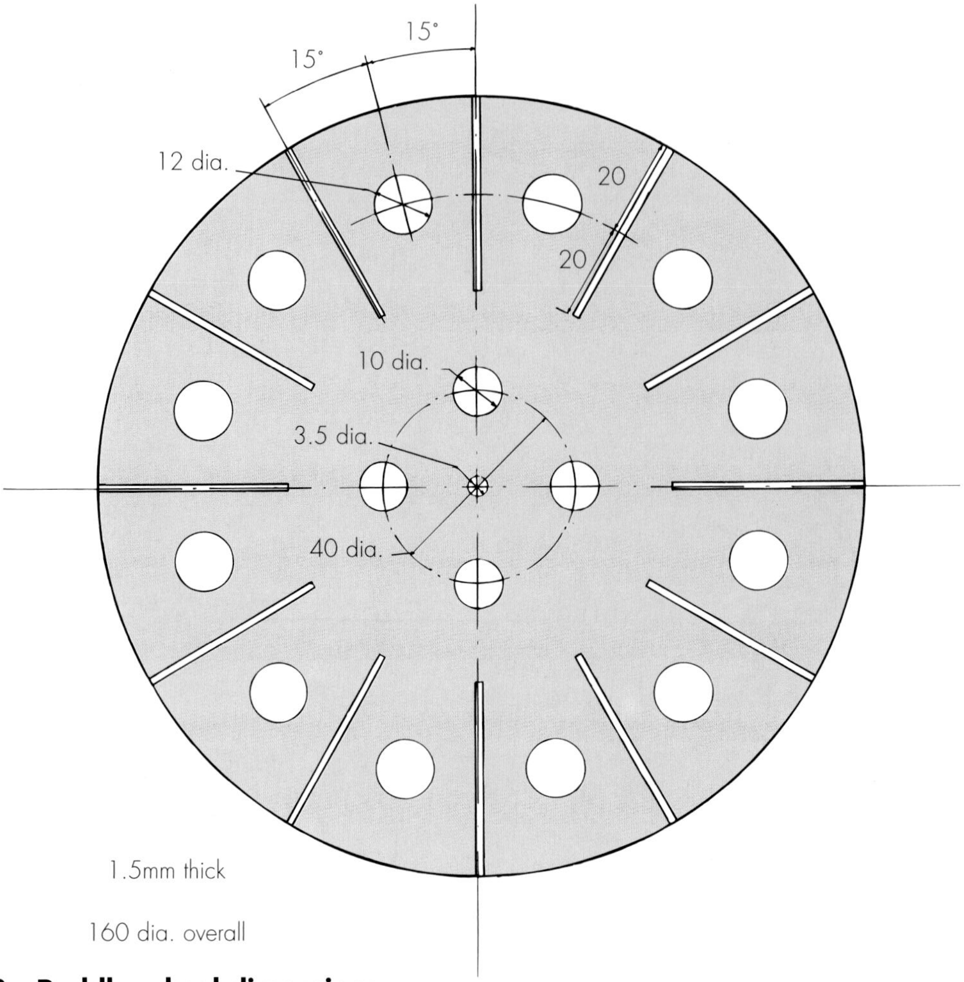

Fig 14.8 Paddle wheel dimensions.

Glue the paddles in position on the wheel. On the back of the wheel, smooth away any protruding paddle edges with a block plane and/or a sanding block.

Dial

Using a compass, mark the outside and inside diameters of the dial on a prepared piece of 3mm (⅛in) birch plywood (*see* Fig 14.1).

Divide the dial into twelve equal segments with the aid of a protractor (each segment being 30° apart). For now, mark the divisions with a pencil only. Cut the dial

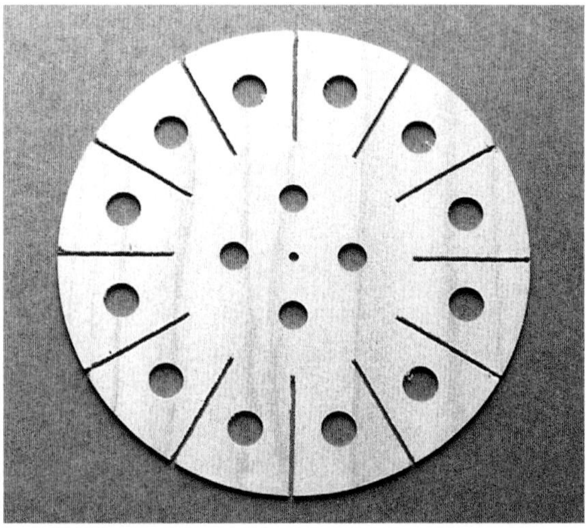

Fig 14.9 The paddle wheel with all the weight-reduction holes drilled and paddle slots cut.

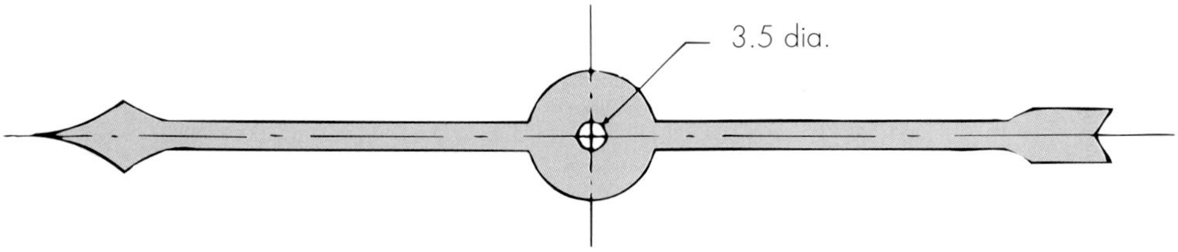

Fig 14.10 Pointer dimensions.

out with a fretsaw. Mark over the pencilled division lines with a fine, blue ballpoint pen.

Pointer/arrow

Transfer the pointer on to 1.5mm (1/16in) birch plywood (*see* Fig 14.10). Drill the centre spindle hole before cutting it out with a fretsaw.

FINISHING

Case

Before finishing the case and its door, punch all pins below the surface and fill the resulting holes with an appropriate coloured filler or stopping. As we chose a dark mahogany hue for our case, we used a medium-mahogany-coloured stopping.

We stained all areas of the case with a spirit-based Victorian mahogany wood stain. On the outside of the case this was followed with three coats of deep-red, mahogany-stained gloss varnish. The front and top of the case were decorated with gold transfers, available at good stationers.

Finally the case was given two coats of clear gloss varnish.

Dial and pointer

Seal six of the dial's segments with two coats of clear gloss varnish. When dry, colour the other segments with a thinned acrylic paint of your choice. (Thin the paint on a palette and test on a scrap piece of birch plywood first.) Give the entire dial three coats of clear gloss varnish.

Now apply the fortunes to the dial. We mainly used gold and black 4mm letter transfers. You could copy ours or make up phrases and sayings of your own. Ours are:

Lucky 7
Make a new friend
Expect the unexpected
Lucky blue
Beware the weather
A treat awaits

Lucky 3
Lend a helping hand
A fresh start
Lucky green
Travel light
Lucky in love

Apply a final coat of clear gloss varnish over the dial to help protect the transfer lettering.

The pointer is coloured with thinned red acrylic paint and then varnished. We embellished ours with gold decoration.

ASSEMBLY

Place the case on its back and place the dial on the front face. With the aid of a square and rule, adjust the dial until it is in the required position. Mark around the inner circumference of the dial with a sharp 2H pencil, so as to slightly indent the varnished surface. Remove the dial, apply adhesive to the back of the dial and glue it on to the case front. Use the indented circle as a guide. Check with a rule and square that the dial is absolutely in its correct position before placing a weight on top of it. Remove the weight when the adhesive has set firm.

Glue a washer over the spindle hole in the interior of the case, and another over the spindle hole on the inside of the door. These washers will help stop the plywood wearing away as the spindle rotates.

Cut a 122mm (4¹³⁄₁₆in) length of 4BA steel studding. Thread the paddle wheel on to the studding, followed by a washer either side. Next, thread a 4BA nut on to either side of the paddle wheel. Position the wheel on the studding so that the paddles will be directly below the coin chute when in position in the case. Ensure that the paddles are facing the door (*see* Fig 14.11). Tighten the nuts so that the paddle wheel is firmly locked on to the studding. Thread two 4BA nuts on to the studding and tighten against the back side (the smooth side) of the paddle wheel. These act as spacers to help stop the rotating wheel from scraping against the case, should the wheel be slightly warped.

Pass the spindle/wheel assembly into the case. Thread the spindle into the spindle hole in the case. While steadying the wheel with one hand, place a washer, then a nut on to the protruding length of spindle at the front of the case with your other hand. Do not tighten the nut against the front face of the case, otherwise the spindle will not turn. Place another washer on the spindle, then the pointer, another washer and finally another nut.

Fit the back door lock and hinges and fix it to the case. If the door does not quite thread on to the spindle when you try to shut it, you should be able to guide the spindle by gently manipulating the pointer as the door is closed.

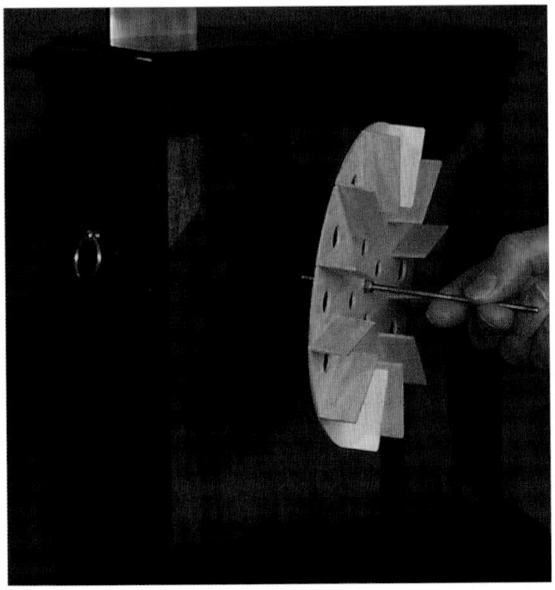

Fig 14.11 Fitting the paddle wheel spindle into the case.

Place the case on its back in order to lock the pointer on to the spindle. The two nuts either side of the pointer must be tightened against each other. Fortunately, they do not have to be tightened too much, just enough so that the pointer rotates with the spindle. We found that finger tight was adequate but, if you can, fit a 4BA spanner on to the nut behind the pointer and a socket, or a spanner, on to the front nut and tighten (*see* Fig 14.12). If you have difficulty with this you can hold the back nut carefully with a pair of long-nosed pliers.

Fig 14.12 Securing the pointer in place.

On each side of the case we fitted 25mm (1in) brass O/D rings. These have a combined woodscrew fitting and are of the type often used for clock cases. Four claw feet are screwed to the base. These rings and feet can be purchased from clock-making suppliers (*see* Fig 14.13).

Fig 14.13 The interior of the completed money box. Note the brass ring and decorative claw feet on the case.

Polish the coin slot and fit it into the slot on top of the case. If you do not glue it into place it may be removed for cleaning.

A piece of cloth, such as felt, could be fitted inside the case at the bottom. This will help deaden the sound of the coins as they drop.

Good fortune!

CHAPTER 15

Corner Dolls' House

★★★

The corner dolls' house has been designed to meet the needs of all dolls' house lovers with limited space. The finished house is attached to the wall, at an appropriate height for its main users, fitting neatly into the corner of a room.

Made to 1/12 scale, all the components are individually made. We purposely avoided using ready-made dolls' house windows, doors, mouldings and so on, in case those chosen were not universally available. A staircase has been omitted in order to maximize the floor space available. Although the facade of the house has been influenced by the Georgian era it is by no means architecturally or historically correct, so feel free to paint, decorate and furnish it in any style you choose.

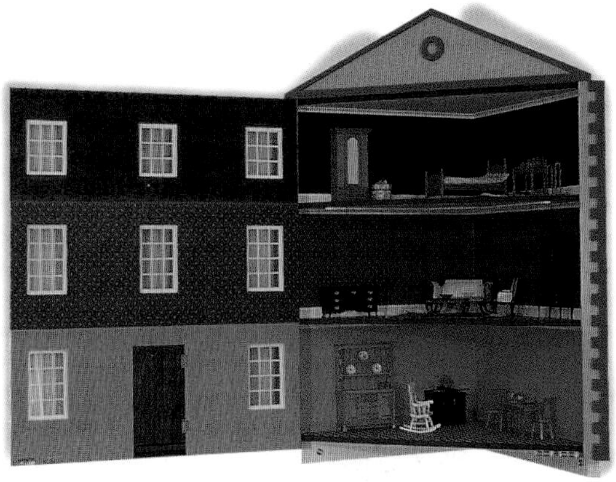

CUTTING LIST

Side wall:	700 x 495 x 12mm (27 9/16 x 19½ x ½in) birch plywood
Side wall:	700 x 483 x 12mm (27 9/16 x 19 x ½in) birch plywood
Small facade section (2):	712 x 50 x 12mm (28 x 2 x ½in) birch plywood
Facade:	712 x 600 x 12mm (28 x 23⅝ x ½in) birch plywood
Floor/ceiling triangular section (4):	483 x 483 x 670 x 12mm (19 x 19 x 26⅜ x ½in) birch plywood
Quoin (2):	712 x 30 x 6mm (28 x 1 3/16 x ¼in) birch plywood
Roof pediment front:	650 x 164 x 12mm (25 9/16 x 6 7/16 x ½in) birch plywood
Roof pediment front border:	650 x 164 x 6mm (25 9/16 x 6 7/16 x ¼in) birch plywood
Roof pediment triangular back piece:	380 x 270 x 270 x 18mm (15 x 10½ x 10½ x ¾in) birch plywood or MDF
Decorative portal:	48mm (1⅞in) diameter x 6mm (¼in) birch plywood
Large windowframe (5):	162 x 96 x 3mm (6⅜ x 3 13/16 x ⅛in) birch plywood
Small windowframe (3):	132 x 96 x 3mm (5 3/16 x 3 13/16 x ⅛in) birch plywood
Windowsills (8):	102 x 6 x 6mm (4 x ¼ x ¼in) hardwood strip
Doorframe:	240 x 136 x 6mm (9 7/16 x 5⅜ x ¼in) birch plywood
Door:	193 x 106 x 12mm (7⅝ x 4 3/16 x ½in) birch plywood
Top step:	136 x 24 x 12mm (5⅜ x 15/16 x ½in) birch plywood
Bottom step:	160 x 24 x 12mm (6 5/16 x 15/16 x ½in) birch plywood
Large windowpane (5):	130 x 76 x 2mm (5⅛ x 3 x 3/32in) acrylic sheet
Small windowpane (3):	100 x 76 x 2mm (3 15/16 x 3 x 3/32in) acrylic sheet

Miscellaneous

25mm (1in) brass butt hinges (2)
712 x 25mm (28 x 1in) piano hinge
Magnetic catches or brass turnbutton catches
Dolls' house brass door knob

CONSTRUCTION

Main frame of the house

In view of the fact that the design is based on, and in fact could be used as, a corner cabinet, 12mm (½in) plywood has been used in the construction as opposed to the more usual 9mm (⅜in) for dolls' houses. The roof is only a pediment and its sole purpose is for show. It can be removed easily to allow for dusting.

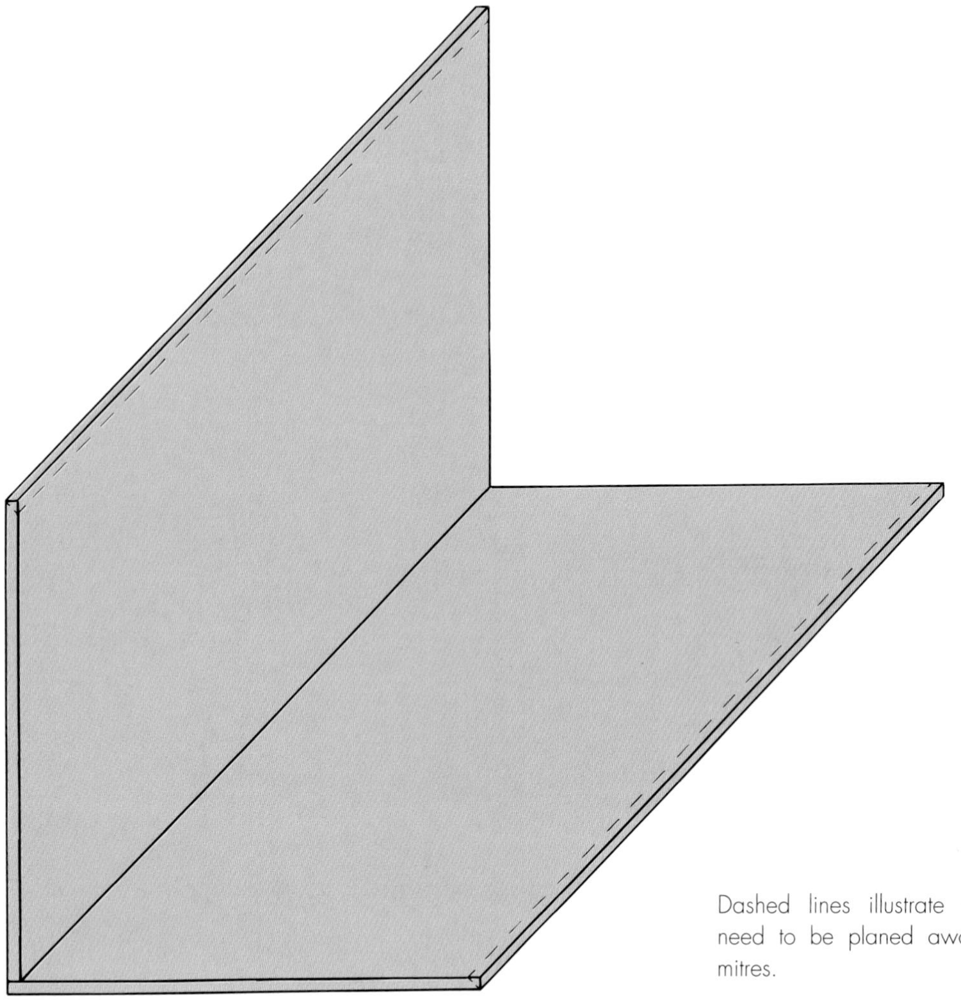

Dashed lines illustrate areas that need to be planed away to form mitres.

Fig 15.1 Side walls.

Join the two side walls of the house using panel pins and glue. Ensure that the wider wall is pinned to the edge of the narrower wall so that, when joined, the width of each wall is an equal distance from the centre.

Plane the vertical outer edge of each wall to an angle of 45°. Using a mitre square (a sliding bevel set at 45° would do as a substitute), mark a line 45° from the outer corner of each wall. Place a marking gauge on the vertical edge of one of the walls, and set it to the point where one of the 45° lines meets the inside of the wall. The gauge will then be set to mark a line on the inside face of each wall (*see* Fig 15.1).

Each area must now be planed away. To do this, clamp the walls to your workbench so that one wall is horizontal and protruding over the edge of the workbench. Use a block plane to plane away the waste areas up to the marked lines. Check the newly mitred edges with the mitre square (or bevel) and adjust if necessary.

Mark the centre lines on the inside surface of each wall, showing where each floor

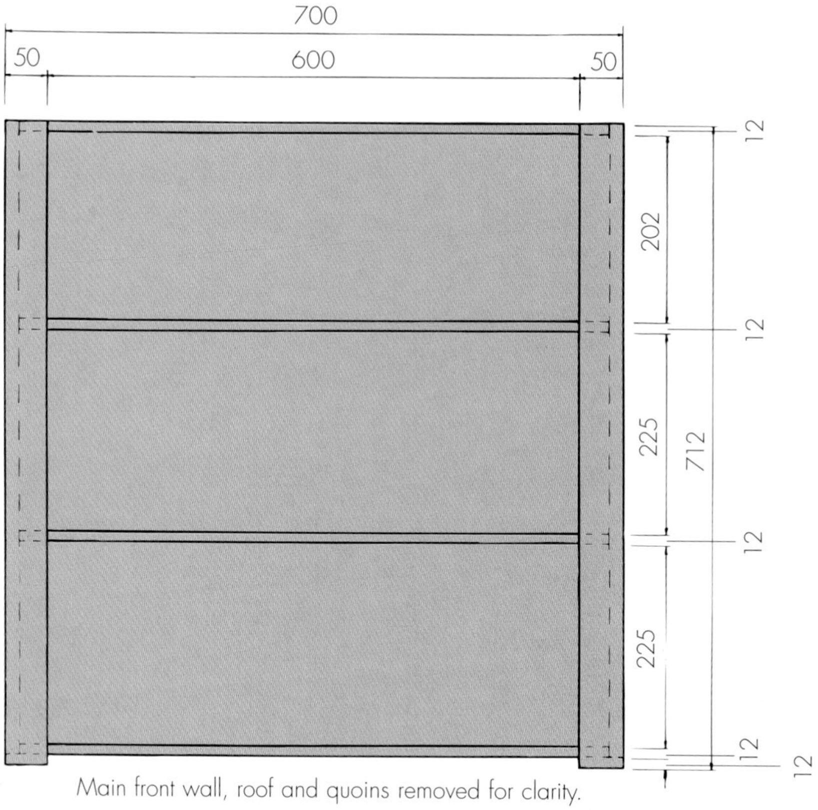

Fig 15.2 Front view showing floor/ceiling heights.

(and the top ceiling/roof) piece will be attached (*see* Fig 15.2). Then drill pin holes (*see* Chapter 3) along each centre line. Glue and pin each floor piece into place. If any of the front edges of the floors protrude you can shave them flush with a block plane.

Glue and pin the two narrow front wall sections into place (*see* Fig 15.2). As they are longer than the carcass of the house, ensure that they both protrude at the same end; this end will now be the base of the house.

Cut out the two quoin lengths with a fretsaw (*see* Fig 15.3). If you have difficulty cutting the centre sections (the throat depth of a hand fretsaw may be inadequate) use a coping saw – the blade can be turned 90°, thus allowing a parallel cut.

To differentiate between the stone blocks of the quoin lengths define them by scoring with a sharp, heavy-duty craft knife between each block. Use a steel straightedge as a guide.

Glue and pin each quoin section into position (*see* Figs 15.4 and 15.5). Ensure that the large base stone of each section is at the foot of the house.

Glue 9mm (⅜in) coving round the wall/ceiling join of each room. Mitre each end of the coving before fixing.

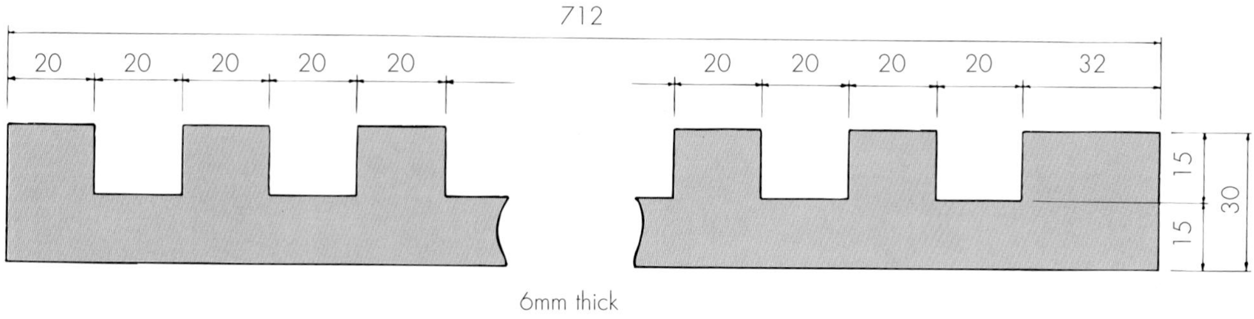

Fig 15.3 Dimensions of the quoins.

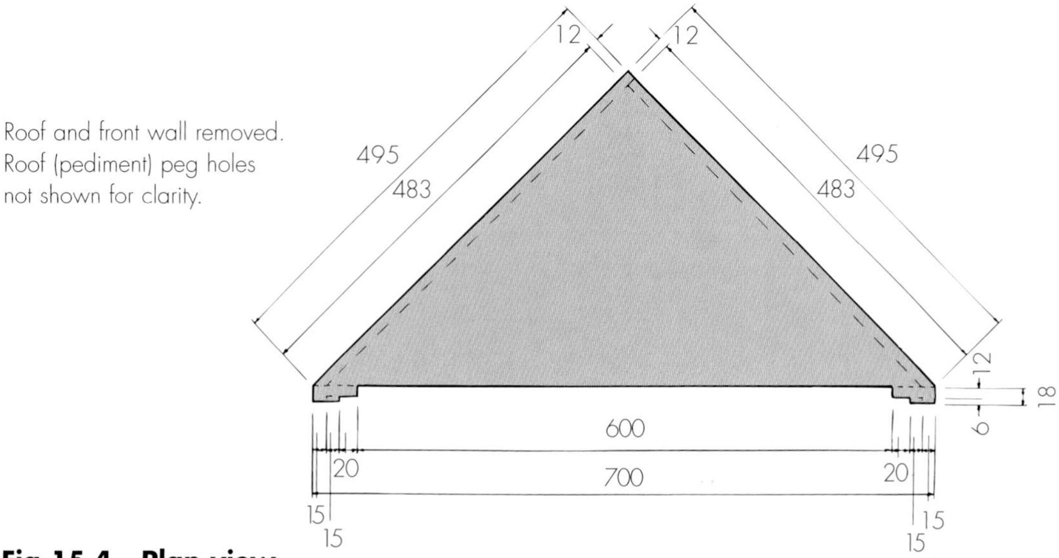

Fig 15.4 Plan view.

The first- and top-floor rooms have skirting boards made from 21 x 9mm (13/16 x 3/8in) standard base moulding (*see* Fig 15.5). We planed away the bottom step of the moulding to make it appear less fussy. As the ground-floor room was to be the kitchen, we felt that the skirting board should be less elaborate. Therefore we used a length of 22 x 6mm (7/8 x 1/4in) ramin strip. We scored a few decorative lines along the top of this with a marking gauge. Attach the skirting boards with pins and glue in a similar manner to the coving.

Fig 15.5 Skirting boards fitted.

We couldn't resist cutting out a decorative piece of ceiling moulding for the first-floor

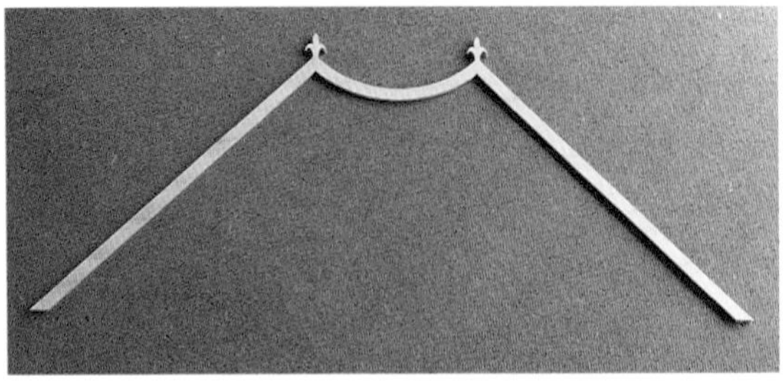

Fig 15.6 Detail of the fleur-de-lis ceiling moulding.

room from 3mm (1/8in) birch plywood (*see* Fig 15.6). We embellished it with two fleurs-de-lis to match our chosen wallpaper. You, of course, could design a pattern of your own choice.

Windows

Cut out each windowframe with a fretsaw (*see* Figs 15.7, 15.8).

For the windowsills you could use standard ready-made 6 x 6mm (1/4 x 1/4in) hardwood strip. However, we had a length of 5mm (3/16in) thick hardwood strip, so we planed this to 6mm (1/4in) wide and used this instead.

The windowpanes are cut from 2mm (3/32in) thick clear acrylic sheet. We did this with a tenon saw, ensuring that the sheet was well supported during cutting.

The glazing bars were created by applying 6mm (1/4in) and 3mm (1/8in) wide strips of white sticky-back plastic to each 'glass' pane (*see* Fig 15.9). Sticky-back plastic can usually be bought from most DIY or hardware stores, and comes in a variety of colours. Use a sharp, fine craft knife and steel straightedge when cutting it.

Alternatively, the glazing bars could be cut from a piece of 1.5mm (1/16in) birch plywood.

Whatever method of producing the glazing bars you choose, we have left their pattern and spacing for you to decide.

Door

The door is made from 12mm (1/2in) birch plywood. As this is the same thickness as the front wall section, it makes a nice flush fit when hinged into place. The bevel-edged panels were carved with a combination of a craft knife and a 6mm (1/4in) chisel. However,

The broken line defines the location of the windowframe over a front wall window aperture.

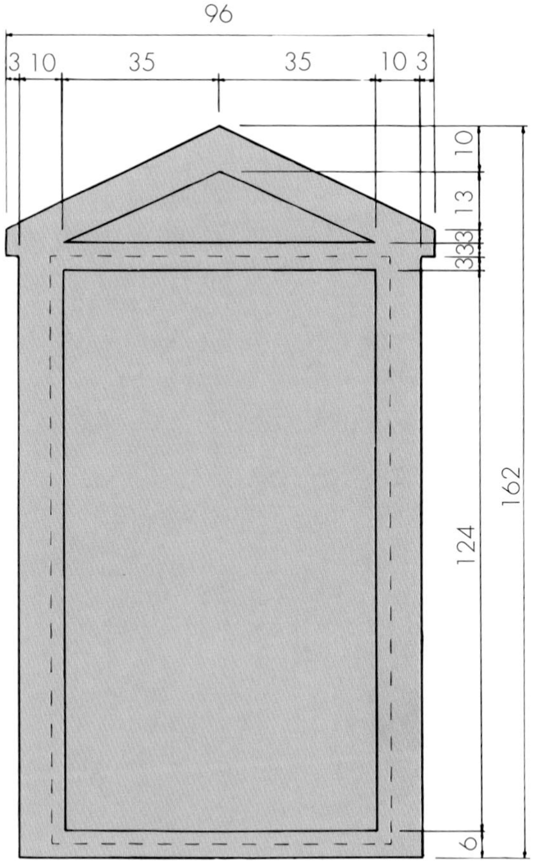

Fig 15.7 Dimensions of the large windowframes.

we would advise against you doing this unless you are confident of your abilities. As an alternative you could make the door from a piece of 9mm (3/8in) and a piece of 3mm (1/8in) birch plywood. Cut a piece to the door's dimensions from each thickness. On the 3mm (1/8in) piece, mark out the panel design you would like, then cut out the panels with a fretsaw. Now glue this fretted sheet on to the 9mm (3/8in) piece. When set, trim the edges with a block pane.

The 'stone' doorframe is fretsawn from 6mm (1/4in) birch plywood (*see* Figs 15.10, 15.11).

Fig 15.9 Applying sticky-back plastic glazing bars to the acrylic windows.

The broken line defines the location of the windowframe over a front wall window aperture.

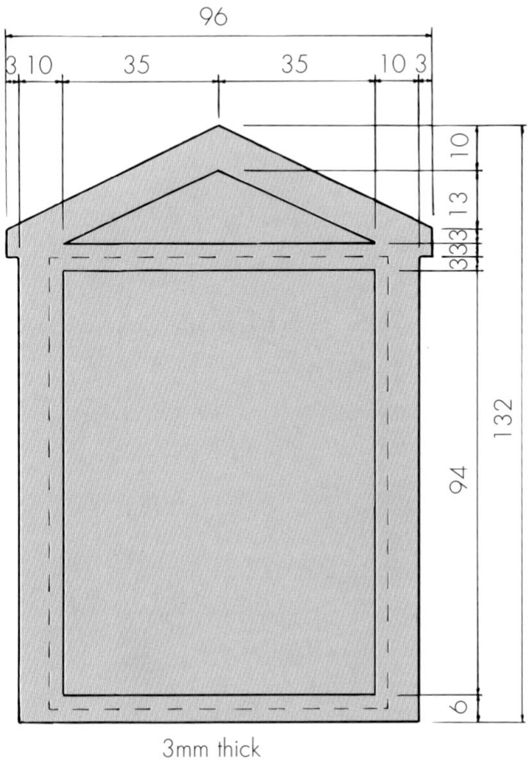

Fig 15.8 Dimensions of the small windowframes.

The broken line defines the location of the doorframe and steps over the door aperture.

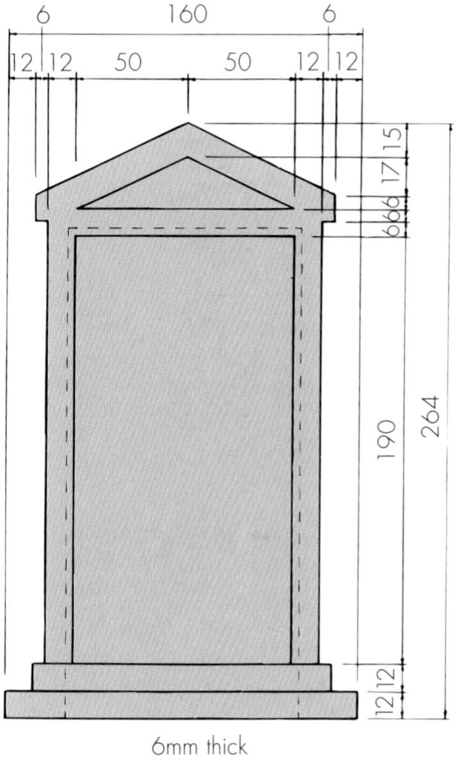

Fig 15.10 Doorframe and steps.

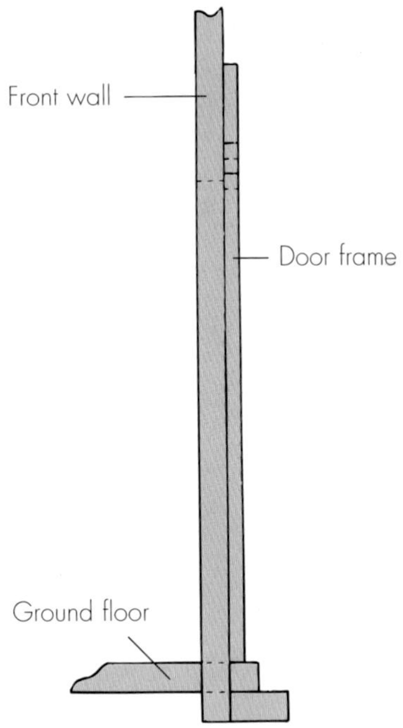

Fig 15.11 Side view of front wall, doorframe and steps.

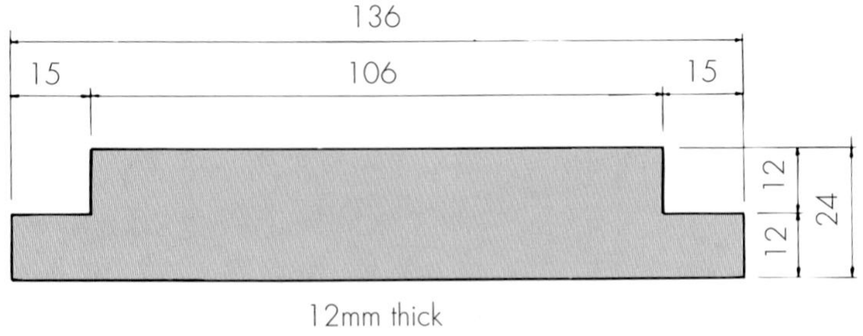

Fig 15.12 Top step dimensions.

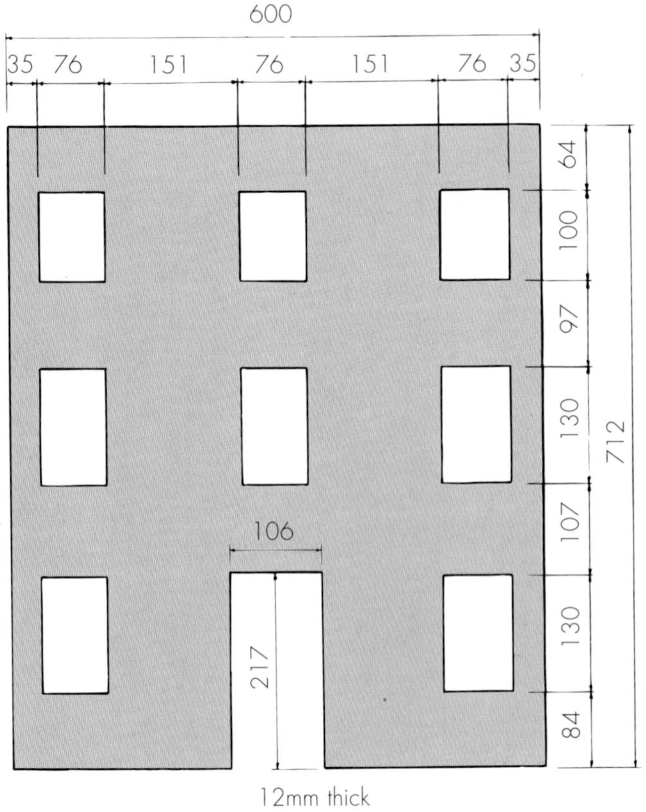

Fig 15.13 Facade: door and window dimensions.

Steps

Cut the steps out ready for attaching later (*see* Fig 15.12).

Facade

If you do not have use of a machine fretsaw (or its capacity is small), cut out the window apertures with a combination of coping saw and hand fretsaw (*see* Fig 15.13). This said, you will probably be unable to cut out the central window. In order to do so, you will have to use either a portable power jigsaw or a padsaw (*see* Fig 15.14).

At this stage it is advisable to hinge the front wall to the house. A 25mm (1in) wide piano hinge is used for strength. We intended to fit a solid brass one until we

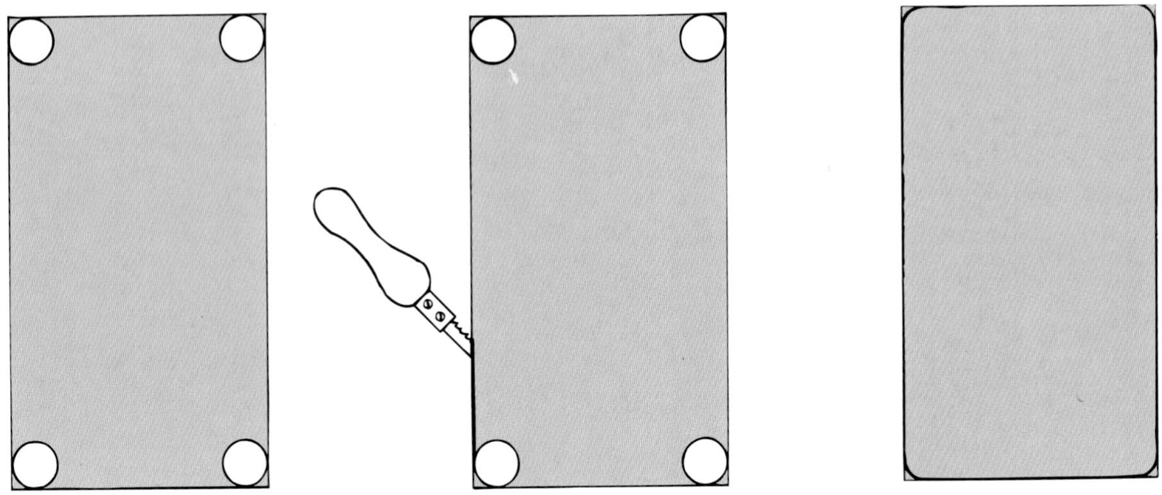
(a) Drill a suitably sized hole in each corner.
(b) Insert the blade in the hole and cut out.
(c) Square the corners with a knife and/or sanding sticks.

Fig 15.14 Alternative method of cutting out the central window aperture.

saw the price! Piano hinges are available in variously sized long lengths. Choose a length that is longer than the facade, and cut the desired length with a hacksaw. File away any resulting sharp edges.

Each flap of the hinge is approximately 11mm ($\frac{7}{16}$in), so they will be screwed flush (not set in) to the edges. However, because the hinge is not set in you will probably find that the facade is now slightly too wide. You will need to plane the edge to the thickness of your piano hinge.

When the facade is hinged and fits correctly, remove it and lay it face up on the workbench. Each 'stone' windowframe and the doorframe/steps may now be glued into position (*see* Figs 15.7, 15.8, 15.10, 15.11, 15.15). Next glue a sill to each windowframe. As an embellishment you could apply a decorative upholstery pin centrally in the pediment of the doorframe (*see* Fig 15.16).

Fig 15.15 A windowframe ready to be glued in place.

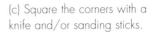

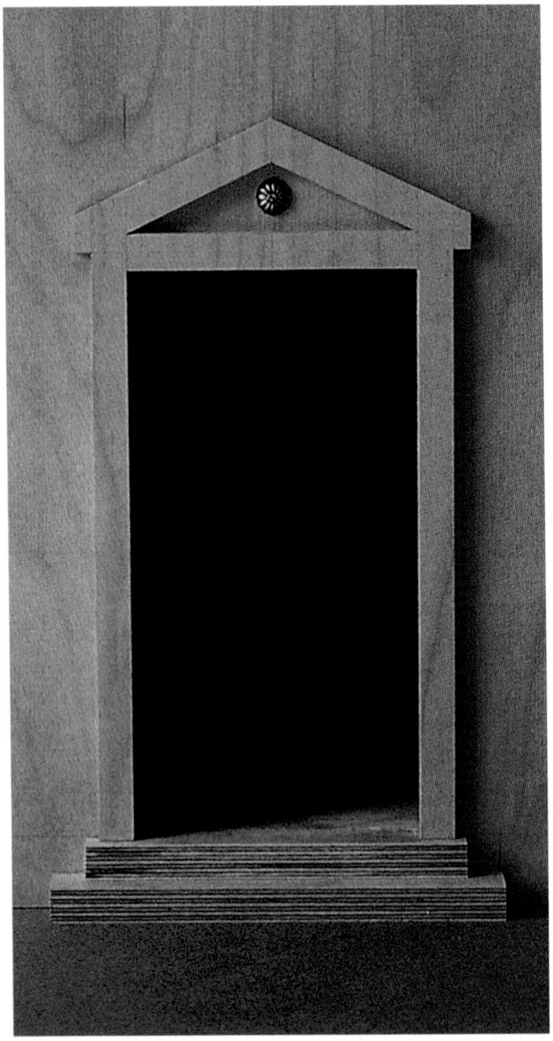

Fig 15.16 Doorframe and steps.

Roof

Firstly, you will need to cut out the roof pediment's border from 6mm (¼in) birch plywood. Then glue and pin this to a piece of 12mm (½in) birch plywood and cut around the perimeter (*see* Fig 15.17). True up the edges with a block plane.

The decorative 'stone' circle is cut from 6mm (¼in) birch plywood. Score any stone block lines before gluing it into position.

Cut the supporting triangular back base of the roof from either 18mm (¾in) birch plywood or MDF. Before gluing and pinning it to the roof, drill the four 6mm (¼in) peg holes. These should be drilled to a depth of no more than 12mm (½in) (*see* Fig 15.18). The back base may now be attached to the roof.

To locate the position of the peg hole centres on the top of the house, use dowel centre points (*see* Fig 3.15 on page 27). Insert these into the peg holes, place the roof into position and press downwards.

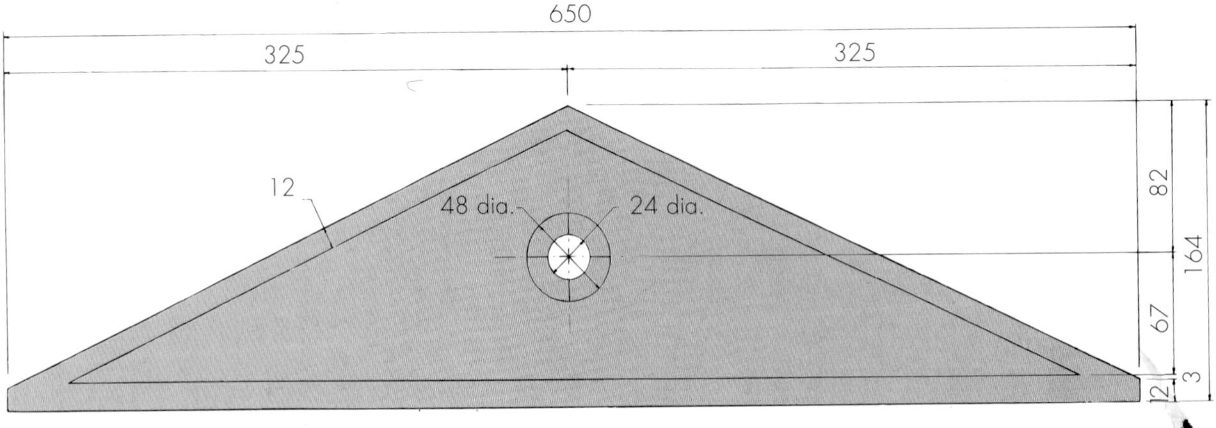

12mm thick ply with 6mm thick ply border and decorative portal

Fig 15.17 Roof pediment dimensions.

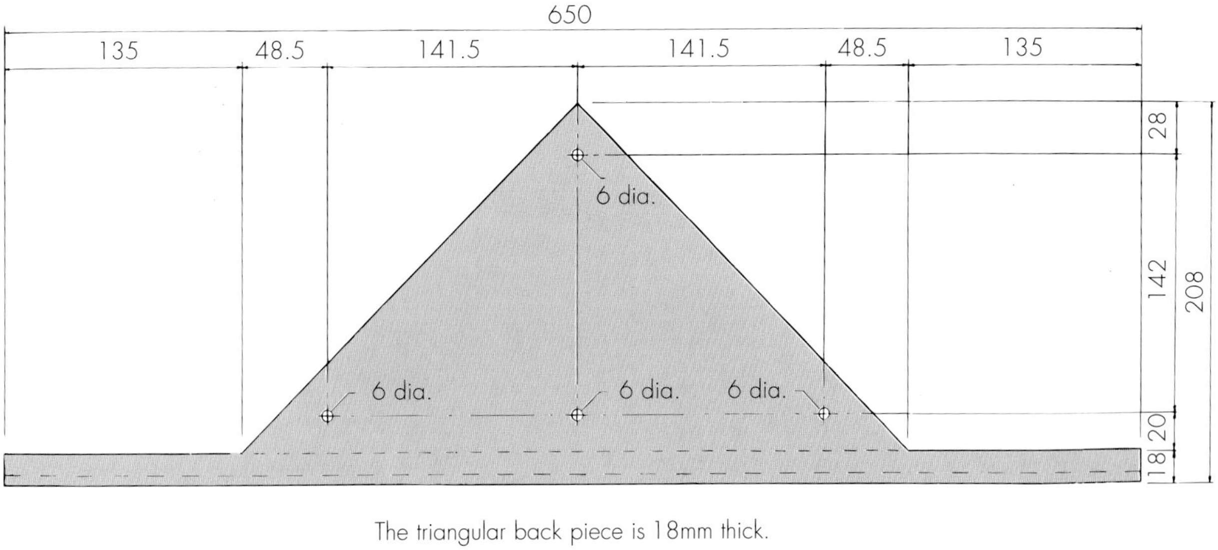

Fig 15.18 Plan of the underside of the roof, showing peg hole positions.

Fig 15.19 Underside of the roof pediment, illustrating the dowel pegs.

The dowel centre points will make small indentations indicating where to drill. Drill these four 6mm (¼in) diameter holes using a wood bit to a depth of no more than 8mm (5⁄16in).

Glue four 20mm (25⁄32in) long, ready-made fluted dowels (you may need to cut these down from longer ones) in the four holes of the triangular base (*see* Fig 15.19). Do not then glue this to the roof top if you require it to be removable!

PAINTING AND FINISHING

Before final assembly, decorate your dolls' house. Remove the facade of the house to make access and finishing easier.

Initially we felt it was rather a shame to paint and decorate the exterior of the house, as the grain pattern of the birch plywood looked so attractive. If you like this option, just give your house a few coats of varnish for protection. In the end we chose to finish the main exterior parts with

Fig 15.20 Painting the facade of the house – cutting in round a top windowframe.

Fig 15.21 The interior, decorated and furnished as a kitchen, drawing room and bedroom.

a soft blue shade of vinyl silk paint. This is solvent free, low odour and safe for children. It is washable, so the odd mark or two can be cleaned away. One aspect of using this type of paint is that it tends to leave brush marks, even when very carefully applied. This needn't be viewed as a drawback, however, as the brush marks can add texture to the wall.

A matt, sand-colour paint was chosen for the exposed stone work (*see* Fig 15.20). This was protected with a couple of coats of matt varnish.

If your dolls' house is to be permanently fixed to a corner of a room, the exterior of the rear walls need not be finished, but they should be sealed with primer for protection.

The front door was stained mahogany and varnished.

For the inside of the house, papers which are stocked by dolls' house specialist suppliers were used for the floors and walls. These were pasted on, but you will need to seal the wood before applying them (*see* Fig 15.21).

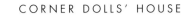

FINAL ASSEMBLY

With the painting and decorating complete, the windowpanes can now be fitted.

Lay the facade of the house face down on the workbench (it is advisable to spread a blanket on the bench first to protect the paintwork). Place a spot of instant-set glue to each corner and, centrally, to each edge of a window aperture. Drop the windowpane into place and apply gentle pressure. This should be sufficient to hold each pane in place.

The front door can now be hinged in place. Lay two 25mm (1in) brass hinges on the back of the door and inside wall, and then screw them down. A door knob can be fitted if desired.

Hinge the facade to the house.

You could fit a hook and eye or a brass cupboard turnbutton to keep the front wall closed when not in use. Alternatively, you could fit one or two magnetic cupboard catches to the underside of the ground floor.

Wall mounting

When mounting the house to the corner walls of a room, you could simply put screws straight through the interior walls of the house. However, unless hidden by strategically placed items of furniture this method is unsightly. We mounted it on a corner shelf. This was constructed by screwing two horizontal battens to the corner of a wall and screwing a top to it: a 6mm (¼in) piece of plywood is sufficient. Use small screws to help hold the base of the dolls' house to the shelf. Ensure that the shelf is 25mm (1in) or so narrower than the dolls' house. This will ensure that the shelf avoids any magnetic catches which may be fitted.

The top of the dolls' house should be attached to the corner walls by a couple of strong mirror plates.

To open the dolls' house, place the palm of a hand underneath the steps with your fingers behind them, and pull the facade open.

Freestanding

If you do not wish to attach your dolls' house to the wall, you will need to screw a couple of battens to the underside. These must be of a thickness that is fractionally greater than the distance between the ground floor to the bottom of the facade, or the facade will not open freely. To open the facade, open the door, hold the door frame and pull towards you.

Alternatively, you could change the design of the dolls' house by extending the depth of the two back walls to that of the front wall (or preferably a millimetre or so longer).

If you do choose to have your dolls' house freestanding, and it is resting on a small table so that the facade, when open, extends over the edge, beware that it does not topple over!

RECOVERY
24hr.
RES Q IT

CHAPTER 16

Breakdown Recovery Truck & Car

★★★

The estate car and its rescuing partner should appeal to most youngsters who enjoy transport toys. The breakdown recovery truck is fitted with a winch which is used to pull the estate car up the ramps and on to the recovery bed. When not in use these ramps are neatly stored away in a compartment underneath the bed. While being transported back to the garage the car is held securely in place on the truck bed by two wheel retaining strips.

ESTATE CAR CUTTING LIST

Chassis:	260 x 88 x 3mm ($10\frac{1}{4}$ x $3\frac{1}{2}$ x $\frac{1}{8}$in) birch plywood
Bonnet block:	80 x 88 x 32mm ($3\frac{1}{8}$ x $3\frac{1}{2}$ x $1\frac{1}{4}$in) hardwood
Rear seat/boot floor:	98 x 88 x 12mm ($3\frac{13}{16}$ x $3\frac{1}{2}$ x $\frac{1}{2}$in) birch plywood
Rear seat back rest:	88 x 28 x 20mm ($3\frac{1}{2}$ x $1\frac{1}{8}$ x $\frac{13}{16}$in) hardwood
Boot lid:	88 x 32 x 6mm ($3\frac{1}{2}$ x $1\frac{1}{4}$ x $\frac{1}{4}$in) birch plywood
Dashboard:	88 x 10 x 10mm ($3\frac{1}{2}$ x $\frac{3}{8}$ x $\frac{3}{8}$in) birch plywood
Gearbox/handbrake console:	76 x 22 x 10mm ($3\frac{1}{32}$ x $\frac{7}{8}$ x $\frac{3}{8}$in) birch plywood
Side (2):	260 x 76 x 6mm ($10\frac{1}{4}$ x 3 x $\frac{1}{4}$in) birch plywood
Front tow hook retaining strip:	88 x 11 x 6mm ($3\frac{1}{2}$ x $\frac{7}{16}$ x $\frac{1}{4}$in) birch plywood
Rear undersill:	88 x 11 x 6mm ($3\frac{1}{2}$ x $\frac{7}{16}$ x $\frac{1}{4}$in) birch plywood
Axle retaining strip (2):	248 x 11 x 6mm ($9\frac{3}{4}$ x $\frac{7}{16}$ x $\frac{1}{4}$in) birch plywood
Rear interior wheel arch (2):	30 x 7 x 6mm ($1\frac{3}{16}$ x $\frac{9}{32}$ x $\frac{1}{4}$in) birch plywood
Bumper, front and rear (2):	112 x 12 x 6mm ($4\frac{7}{16}$ x $\frac{1}{2}$ x $\frac{1}{4}$in) birch plywood
Bumper side (4):	12 x 12 x 6mm ($\frac{1}{2}$ x $\frac{1}{2}$ x $\frac{1}{4}$in) birch plywood
Roof:	150 x 88 x 6mm ($5\frac{15}{16}$ x $3\frac{1}{2}$ x $\frac{1}{4}$in) birch plywood
Front seat base (2):	45 x 33 x 12mm ($1\frac{3}{4}$ x $1\frac{9}{32}$ x $\frac{1}{2}$in) birch plywood
Front seat back rest (2):	33 x 28 x 20mm ($1\frac{9}{32}$ x $1\frac{1}{8}$ x $\frac{13}{16}$in) hardwood
Front seat headrest (2):	20 x 8 x 6mm ($\frac{13}{16}$ x $\frac{5}{16}$ x $\frac{1}{4}$in) hardwood
Radiator/lights:	Scraps of 1.5mm ($\frac{1}{16}$in) birch plywood

Miscellaneous

42mm ($1\frac{5}{8}$in) wheels (4)
2mm ($\frac{3}{32}$in) axle rods (2)
Spring hubcaps (4)
Snap rivets for gearstick and handbrake (2)
3mm ($\frac{1}{8}$in) hardwood dowels (2)
6mm ($\frac{1}{4}$in) diameter brass screw eyelet

CONSTRUCTION

Chassis, bonnet and boot sections

Cut out and prepare the chassis (*see* Fig 16.1).

Shape the bonnet block from suitable hardwood such as beech (*see* Fig 16.3). We actually used lime, which is easier to work but less hard-wearing.

Glue and pin to the chassis the 12mm ($\frac{1}{2}$in) birch plywood which forms the rear seat/boot floor section (*see* Figs 16.1, 16.2).

A: Bonnet block **B**: Dashboard **C**: Gearbox/handbrake console **D**: Chassis
E: Rear seat/boot floor **F**: Rear seat **G**: Boot lid

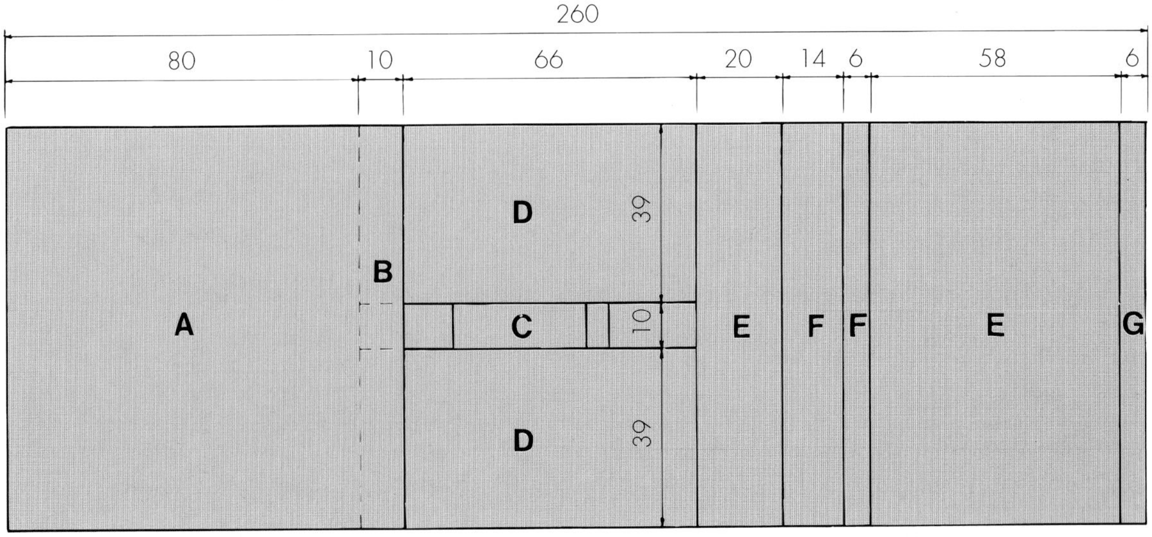

Fig 16.1 Plan view of the car chassis before attaching the sides.

Cross-sectional view of the car, taken from the centre (lengthways). Gear lever, handbrake and towing eyelet not shown.

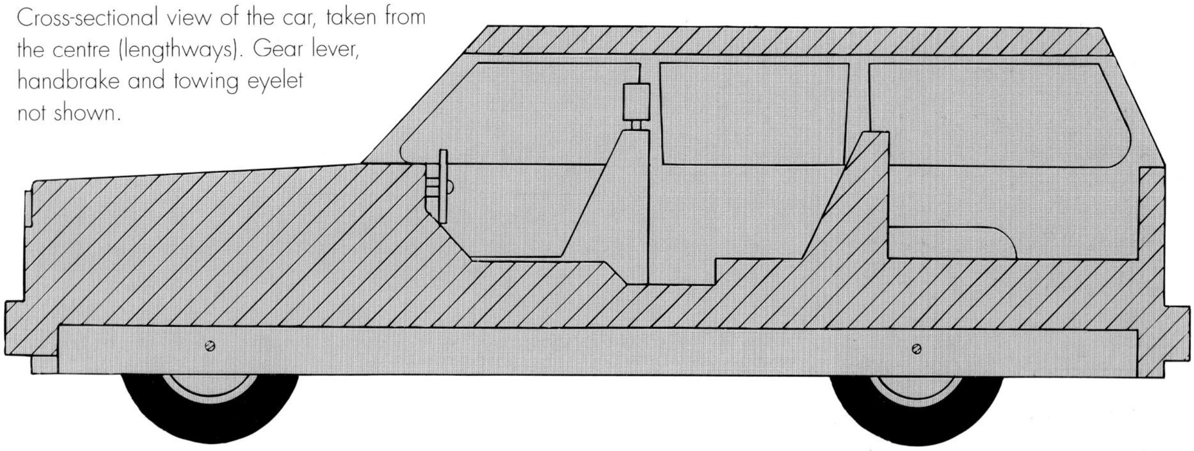

Fig 16.2 Cross-section of the car.

Gearbox and handbrake

With a fretsaw (preferably powered), cut out the gearbox/handbrake console (*see* Fig 16.4).

The gear lever and handbrake are made from the centre pins of snap rivets. To make the gear lever, choose the size of snap

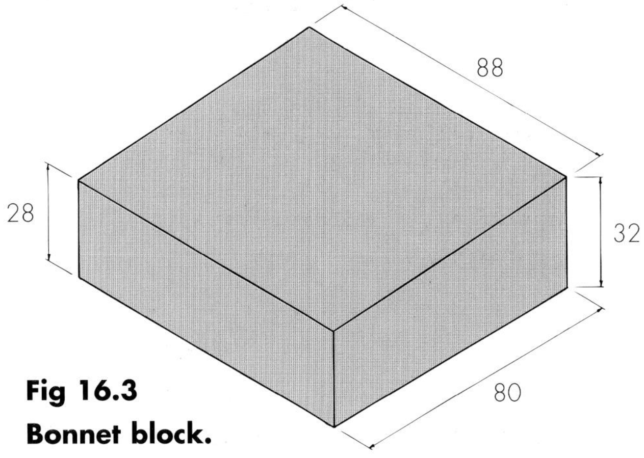

Fig 16.3
Bonnet block.

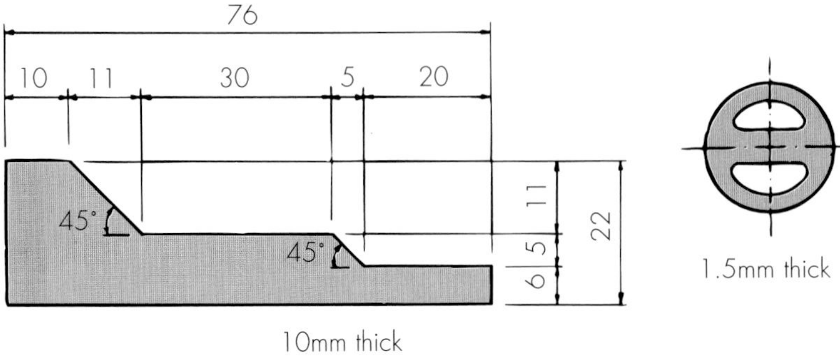

Fig 16.4 Gearbox/handbrake central console and steering wheel.

rivet you wish to use and place it, shank down, between the jaws of a metalwork vice – do not tighten. Remove the centre pin by gently tapping it with a hammer. Cut the pin to the length required with a junior hacksaw. Remember to include 3–4mm (about ⅛in) for fixing. Drill a hole in the console to accommodate the gear lever, ensuring a snug fit. A spot or two of adhesive will secure it in place.

Prepare the pin you have chosen for the handbrake in a similar manner, except that it will need to be bent before fixing to the console. To bend it, clamp it securely in the vice and tap it repeatedly with a hammer until you achieve the degree of bend you desire. Fix in place in the same manner as the gear lever.

Steering wheel and dashboard

Transfer the pattern of the steering wheel (*see* Fig 16.4) on to 1.5mm (1/16in) birch plywood. Drill the central screw hole before cutting out with a fretsaw. The diameter of the hole will be dependent upon the size of screw you use. We used a No. 2 x 12mm (½in) brass round-head screw.

Cut out and prepare the dashboard (*see* Fig 16.5). Drill a pilot hole for the steering wheel fixing screw. It is a good idea to screw the screw a little way into the hole and then remove it. This will make fitting the steering wheel to the dashboard easier later on.

Glue the dashboard into position on the bonnet block (*see* Figs 16.1, 16.2).

Back seat, boot lid and car body sides

Cut and shape the rear seat back rest from a piece of suitable hardwood (*see* Fig 16.6), and glue it into position.

Prepare the boot 'lid' and glue and pin it into position (*see* Figs 16.1, 16.2).

Cut out the two long side shapes of the car body (*see* Fig 16.7). Before fixing them to the car with pins and glue, ensure that each side of the engine block/chassis/rear seat/ boot (trunk) floor and lid are smooth and exactly at a right angle to the chassis underside. Rectify any erroneous high spots with a finely set block plane.

Front tow hook retaining strip and rear undersill

Cut out and prepare the towing eyelet retaining strip (*see* Fig 16.5). Glue it into position at the front underside of the chassis. Then prepare the rear undersill strip and glue this into position on the rear underside of the chassis.

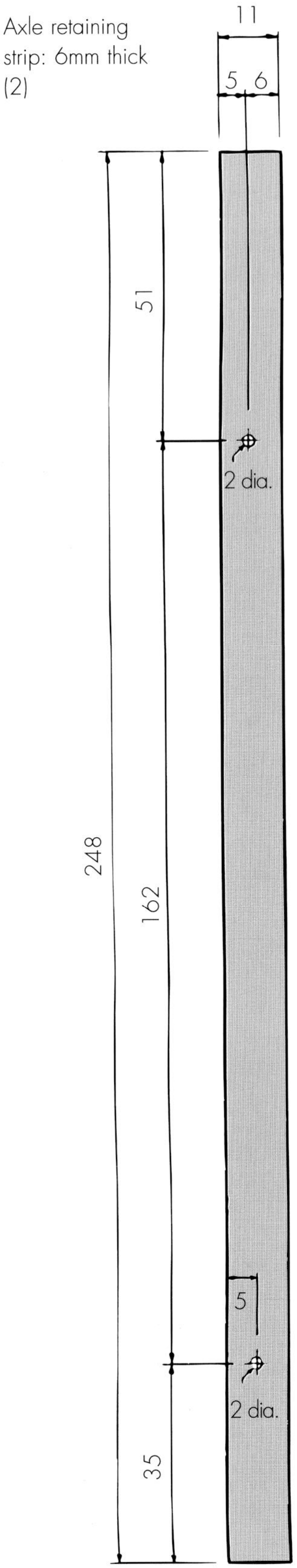

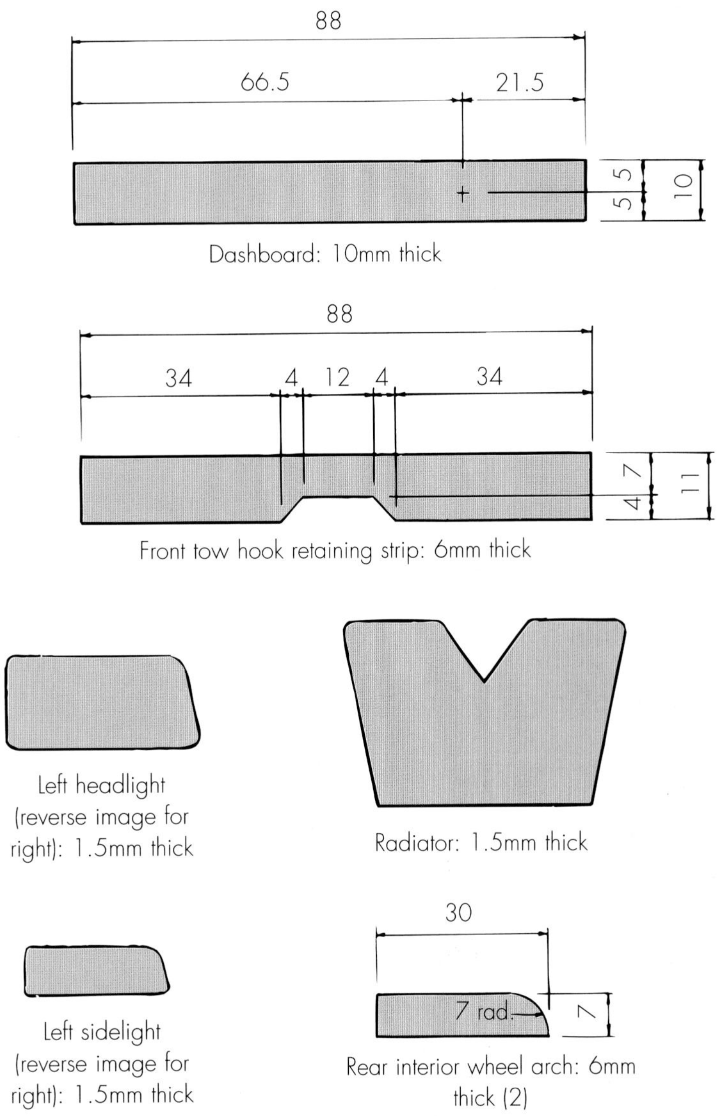

Fig 16.5 Various car components.

Axle retaining strips

The axle retaining strips now need to be prepared (*see* Fig 16.5). The axle holes should be of a size that will accommodate the 2mm axle rod freely.

Assemble the axle retaining strips 'dry' first, so that you can check that each axle hole is positioned centrally in its wheel arch, thus allowing the wheel to turn freely when fitted. Remove the strips, apply glue and reassemble.

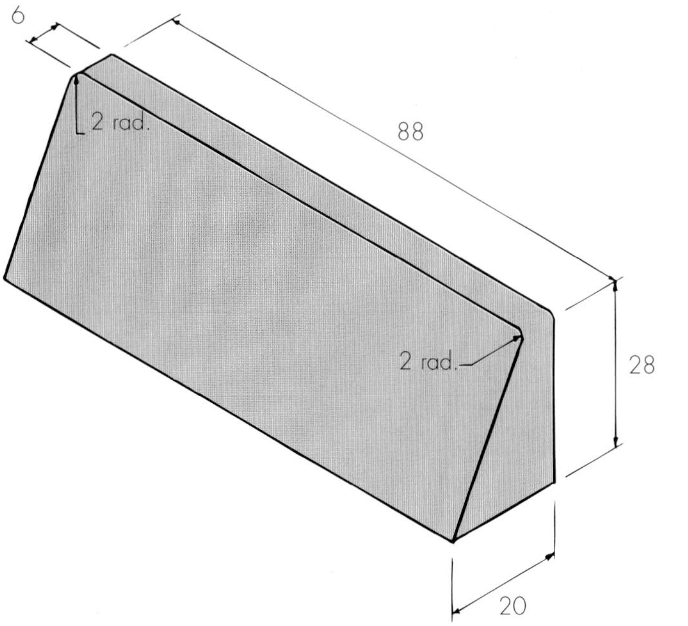

Fig 16.6 Rear seat back rest.

Wheel arch covers and bumpers

Using a block plane and/or sanding sticks, generally clean up any unevenness from the front, back and chassis underside of the car.

Using a fretsaw cut out the two wheel arch covers for the boot with a fretsaw (*see* Fig 16.5) and glue them in position.

Prepare the component pieces that will form the front and rear bumpers, and glue them in position.

Lights and radiator grille

Transfer the front headlights, indicator/side lights and radiator grille profiles on to 1.5mm (1/16in) birch plywood and cut them out using a fretsaw (*see* Fig 16.5).

We used a sharp, heavy-duty craft knife to score the pattern of the radiator grille. We

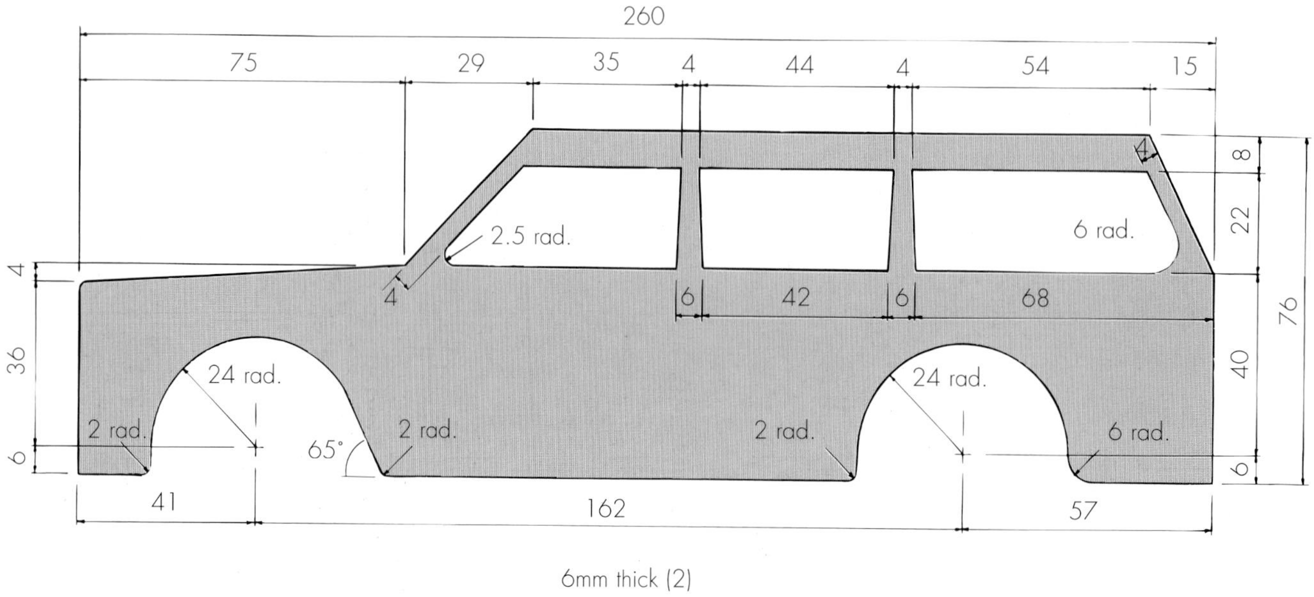

Fig 16.7 The side of the car.

suggest that you do this only if you are confident and conversant with the use of these knives.

Before gluing the radiator and lights into position you may wish to shape the front wings of the car. On our car, we gently rounded them with various grades of sanding stick.

When the bumpers have been attached you may round their corners, again using sanding sticks. You may also wish to slightly round the front and back corners of the car body (*see* Fig 16.8).

Front seats

Cut out the seat base.

Prepare the back rest from a suitable piece of hardwood (*see* Fig 16.9). We used lime as it is easy to shape. Glue the back rest to the seats' base. When the glue has dried clean up any unevenness.

Prepare the headrest and join it to the top of the back rest with a 3mm (⅛in) hardwood dowel (*see* Fig 16.9, 16.10).

Paint the two seats before you fix them into the car. Do not paint the underside of the

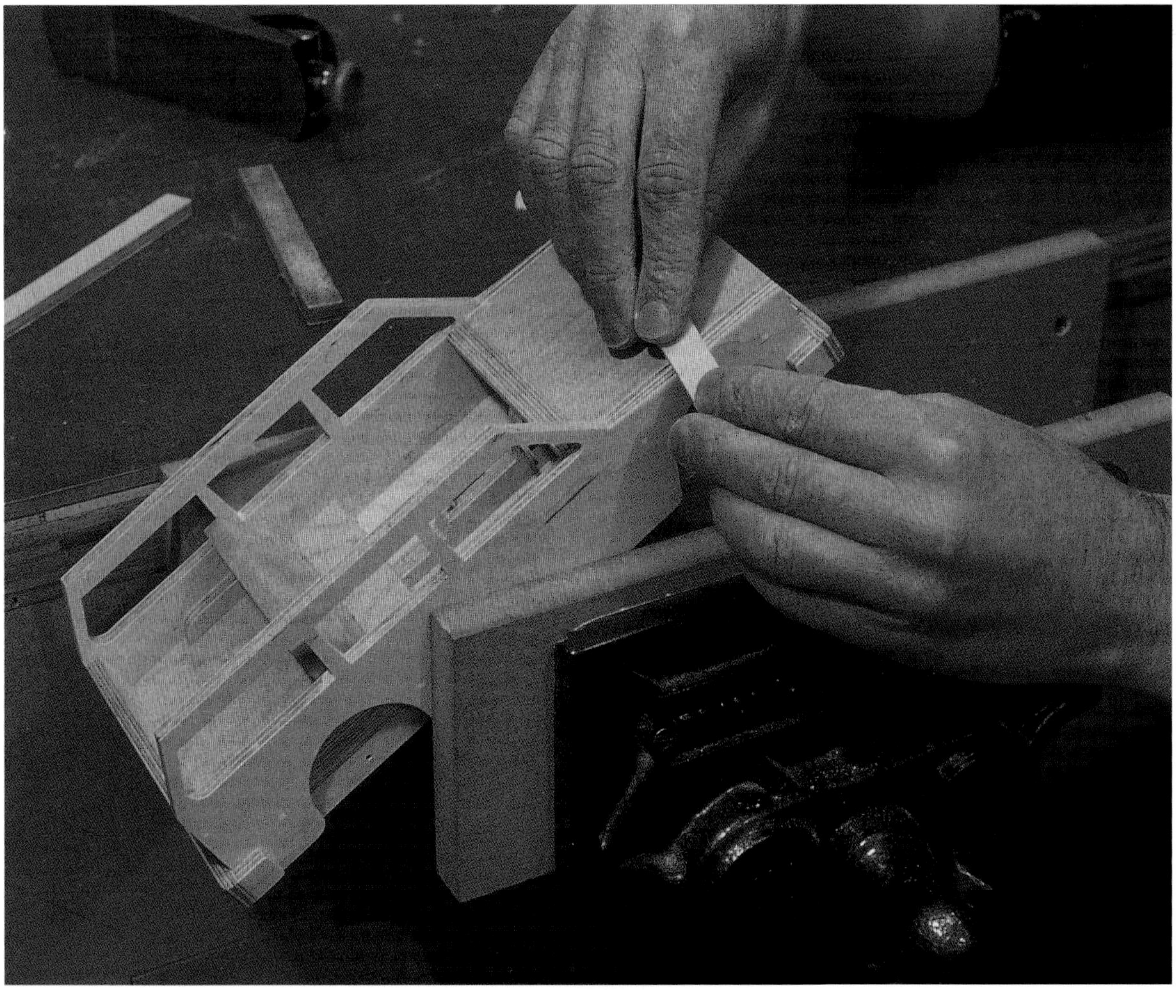

Fig 16.8 Shaping a front wing with a sanding stick.

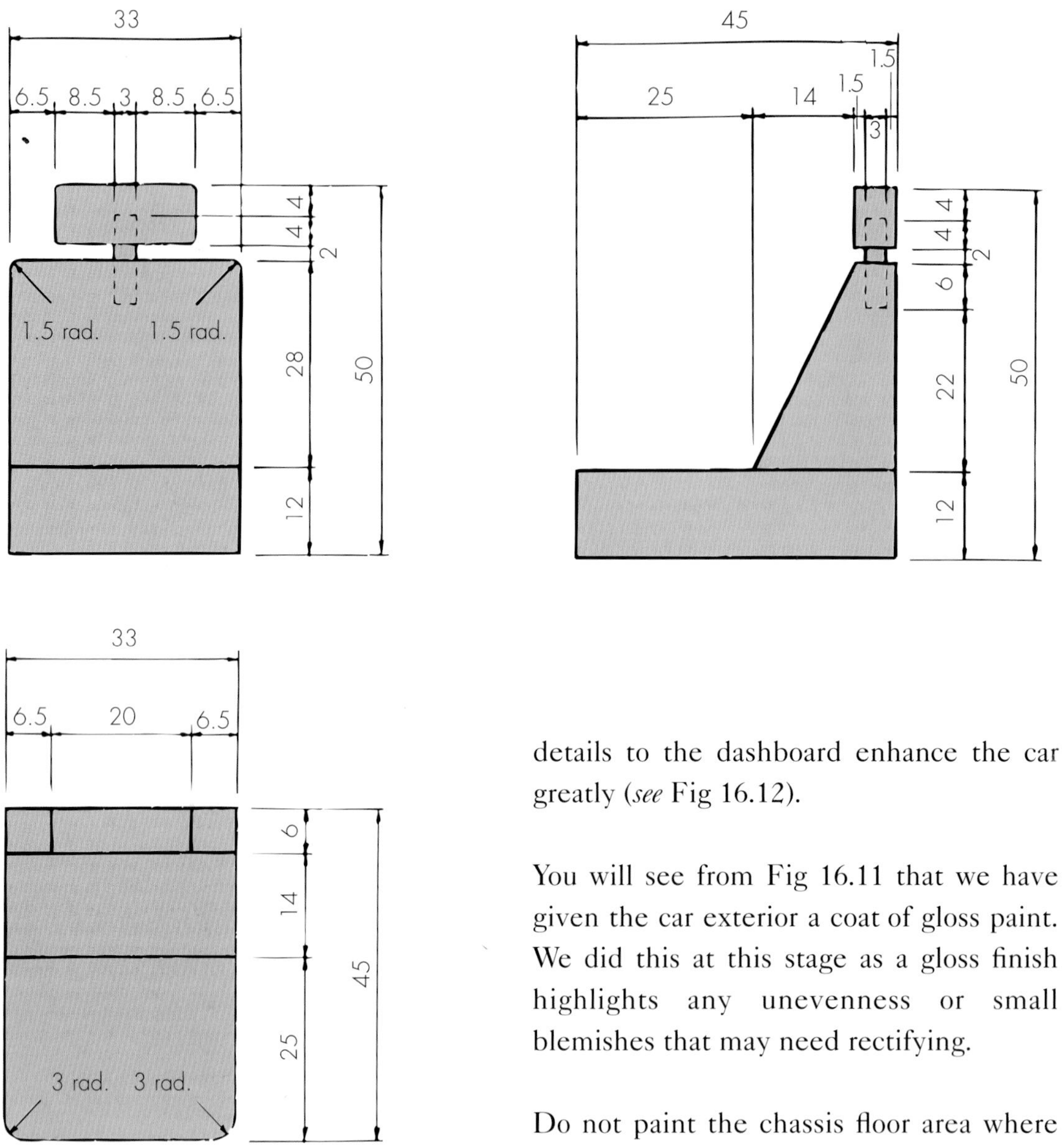

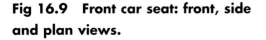

Fig 16.9 Front car seat: front, side and plan views.

seat bases, as you will need these bare in order to glue them down.

Car interior

Paint and decorate the interior of the car before you fit the roof (*see* Fig 16.11). How intricately you choose to decorate the interior is up to you, but some dials and details to the dashboard enhance the car greatly (*see* Fig 16.12).

You will see from Fig 16.11 that we have given the car exterior a coat of gloss paint. We did this at this stage as a gloss finish highlights any unevenness or small blemishes that may need rectifying.

Do not paint the chassis floor area where the front seats will be glued (*see* Fig 16.12). The bare wood will allow a better glue join. Similarly, do not paint the top edges of the side windows where the roof will be fitted.

Fix the steering wheel into place on the dashboard. You may like to fit a brass nut to represent a steering column.

When all the paint is dry, glue the two front seats into position (*see* Fig 16.13).

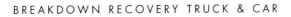

Fig 16.10 Car chassis, illustrating the interior components.

Roof

Prepare the car roof piece. Initially, you should cut this slightly oversize in length. This is so that when it is fitted you can plane its front and back edges to match the slopes of the front and rear window struts. Paint the underside before it is fitted.

Fix the roof into place with pins and glue. If you wish to round the top edges, do this gently with sanding sticks.

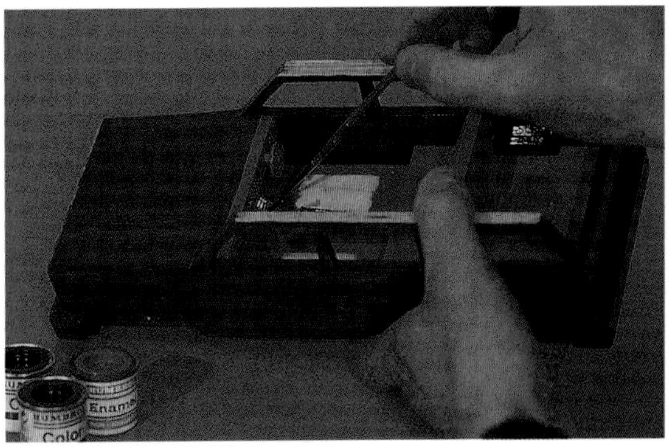

Fig 16.11 Painting the car interior.

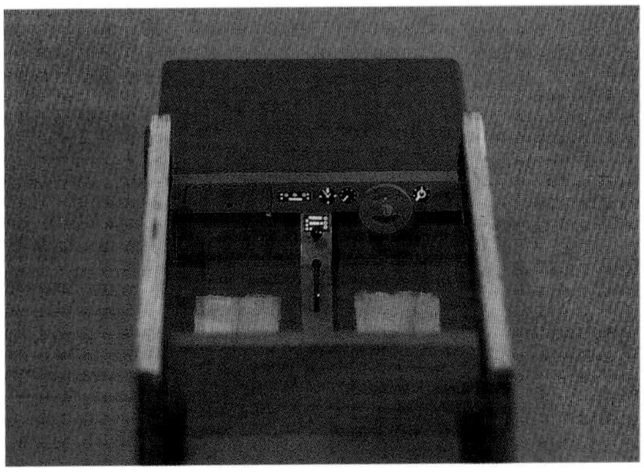

Fig 16.12 The car interior, illustrating the unpainted areas where the seats and roof will be glued.

EXTERIOR FINISHING

The entire exterior of the car may now be painted and decorated.

Fit a 6mm (¼in) eyelet to the centre of the front tow hook retaining strip (*see* Figs 16.5, 16.14).

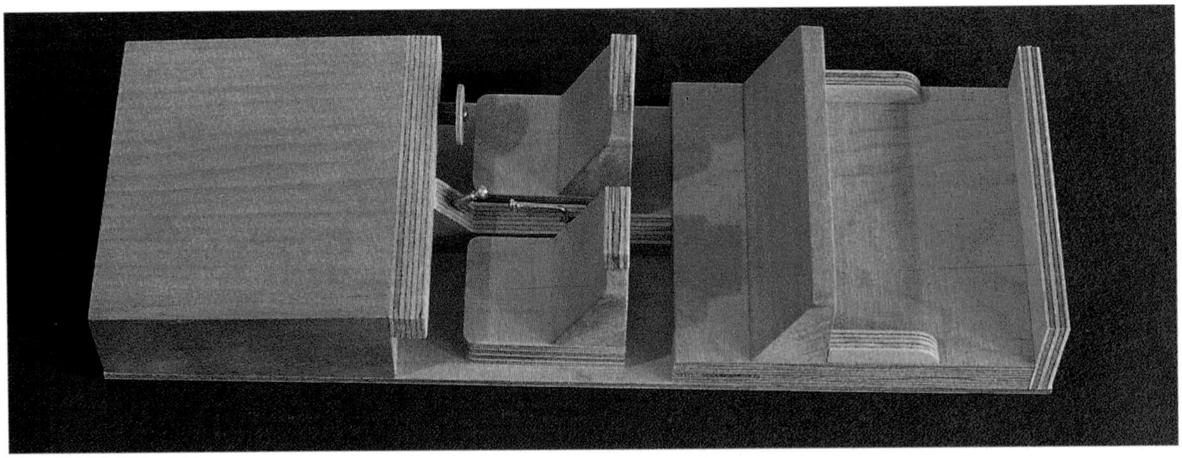

Fig 16.13 Car chassis, illustrating the positions of the front seats.

Wheels

The ready-made rubber-tyred wheels we used came with red centres. As these did not quite complement our chosen colour scheme, we painted them silver.

Fitting plastic wheels is done in a similar manner to wooden wheels, except that steel axle rods are used and spring hubcaps are fixed to the end so that the axles retain the wheels.

Follow the directions given on pages 62–63 for fitting the wheels to Chris Clown's Tricky Trike. Use a junior hacksaw blade to cut the axle rod, and remember to allow axle length for the spring hubcaps, and to file away any sharp edges.

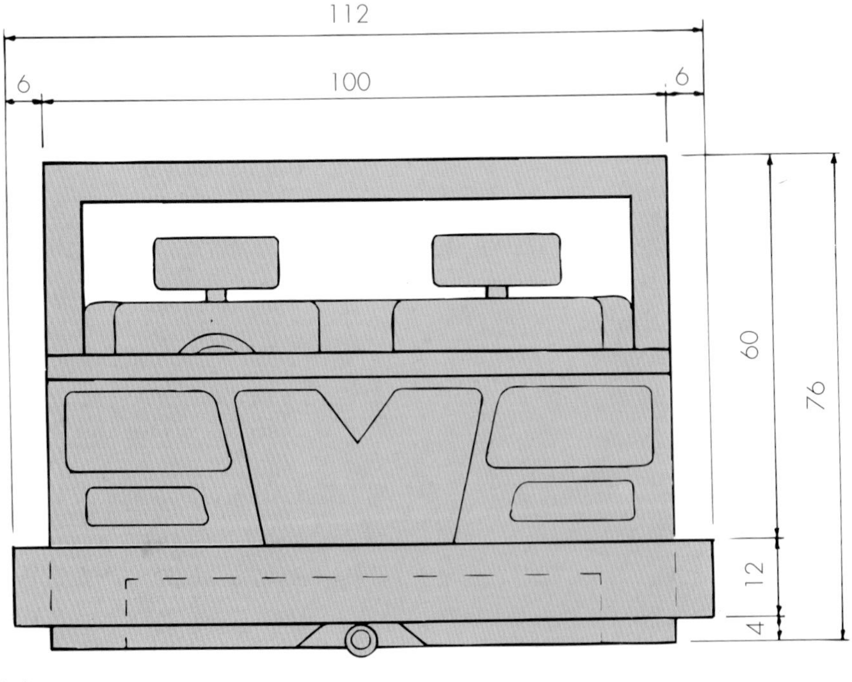

Corners and edges not rounded or shaped for reasons of clarity; similarly, wheels omitted.

Fig 16.14 Front view of the car.

CONSTRUCTION

For the complete plan, and side and front elevations of the recovery truck, see Figs 16.34, 16.35, 16.36.

Chassis and axle holes

Cut out and prepare the chassis bed (*see* Fig 16.15). Fix the chassis supports to the chassis bed underside with pins and glue.

Drill the axle holes into the chassis side strips. Ensure that the 5mm ($\frac{3}{16}$in) diameter axle rod fits comfortably through them.

Fit the chassis sides to the chassis with pins and glue.

Before going any further you need to check that the axle holes are correctly positioned so that all six wheels will touch the ground when fitted. To do this, slide a suitable

BREAKDOWN RECOVERY TRUCK CUTTING LIST

Chassis	
Bed:	412 x 106 x 6mm ($16\frac{1}{4}$ x $4\frac{3}{16}$ x $\frac{1}{4}$in) birch plywood
Supports (3):	106 x 16 x 12mm ($4\frac{3}{16}$ x $\frac{5}{8}$ x $\frac{1}{2}$in) birch plywood
Side strips (2):	412 x 38 x 12mm ($16\frac{1}{4}$ x $1\frac{1}{2}$ x $\frac{1}{2}$in) birch plywood
Cab	
Cab front:	130 x 75 x 12mm ($5\frac{1}{8}$ x 3 x $\frac{1}{2}$in) birch plywood
Dashboard:	130 x 54 x 12mm ($5\frac{1}{8}$ x $2\frac{1}{8}$ x $\frac{1}{2}$in) birch plywood
Seat base:	130 x 48 x 20mm ($5\frac{1}{8}$ x $1\frac{7}{8}$ x $\frac{13}{16}$in) hardwood
Seat back rest:	130 x 48 x 45mm ($5\frac{1}{8}$ x $1\frac{7}{8}$ x $1\frac{3}{4}$in) hardwood
Cab side (2):	122 x 88 x 6mm ($4\frac{13}{16}$ x $3\frac{1}{2}$ x $\frac{1}{4}$in) birch plywood
Wheel arch (2):	94 x 50 x 6mm ($3\frac{3}{4}$ x 2 x $\frac{1}{4}$in) birch plywood
Front bumper:	142 x 18 x 6mm ($5\frac{5}{8}$ x $\frac{3}{4}$ x $\frac{1}{4}$in) birch plywood
Cab back:	130 x 100 x 6mm ($5\frac{1}{8}$ x 4 x $\frac{1}{4}$in) birch plywood
Cab roof:	130 x 78 x 9mm ($5\frac{1}{8}$ x $3\frac{1}{16}$ x $\frac{3}{8}$in) birch plywood
Steering wheel:	24 x 1.5mm (1 x $\frac{1}{16}$in) birch plywood
Radiator/headlights:	142 x 20 x 6mm ($5\frac{5}{8}$ x $\frac{13}{16}$ x $\frac{1}{4}$in) birch plywood
Flashing light unit:	80 x 18 x 18mm ($3\frac{1}{8}$ x $\frac{3}{4}$ x $\frac{3}{4}$in) hardwood
Rear bed	
Main base:	346 x 154 x 6mm ($13\frac{5}{8}$ x $6\frac{1}{16}$ x $\frac{1}{4}$in) birch plywood
Top centre strip:	346 x 85 x 3mm ($13\frac{5}{8}$ x $3\frac{3}{8}$ x $\frac{1}{8}$in) birch plywood
Side strips (2):	346 x 19.5 x 3mm ($13\frac{5}{8}$ x $\frac{25}{32}$ x $\frac{1}{8}$in) birch plywood
Wheel chocks (2):	15 x 10 x 3mm ($\frac{19}{32}$ x $\frac{3}{8}$ x $\frac{1}{8}$in) birch plywood

continued overleaf

CUTTING LIST CONTINUED

Winch box

Side (2):	30 x 30 x 12mm (1 3/16 x 1 3/16 x 1/2in) birch plywood
Front:	85 x 30 x 3mm (3 3/8 x 1 3/16 x 1/8in) birch plywood
Top:	85 x 33 x 3mm (3 3/8 x 1 5/16 x 1/8in) birch plywood
Winch bar:	86 x 9mm (3 13/32 x 3/8in) diameter ramin dowel
Winch bar end:	20 x 3mm (13/16 x 1/8in) diameter birch plywood
Handle base:	20 x 6mm (13/16 x 1/4in) diameter birch plywood
Handle shaft:	42 x 2mm (1 5/8 x 3/32in) diameter steel (axle) rod
Handle:	12mm (1/2in) diameter wooden ball
Ramps (2):	267 x 18mm (10 1/2 x 3/4in) birch plywood

Miscellaneous

50mm (2in) wheels (6)
Lengths of 5mm (3/16in) axle rod (3)
Spring hubcaps (6)
Brass chain link for towing hook
Cord
No. 2 x 12mm (1/2in) brass round-headed screw
No. 2 x 9mm (3/8in) brass round-headed screws (2)
Small brass eyelets (2)
No. 4 x 18mm (3/4in) brass countersink screws (2)

length of axle rod through each set of holes. Then fit a wheel on each end. Place the chassis on a smooth, flat surface and gently move it backwards and forwards (*see* Fig 16.16). If one or more of the wheels do not turn this indicates that the axle holes are out of alignment.

This may be due to the fact that they have been marked and drilled incorrectly, or that the chassis sides have been fitted incorrectly.

Slight misalignment may be rectified by either of the following methods:

1. Enlarging the central pair of axle holes with a marginally larger drill bit;
2. Filing the top of each central pair of axle holes with a small round file.

If the wheels prove to be wildly out of true, then it may prove easier to make the chassis again rather than waste time on a lost cause! After all, if the chassis is out of true then the rest of the truck will be.

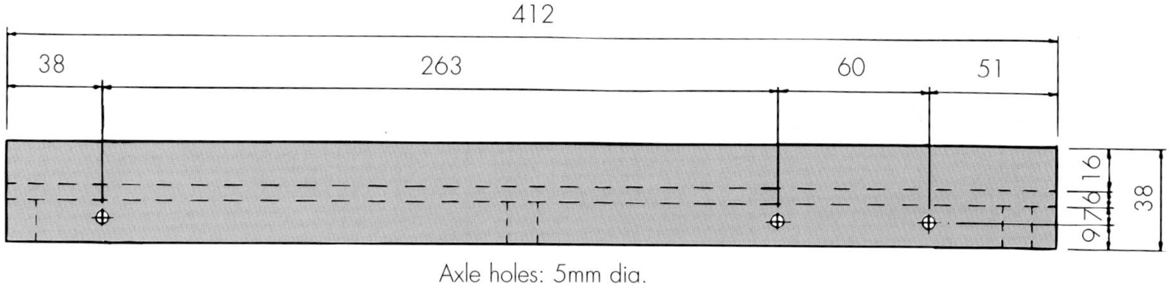

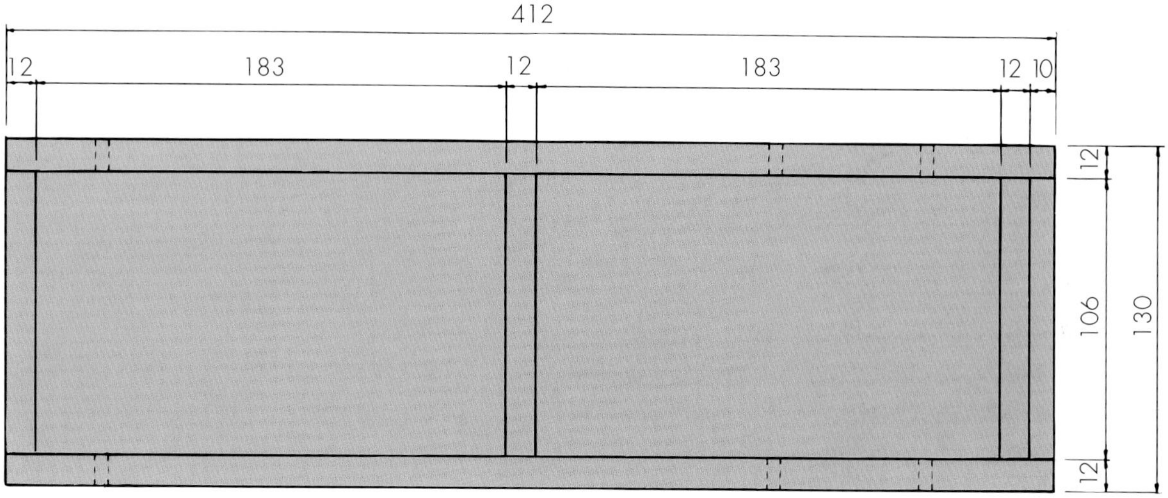

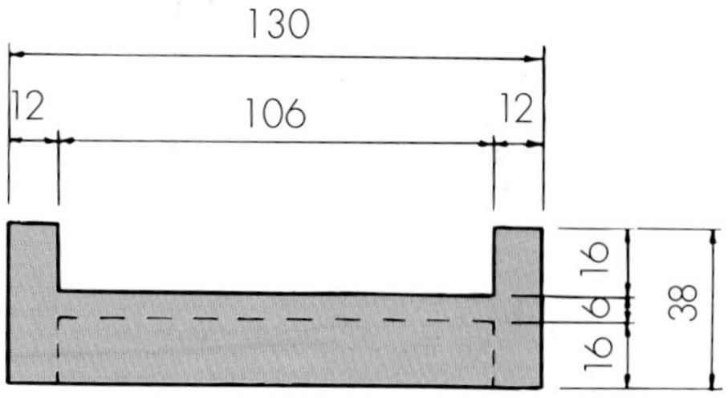

Fig 16.15 Breakdown recovery truck chassis: side, front and underside views.

Dashboard and seat

Prepare the piece of 12mm (½in) birch plywood for the dashboard section (*see* Fig 16.17). Mark and cut out the bottom slots, so that it will fit over the chassis sides, with a fine-toothed saw (a gent's or dovetail saw is ideal). Mark the slope of the instrument panel and shape to size with a block plane. Similarly, prepare the seat base and cut the bottom slots (*see* Fig 16.18).

Next, prepare the seat back. For both the seat base and back we used lime.

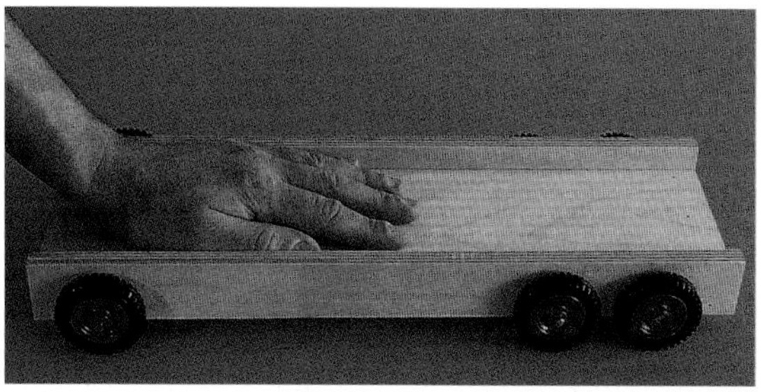

Fig 16.16 Moving the chassis backwards and forwards to check that all six wheels are correctly aligned and roll along.

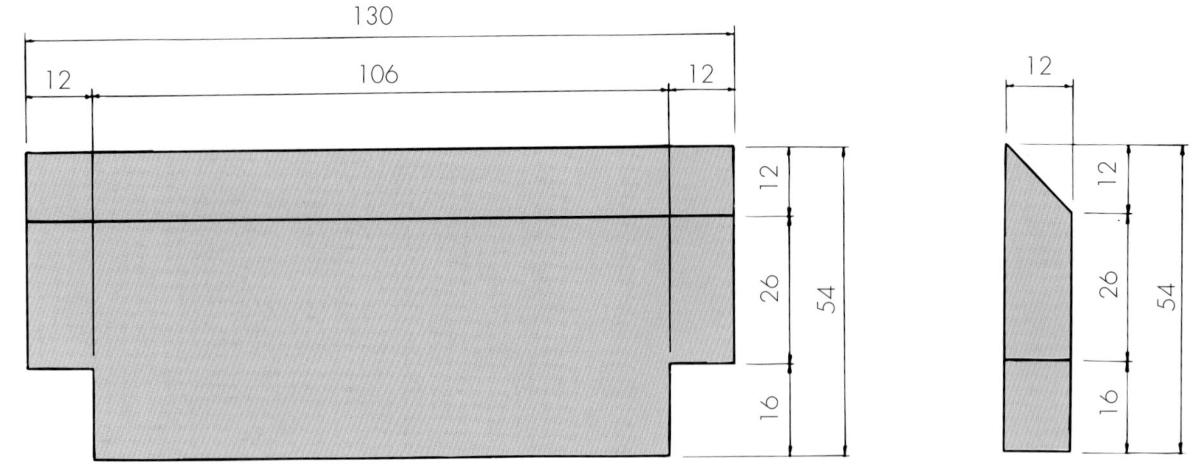

Fig 16.17 Dashboard dimensions.

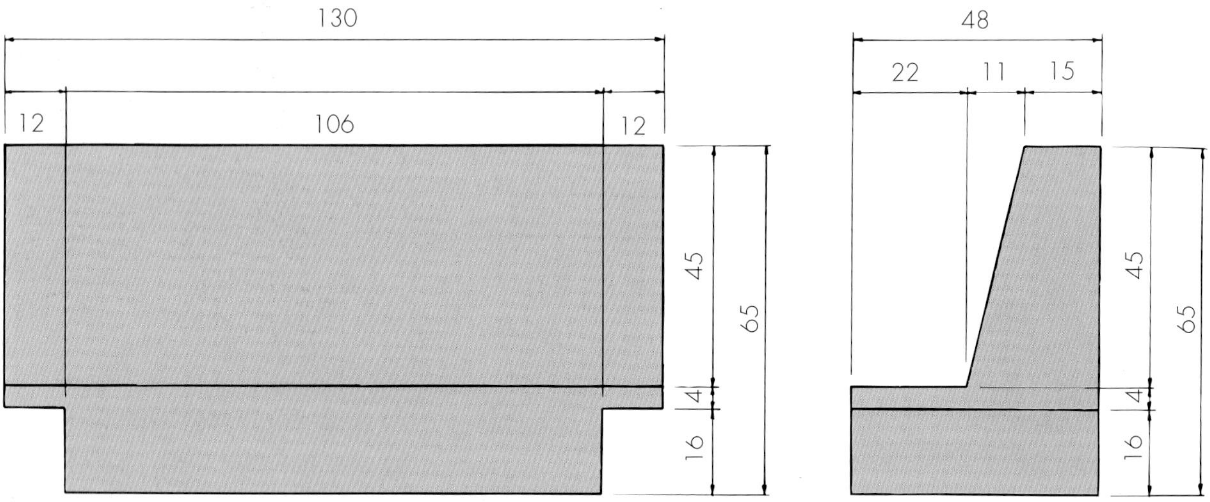

Fig 16.18 Front and side views of the seat.

Glue and pin the dashboard section and seat base into position. Then glue the seat back on to the seat base.

Fig 16.19 Steering wheel.

Cab, steering wheel and bumper sections

Prepare the front piece of the cab and fix it with glue and pins.

The steering wheel is cut from 1.5mm (1/16in) birch plywood (*see* Fig 16.19). Drill the central screw hole first and ensure that it will spin freely on the shank of a No. 2 x 12mm (½in) brass round-headed screw.

Using a hand drill, drill a pilot hole for the screw in the dashboard in the required position. Screw the screw partway into the

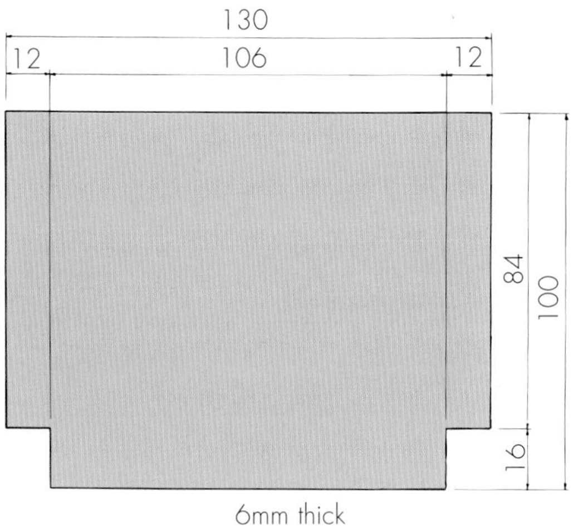

Fig 16.20 Cab back piece.

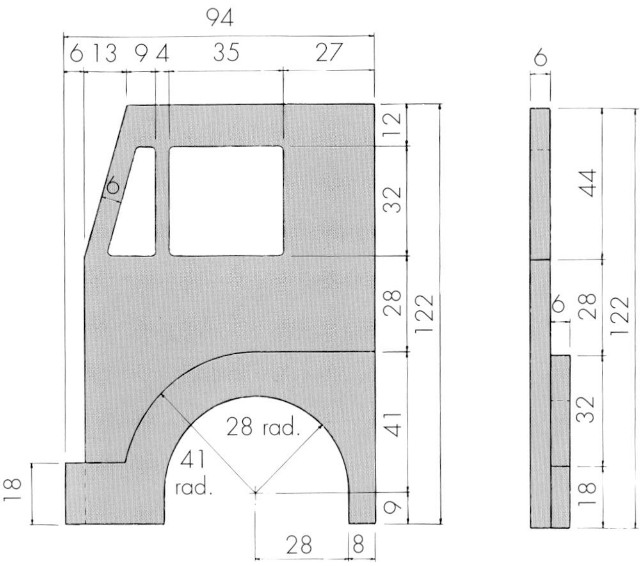

Fig 16.22 Cab side: side and front views (incorporating the wheel arch and the side of the front bumper).

pilot hole, then remove it. This will help you to fit the steering wheel later. The steering wheel can now be painted.

Prepare and fit the back piece of the cab (*see* Figs 16.20, 16.21).

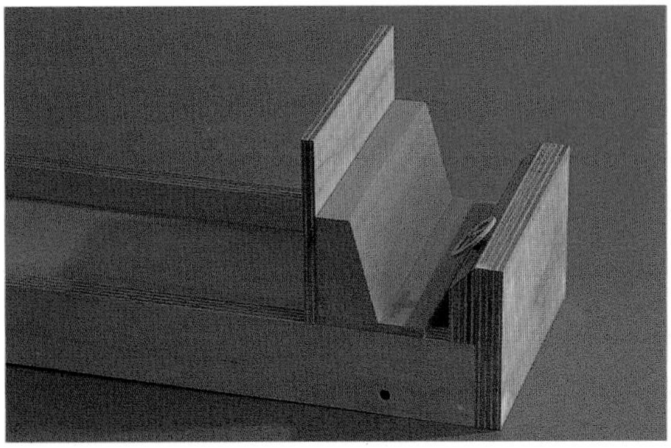

Fig 16.21 The truck cab's interior components when fitted to the chassis.

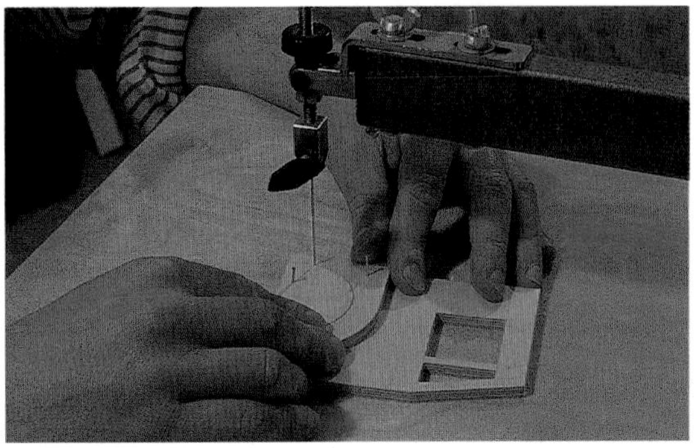

Fig 16.23 Cutting the wheel arch on one of the cab side pieces.

Prepare the cab sides and cut out the windows from both with a fretsaw (*see* Fig 16.22). At this stage do not cut the wheel arches.

Cut out both side wheel arch/bumper sections from 6mm (¼in) birch plywood. Again, do not cut the wheel arches from these yet.

Attach a side wheel arch/bumper section to each of the cab sides with 18mm (¾in) pins and glue. Longer pins are used so that they can be easily removed later.

Cut out the wheel arches (*see* Fig 16.23). Remove the pins when the glue has

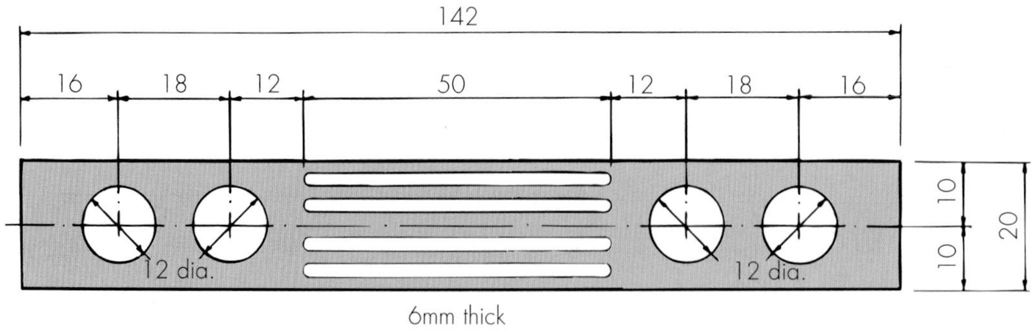

Fig 16.24 Headlights/radiator section.

completely set. Then fit the cab sides with pins and glue.

Front bumper, lights and radiator

Prepare and attach the front bumper.

The headlight and radiator section (*see* Fig 16.24) is constructed from a single piece of 6mm (¼in) birch plywood.

The radiator slits are made by drilling a 2mm (3/32in) diameter hole at each end, feeding a fine-grade fretsaw blade through one of the holes, and then cutting from one end to the other and back again (*see* Fig 16.25).

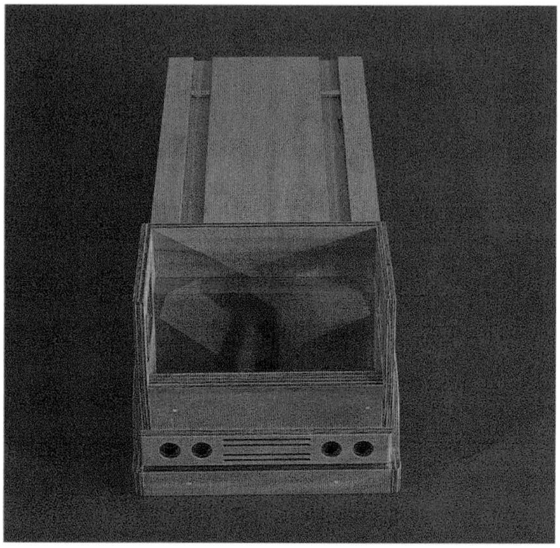

Fig 16.25 Front view of the unfinished truck, highlighting the radiator and lights.

The headlights are simply 12mm (½in) diameter holes.

When fitted, round the side corner edges of the bumper and headlight/radiator grille sections with sanding sticks.

Truck bed

Prepare and fit the base piece of the bed to the chassis.

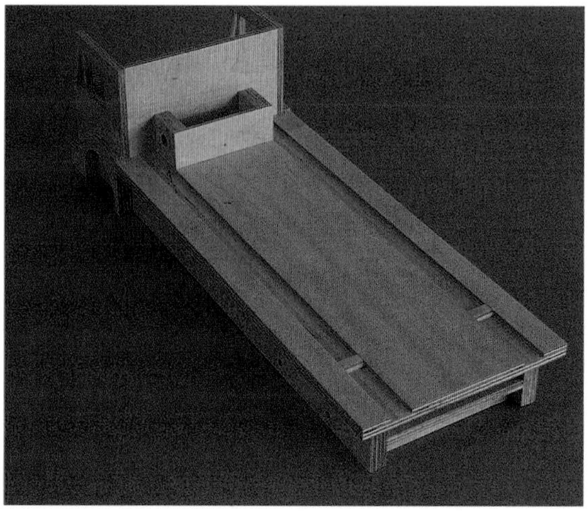

Fig 16.26 Rear view of the truck, illustrating the car wheel retaining strips.

Prepare the bed's top strips (which guide and retain lateral movement of the car

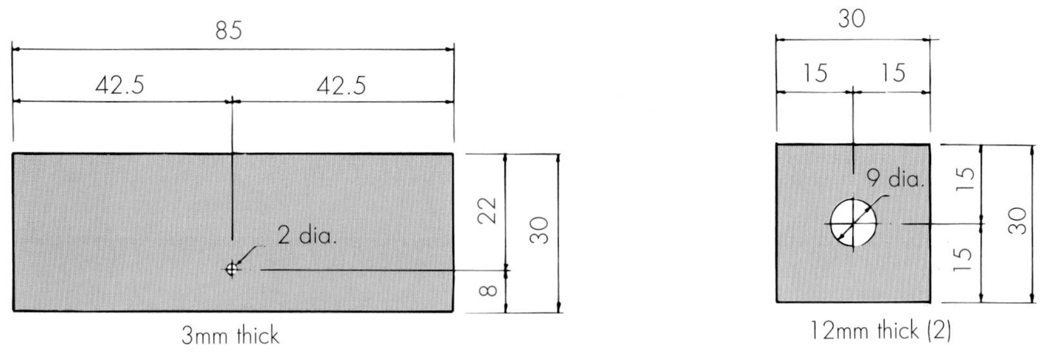

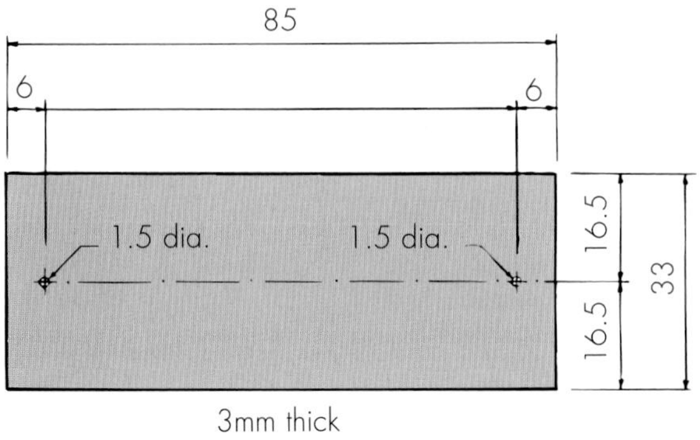

Fig 16.27 Winch box: front, side and top pieces.

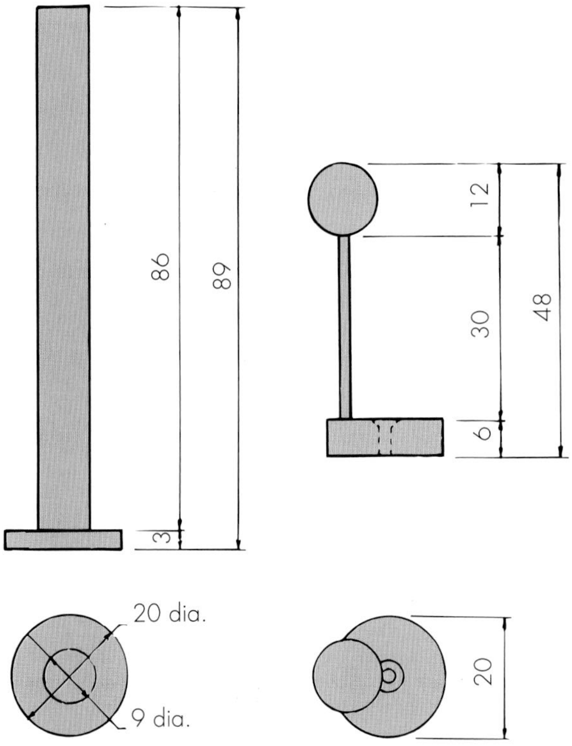

Fig 16.28 Front elevation and plans of the winch bar and handle.

wheels) and glue them into position (*see* Fig 16.26). These strips can be held in place with 18mm (¾in) pins – do not drive them too deep or you will find it difficult to remove them when the glue has set.

Prepare the bed wheel retainers, or chocks. The chamfers are shaped with sanding sticks before fitting.

Winch box

Prepare all the component pieces for the winch box (*see* Fig 16.27). Attach the front of the winch box to its sides with pins and glue. Then glue the winch box to the truck box. Fixing with a good adhesive should be sufficient. However, as an extra precaution you could dowel joint the winch box to the bed. Use 33mm (⅛in) dowels, two to the bottom of each side of the box.

The winch bar is cut from a length of 9mm (⅜in) diameter ramin dowel. The retaining disc is screwed on in case the winch bar ever needs to be removed from the winch box.

Glue together the components to make the winch bar handle (*see* Fig 16.28).

Cab roof

Prepare the cab roof. Cut it a fraction wider

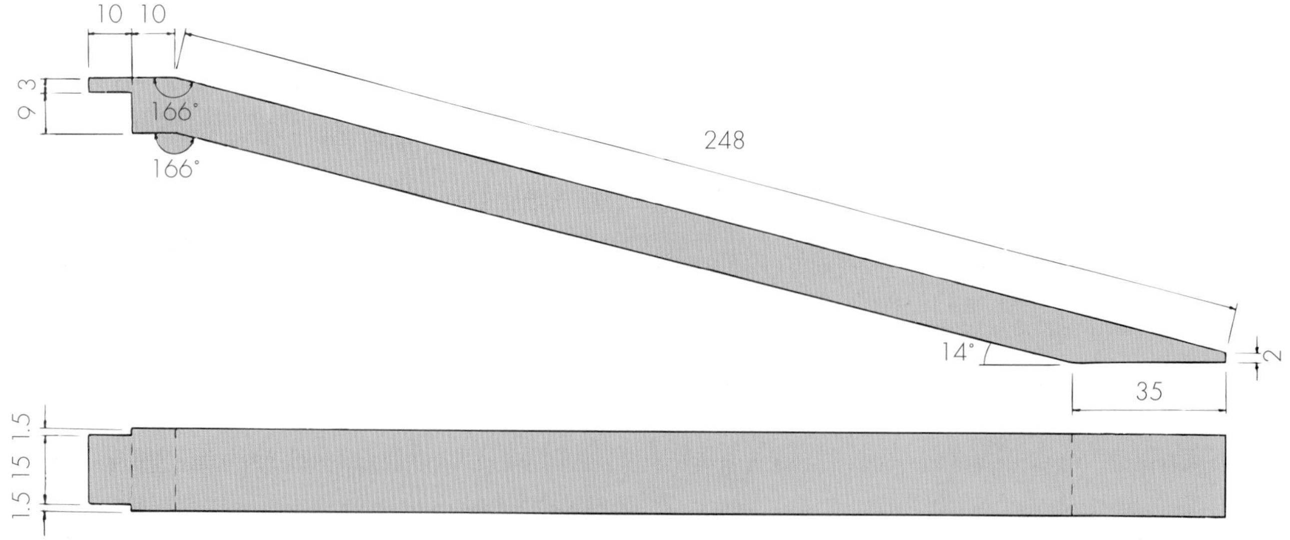

Fig 16.29 Plan and side elevation of the ramp.

Fig 16.30 Rear view of the truck, illustrating the ramp storage.

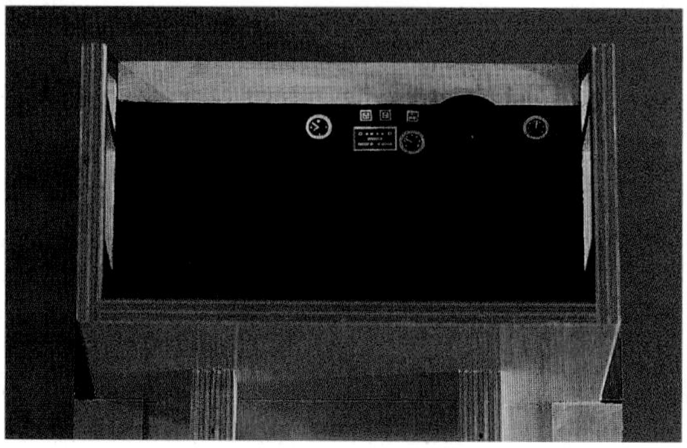

Fig 16.31 Cab interior, showing dashboard decoration.

than you require as it is trimmed to match the slope of the windscreen side frame bars when fitted into position.

Ramps

Cut out the two ramps (*see* Fig 16.29). If you do not have 18mm (¾in) birch plywood available, glue together some 12mm (½in) and 6mm (¼in) birch plywood.

Ensure that the tenoned end of each ramp fits snugly into the truck bed wheel wells. Screw a small brass eyelet to the flat underside of the tenoned end. This will stop the ramps from sliding too far into their storage box under the truck bed (*see* Fig 16.30).

PAINTING AND FINAL ASSEMBLY

The truck can now be primed and the interior of the cab and underside of the roof can be painted and decorated. Ours is finished with matt black paint with a protective coat of satin varnish.

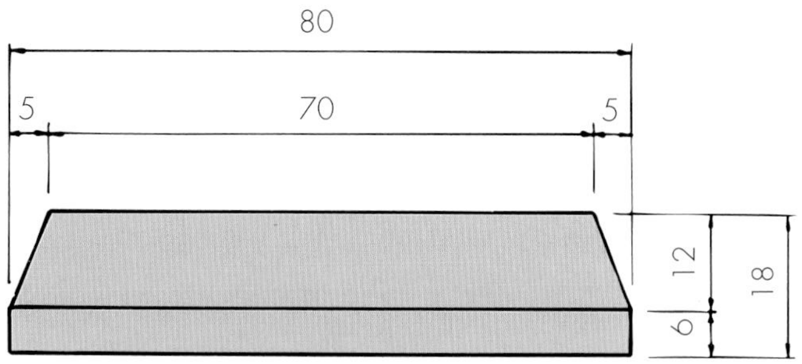

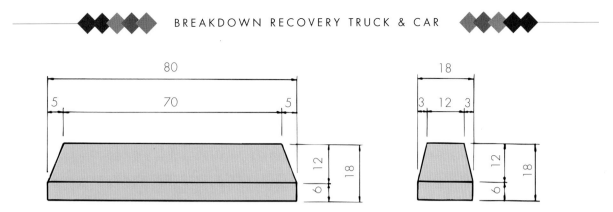

Fig 16.32 Front and end views of the flashing light unit.

Fit the steering wheel to the dashboard. We fitted a small brass nut between ours and the dashboard to act as a steering column. Do not tighten the screw completely if you want the steering wheel to turn. Decorate the dashboard as you choose (*see* Fig 16.31).

Glue and pin the cab roof into position. Shape the front edge with a block plane to match the front slope of the windscreen side frame bars.

Round the edges of the cab roof with sanding sticks.

The flashing light unit is shaped from a piece of beech (*see* Fig 16.32). Attach it to the roof with glue (*see* Fig 16.33).

Paint and decorate the truck in a style of your choice. Bear in mind that breakdown trucks tend to have a highly visible colour scheme. You may wish to use fluorescent tape on certain sections, just like its real-life counterparts.

The plastic wheels had red centres, so we painted ours white to complement our chosen colour scheme.

With the painting and decorating complete, fit the winch bar to the winch box. The handle is now screwed and glued (using a very strong adhesive) to the winch bar. Thread a suitable length of cord through the hole in the front of the winch box and secure it to the winch bar (*see* Fig 16.33). At the other end of the cord attach a hook which will fit into the towing eyelet on the estate car.

Screw the top of the winch box into position using two No. 2 x 9mm (⅜in) brass round-head screws.

Fit the axles and wheels in the same way that the car wheels were fitted.

Fig 16.33 Detail of the winch box interior and the flashing light unit.

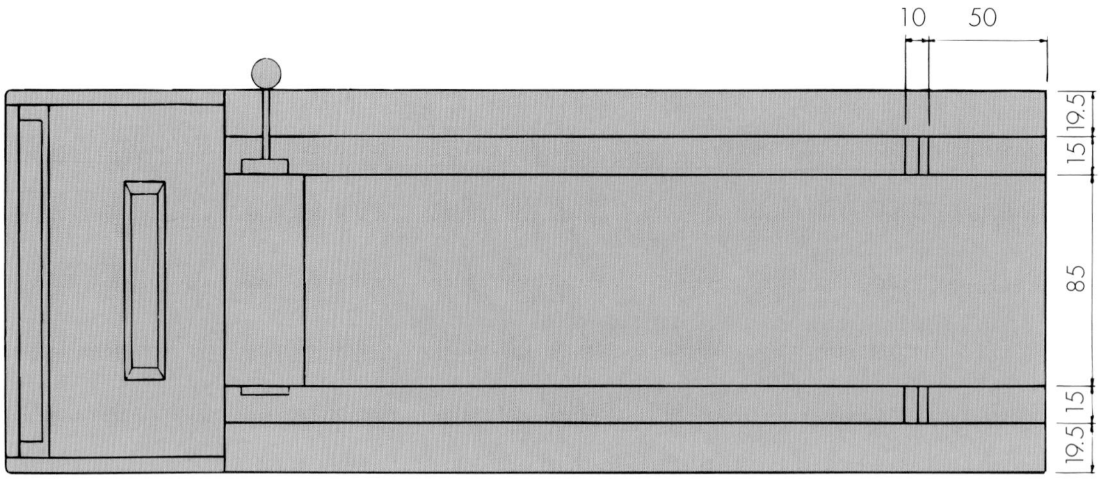

Fig 16.34 Breakdown recovery truck plan.

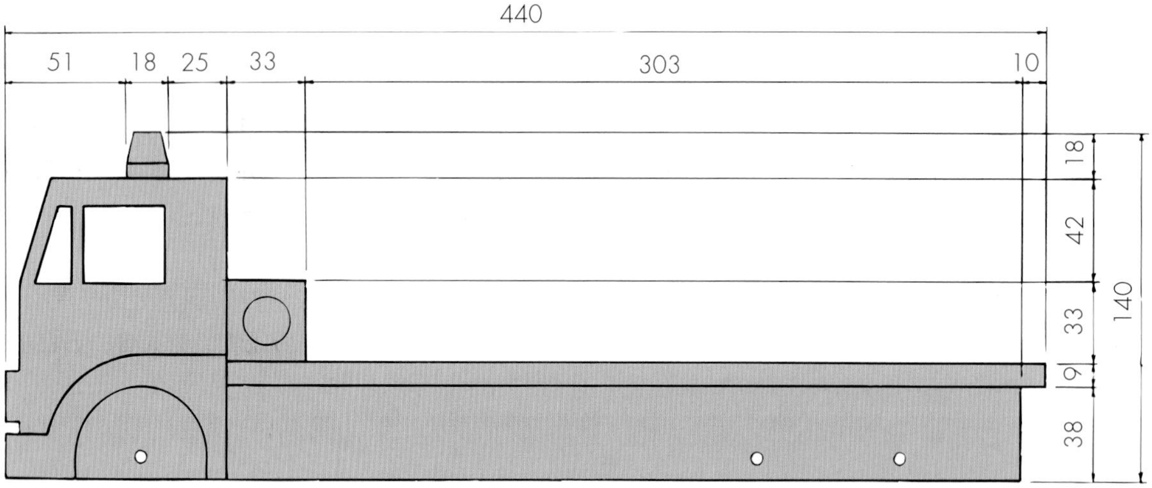

Fig 16.35 Breakdown recovery truck side elevation.

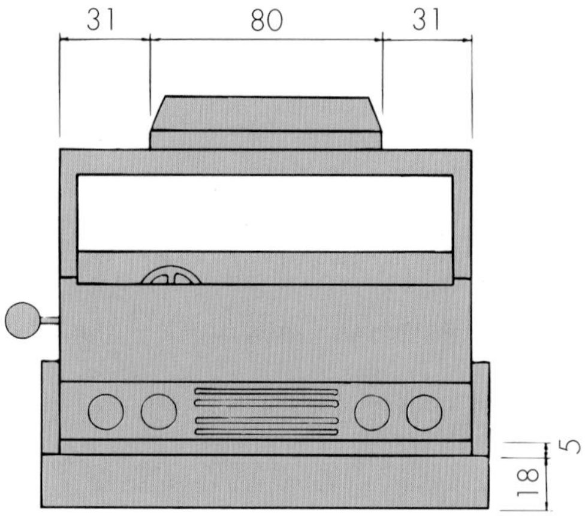

Fig 16.36 Breakdown recovery truck front elevation.

Glossary

Axle
A spindle on which a wheel rotates, or which rotates with the wheel. Sometimes a rod connecting two wheels.

Butt joint
Or butted joint. A simple joint where two items to be joined are placed together, with no interlocking parts, and fixed.

Clean up
Term that describes the smoothing of a sawn edge or surface of a workpiece.

De-nibb
To lightly scour away, with a fine abrasive medium, any imperfections or general roughness from a finish before applying the final coat.

Diameter
The length of a straight line passing through the centre of a circle, and touching the circumference of the circle at each end.

End grain
After cutting across the fibres (or grain) of a piece of wood, the exposed surface is termed the end grain.

Flush finish
A level finish. For example, where two or more components are joined on the same plane, their joins may be detected visually but not by touch.

Fluted
An item (for example a dowel) that has many long concave grooves.

Jig
A device which enables a repetitive operation to be carried out, usually without the need for major adjustment and measurement.

Kerf
The slot created by sawing into a piece of timber or similar material.

MDF
Medium-density fibreboard. Manufactured fibreboard with two smooth surfaces. In some instances, it may be used as a substitute for solid wood or plywood.

Mitre joint
Where two pieces of wood have each been cut at an angle, usually 45°, and joined.

Moulding
In the context of this book, a length of decorative edging usually made in a series of curves and beads.

Pare
As in 'pare away'. The fine removal of wood shavings with a knife or chisel.

Pilot hole
Usually a hole in the workpiece the diameter of which will act as a guide for a screw's thread. It also helps to reduce pressure on the screw, and the grain of the timber (workpiece), during insertion. Thus the screw is less likely to shear under tension and the timber less prone to split.

Plys
The layers of veneer used to form plywood.

Primer
A paint-like substance which seals the grain of the timber so that subsequent coats are not absorbed.

Rivet set
A metal tool that has a cup-like depression set into part of it. This helps to hold a rivet head while the other end of the rivet is worked with a hammer, or a combination of hammer and another set.

Rivet shank
The cylindrical part of the rivet that is situated behind the rivet's convex head.

Screw eyelet
A metal screw with a circular looped end.

Template
A type of jig. In this book, it is a sheet of thin material (cardboard, hardboard or plywood) shaped to the profile of a component required. By placing it on the work material and marking round its edge many components can be repetitively drawn quickly and accurately.

TPI
Teeth per inch. Term used to denote how many saw tooth points there are per inch.

Treadle
Lever that is activated by a foot or feet in a repetitive manner in order to drive the mechanism of a machine.

Veneer
A thin slice of wood used to cover a relatively inexpensive wood or man-made board. Numerous sheets of veneer are bonded together in the manufacture of plywood.

Washer
A flat metal disc, usually with a central hole, which is placed between components. In this book, usually to alleviate friction between wheels and toy vehicle.

METRIC CONVERSION TABLE

inches to millimetres and centimetres

mm = millimetres   cm = centimetres

inches	mm	cm	inches	cm	inches	cm
⅛	3	0.3	9	22.9	30	76.2
¼	6	0.6	10	25.4	31	78.7
⅜	10	1.0	11	27.9	32	81.3
½	13	1.3	12	30.5	33	83.8
⅝	16	1.6	13	33.0	34	86.4
¾	19	1.9	14	35.6	35	88.9
⅞	22	2.2	15	38.1	36	91.4
1	25	2.5	16	40.6	37	94.0
1¼	32	3.2	17	43.2	38	96.5
1½	38	3.8	18	45.7	39	99.1
1¾	44	4.4	19	48.3	40	101.6
2	51	5.1	20	50.8	41	104.1
2½	64	6.4	21	53.3	42	106.7
3	76	7.6	22	55.9	43	109.2
3½	89	8.9	23	58.4	44	111.8
4	102	10.2	24	61.0	45	114.3
4½	114	11.4	25	63.5	46	116.8
5	127	12.7	26	66.0	47	119.4
6	152	15.2	27	68.6	48	121.9
7	178	17.8	28	71.1	49	124.5
8	203	20.3	29	73.7	50	127.0

About the Authors

Jeff Loader's woodworking career led him to help set up and run a wooden-toy-making workshop. This not only involved design and manufacture, but also the instruction of novices in various workshop practices and methods. Through this work he soon realized the love and joy of making, and playing with, wooden toys.

Jeff regularly writes articles for various magazines, as well as co-writing *Making Board, Peg and Dice Games* and *Making Wooden Toys and Games* (both GMC Publications Ltd) with his partner, Jennie. Wooden toys and games apart, Jeff's many interests and activities include furniture history and design, sport and playing (coping?!) with his children.

Jennie Loader has a keen and active interest in many aspects of art, craft and design. She has studied photography and leisure management. Her career has mainly involved organizing drama, creative play, sporting and other pastime activities for varying groups of children, including those with special needs.

Jeff and Jennie were both born in the West Country and now live in Glastonbury with their two young children.

TITLES AVAILABLE FROM

GMC PUBLICATIONS

BOOKS

WOODWORKING

40 More Woodworking Plans & Projects	*GMC Publications*
Bird Boxes and Feeders for the Garden	*Dave Mackenzie*
Complete Woodfinishing	*Ian Hosker*
David Charlesworth's Furniture-making Techniques	*David Charlesworth*
Electric Woodwork	*Jeremy Broun*
Furniture & Cabinetmaking Projects	*GMC Publications*
Furniture Projects	*Rod Wales*
Furniture Restoration (Practical Crafts)	*Kevin Jan Bonner*
Furniture Restoration and Repair for Beginners	*Kevin Jan Bonner*
Furniture Restoration Workshop	*Kevin Jan Bonner*
Green Woodwork	*Mike Abbott*
Making & Modifying Woodworking Tools	*Jim Kingshott*
Making Chairs and Tables	*GMC Publications*
Making Fine Furniture	*Tom Darby*
Making Little Boxes from Wood	*John Bennett*
Making Shaker Furniture	*Barry Jackson*
Making Woodwork Aids and Devices	*Robert Wearing*
Pine Furniture Projects for the Home	*Dave Mackenzie*
Router Magic: Jigs, Fixtures and Tricks to Unleash your Router's Full Potential	*Bill Hylton*
Routing for Beginners	*Anthony Bailey*
The Scrollsaw: Twenty Projects	*John Everett*
Sharpening Pocket Reference Book	*Jim Kingshott*
Sharpening: The Complete Guide	*Jim Kingshott*
Space-Saving Furniture Projects	*Dave Mackenzie*
Stickmaking: A Complete Course	*Andrew Jones & Clive George*
Stickmaking Handbook	*Andrew Jones & Clive George*
Test Reports: *The Router* and *Furniture & Cabinetmaking*	*GMC Publications*
Veneering: A Complete Course	*Ian Hosker*
Woodfinishing Handbook (Practical Crafts)	*Ian Hosker*
Woodworking Plans and Projects	*GMC Publications*
Woodworking with the Router: Professional Router Techniques any Woodworker can Use	*Bill Hylton & Fred Matlack*
The Workshop	*Jim Kingshott*

WOODTURNING

Adventures in Woodturning	*David Springett*
Bert Marsh: Woodturner	*Bert Marsh*
Bill Jones' Notes from the Turning Shop	*Bill Jones*
Bill Jones' Further Notes from the Turning Shop	*Bill Jones*
Colouring Techniques for Woodturners	*Jan Sanders*
The Craftsman Woodturner	*Peter Child*
Decorative Techniques for Woodturners	*Hilary Bowen*
Essential Tips for Woodturners	*GMC Publications*
Faceplate Turning	*GMC Publications*
Fun at the Lathe	*R.C. Bell*
Illustrated Woodturning Techniques	*John Hunnex*
Intermediate Woodturning Projects	*GMC Publications*
Keith Rowley's Woodturning Projects	*Keith Rowley*
Make Money from Woodturning	*Ann & Bob Phillips*
Multi-Centre Woodturning	*Ray Hopper*
Pleasure and Profit from Woodturning	*Reg Sherwin*
Practical Tips for Turners & Carvers	*GMC Publications*
Practical Tips for Woodturners	*GMC Publications*
Spindle Turning	*GMC Publications*
Turning Miniatures in Wood	*John Sainsbury*
Turning Wooden Toys	*Terry Lawrence*
Understanding Woodturning	*Ann & Bob Phillips*
Useful Techniques for Woodturners	*GMC Publications*
Useful Woodturning Projects	*GMC Publications*
Woodturning: Bowls, Platters, Hollow Forms, Vases, Vessels, Bottles, Flasks, Tankards, Plates	*GMC Publications*
Woodturning: A Foundation Course	*Keith Rowley*
Woodturning: A Source Book of Shapes	*John Hunnex*
Woodturning Jewellery	*Hilary Bowen*
Woodturning Masterclass	*Tony Boase*
Woodturning Techniques	*GMC Publications*
Woodturning Tools & Equipment Test Reports	*GMC Publications*
Woodturning Wizardry	*David Springett*

WOODCARVING

The Art of the Woodcarver	*GMC Publications*
Carving Birds & Beasts	*GMC Publications*
Carving on Turning	*Chris Pye*
Carving Realistic Birds	*David Tippey*
Decorative Woodcarving	*Jeremy Williams*
Essential Tips for Woodcarvers	*GMC Publications*
Essential Woodcarving Techniques	*Dick Onians*
Lettercarving in Wood: A Practical Course	*Chris Pye*
Power Tools for Woodcarving	*David Tippey*
Practical Tips for Turners & Carvers	*GMC Publications*
Relief Carving in Wood: A Practical Introduction	*Chris Pye*
Understanding Woodcarving	*GMC Publications*
Understanding Woodcarving in the Round	*GMC Publications*
Useful Techniques for Woodcarvers	*GMC Publications*
Wildfowl Carving - Volume 1	*Jim Pearce*
Wildfowl Carving - Volume 2	*Jim Pearce*
The Woodcarvers	*GMC Publications*
Woodcarving: A Complete Course	*Ron Butterfield*
Woodcarving: A Foundation Course	*Zoë Gertner*
Woodcarving for Beginners	*GMC Publications*
Woodcarving Tools & Equipment Test Reports	*GMC Publications*
Woodcarving Tools, Materials & Equipment	*Chris Pye*

UPHOLSTERY

Seat Weaving (Practical Crafts)	*Ricky Holdstock*
Upholsterer's Pocket Reference Book	*David James*
Upholstery: A Complete Course	*David James*
Upholstery Restoration	*David James*
Upholstery Techniques & Projects	*David James*

Toymaking

Designing & Making Wooden Toys *Terry Kelly*
Fun to Make Wooden Toys & Games *Jeff & Jennie Loader*
Making Board, Peg & Dice Games *Jeff & Jennie Loader*
Making Wooden Toys & Games *Jeff & Jennie Loader*
Restoring Rocking Horses *Clive Green & Anthony Dew*
Scrollsaw Toy Projects *Ivor Carlyle*
Wooden Toy Projects *GMC Publications*

Dolls' Houses & Miniatures

Architecture for Dolls' Houses *Joyce Percival*
Beginners' Guide to the Dolls' House Hobby *Jean Nisbett*
The Complete Dolls' House Book *Jean Nisbett*
The Dolls' House 1/24 Scale: A Complete Introduction *Jean Nisbett*
Dolls' House Accessories, Fixtures and Fittings *Andrea Barham*
Dolls' House Bathrooms: Lots of Little Loos *Patricia King*
Dolls' House Fireplaces and Stoves *Patricia King*
Easy to Make Dolls' House Accessories *Andrea Barham*
Heraldic Miniature Knights *Peter Greenhill*
Make Your Own Dolls' House Furniture *Maurice Harper*
Making Dolls' House Furniture *Patricia King*
Making Georgian Dolls' Houses *Derek Rowbottom*
Making Miniature Gardens *Freida Gray*
Making Miniature Oriental Rugs & Carpets *Meik & Ian McNaughton*
Making Period Dolls' House Accessories *Andrea Barham*
Making Period Dolls' House Furniture *Derek & Sheila Rowbottom*
Making Tudor Dolls' Houses *Derek Rowbottom*
Making Unusual Miniatures *Graham Spalding*
Making Victorian Dolls' House Furniture *Patricia King*
Miniature Bobbin Lace *Roz Snowden*
Miniature Embroidery for the Victorian Dolls' House *Pamela Warner*
Miniature Needlepoint Carpets *Janet Granger*
The Secrets of the Dolls' House Makers *Jean Nisbett*

Crafts

American Patchwork Designs in Needlepoint *Melanie Tacon*
A Beginners' Guide to Rubber Stamping *Brenda Hunt*
Celtic Knotwork Designs *Sheila Sturrock*
Celtic Knotwork Handbook *Sheila Sturrock*
Collage from Seeds, Leaves and Flowers *Joan Carver*
Complete Pyrography *Stephen Poole*
Creating Knitwear Designs *Pat Ashforth & Steve Plummer*
Creative Doughcraft *Patricia Hughes*
Creative Embroidery Techniques Using Colour Through Gold *Daphne J. Ashby & Jackie Woolsey*
Cross Stitch Kitchen Projects *Janet Granger*
Cross Stitch on Colour *Sheena Rogers*
Designing and Making Cards *Glennis Gilruth*
Embroidery Tips & Hints *Harold Hayes*
An Introduction to Crewel Embroidery *Mave Glenny*
Making Character Bears *Valerie Tyler*
Making Greetings Cards for Beginners *Pat Sutherland*
Making Hand-Sewn Boxes: Techniques and Projects *Jackie Woolsey*
Making Knitwear Fit *Pat Ashforth & Steve Plummer*
Needlepoint: A Foundation Course *Sandra Hardy*
Pyrography Designs *Norma Gregory*
Pyrography Handbook (Practical Crafts) *Stephen Poole*
Ribbons and Roses *Lee Lockheed*
Tassel Making for Beginners *Enid Taylor*
Tatting Collage *Lindsay Rogers*
Temari: A Traditional Japanese Embroidery Technique *Margaret Ludlow*
Theatre Models in Paper and Card *Robert Burgess*
Wool Embroidery & Design *Lee Lockheed*

The Home & Gardening

Home Ownership: Buying and Maintaining *Nicholas Snelling*
The Living Tropical Greenhouse *John and Maureen Tampion*
Security for the Householder: Fitting Locks and Other Devices *E. Phillips*
The Birdwatcher's Garden *Hazel and Pamela Johnson*

VIDEOS

Drop-in and Pinstuffed Seats *David James*
Stuffover Upholstery *David James*
Elliptical Turning *David Springett*
Woodturning Wizardry *David Springett*
Turning Between Centres: The Basics *Dennis White*
Turning Bowls *Dennis White*
Boxes, Goblets and Screw Threads *Dennis White*
Novelties and Projects *Dennis White*
Classic Profiles *Dennis White*
Twists and Advanced Turning *Dennis White*
Sharpening the Professional Way *Jim Kingshott*
Sharpening Turning & Carving Tools *Jim Kingshott*
Bowl Turning *John Jordan*
Hollow Turning *John Jordan*
Woodturning: A Foundation Course *Keith Rowley*
Carving a Figure: The Female Form *Ray Gonzalez*
The Router: A Beginner's Guide *Alan Goodsell*
The Scroll Saw: A Beginner's Guide *John Burke*

MAGAZINES

Woodturning • Woodcarving • Furniture & Cabinetmaking • The Dolls' House Magazine
The Router • The ScrollSaw • Creative Crafts for the Home • BusinessMatters

---

The above represents a full list of all titles currently published or scheduled to be published.
All are available direct from the Publishers or through bookshops, newsagents and specialist retailers.
To place an order, or to obtain a complete catalogue, contact:

GMC Publications
Castle Place, 166 High Street, Lewes, East Sussex BN7 1XU, United Kingdom Tel: 01273 488005 Fax: 01273 478606

Orders by credit card are accepted